改訂版

やっておきたい

英語長文

1000

［問題編］

河合塾講師

杉山 俊一
塚越 友幸
山下 博子

［共著］

河合出版

河合塾
SERIES

改訂版

やっておきたい

英語長文

1000

［問題編］

河合塾講師

杉山 俊一
塚越 友幸
山下 博子

［共著］

河合出版

次の英文を読んで，設問に答えなさい。

(1)The idea that animals feel emotions remains controversial among many scientists. Researchers' doubt is fueled in part by the very nonscientific tendency to attribute human qualities to nonhumans. Many scientists also say that standard scientific methods cannot prove the existence of emotions in animals. Today, however, with mounting evidence to the contrary, "the tide is turning radically and rapidly," says biologist Marc Bekoff, who is at the forefront of this movement.

(2)Even those who do not believe in animal passion agree that many creatures experience fear — which some scientists define as a primary emotion that contrasts with secondary emotions such as love and grief. Unlike these more complex feelings, fear is instinctive, they say, and requires no conscious thought.

But beyond such instinctive emotions, the possibility of more complex animal feelings is difficult to demonstrate. "I can't even prove that another human being is feeling happy or sad," says Bekoff, "but I can deduce how they're feeling through body language and facial expression." As a scientist who has conducted field studies of coyotes and foxes for the past three decades, Bekoff also believes he can accurately tell what these animals are feeling by observing their behavior. He adds that animal emotions may actually be more knowable than those of humans, because (3)they don't filter their feelings the way we do.

Yet because feelings are *intangible and difficult to study scientifically, "most researchers don't even want to talk about animal emotions," says *neuroscientist Jaak Panksepp. Within his field, Panksepp is a rare exception. Focusing on similarities between the brains of humans and those of other animals, he suggests that at least some creatures have true feelings. "Imagine where we'd be in physics if we hadn't guessed what's inside the atom," says Panksepp. "Most of what goes on in nature is invisible, yet we don't deny that it exists." The new case for animal emotions comes in part from the growing acceptability of field observations. The latest contribution to this body of knowledge is a book, *The Smile of a Dolphin*, which presents personal reports from more than

50 researchers who have spent their careers studying animals — from cats, dogs, bears and chimpanzees to birds, iguanas, and fish. Edited by Bekoff, the volume already has caught scientific attention.

One of the most obvious animal emotions is (4a). Anyone who has ever been greeted by a bounding, barking, tail-wagging dog knows that animals often appear to be happy. Beastly joy seems particularly apparent when the animals are playing with one another or sometimes, in the case of pets, with people.

(4b) also seems to be common in the wild, particularly following the death of a mate, parent, offspring, or even close companion. When a goose, which mates for life, loses its partner, the bird's head and body droop disappointedly. Jane Goodall, who has studied chimpanzees in Tanzania for four decades, saw a young chimpanzee starve after his mother died. Goodall maintains that the animal died of grief.

There is hard scientific evidence for animal feelings as well. Scientists who study the biology of emotions, a field still in its infancy, are discovering many similarities between the brains of humans and those of other animals. $_{(5)}$<u>In animals studied so far, including humans, emotions seem to arise from ancient parts of the brain, regions that have been saved across many species throughout evolution.</u>

The most important emotional site identified so far is the *amygdala, an almond-shaped structure in the center of the brain. Working with rats, neuroscientists have discovered that stimulating a certain part of the amygdala induces a state of intense fear. In humans, brain-imaging studies show that when people experience fear, their amygdalas, too, are made active. And just like the rats, people whose amygdalas are damaged by accident or disease seem unable to be afraid when $_{(6)}$<u>the situation warrants it</u>. In humans and rats, at least, amygdalas are "basically wired the same way," says neuroscientist Joseph LeDoux. He adds that, beyond (4c), the evidence is less clear, but the amygdala has a connection with other emotions as well.

The case for animal emotions is also supported by recent studies of brain chemistry. Steven Siviy has found that when rats play, their brains release large amounts of *dopamine, a chemical that is associated with pleasure and excitement in humans.

Doubtful scientists remain unconvinced. "A whale may behave as if it's in love, but you can't prove what it's feeling, if anything," says LeDoux. He maintains

3

that the question of feelings boils down to whether or not animals are conscious. And though animals "may have snapshots of self-awareness," he says, "the movie we call consciousness is not there."

The most convincing argument, perhaps, comes from the theory of evolution, widely accepted by biologists of all types. Citing similarities in the brain structure and chemistry of humans and other animals, neuroscientist Siviy asks: "If you believe in evolution by natural selection, how can you believe that feelings suddenly appeared, out of the blue, with human beings?" Goodall says it is illogical for scientists to use animals to study the human brain and then deny that animals have feelings.

In the end, what difference does it really make? According to many scientists, resolving the debate over animal emotions could turn out to be much more than an intellectual exercise. ₍₇₎If animals do indeed experience a wide range of feelings, it has profound implications for how humans and animals interact in the future. Bekoff hopes that greater understanding of what animals are feeling will spur more strict rules on how animals should be treated, everywhere from zoos and circuses to farms and backyards.

(注)　intangible：触れることができない　　neuroscientist：神経科学者　　amygdala：扁桃体
dopamine：ドーパミン（脳内の神経伝達物質）

（同志社大）

問1　下線部(1)に関して，最も説得力があると考えられる論拠を90字以内の日本語で述べなさい。

問2　下線部(2)を日本語に訳しなさい。

問3　下線部(3)とほぼ同じ意味を表すものを，次のア〜エから1つ選びなさい。

　　ア．animals modify their feelings as much as humans do

　　イ．animals hide their feelings as effectively as humans do

　　ウ．animals control their feelings more easily than humans do

　　エ．animals express their feelings more directly than humans do

問4　空所（　4a　）（　4b　）（　4c　）に入れるのに最も適当な組み合わせを，次のア〜カから1つ選びなさい。ただし，文頭にくるべき語も小文字で始められている。

ア．despair — fear — anger　　　　イ．pleasure — grief — fear

ウ．anger — fear — pleasure　　　　エ．despair — anger — grief

オ．pleasure — despair — fear　　　カ．anger — grief — despair

問5　下線部(5)を日本語に訳しなさい。

問6　下線部(6)とほぼ同じ意味を表すものを，次のア〜エから1つ選びなさい。

ア．the damage is serious enough

イ．the neuroscientists cannot analyze the situation

ウ．feelings of fear are appropriate

エ．the people reveal feelings of pleasure

問7　下線部(7)を日本語に訳しなさい。

2

次の英文を読んで，設問に答えなさい。

Globalization is often seen as global Westernization. On this point, there is substantial agreement among many proponents and opponents. Those who take an upbeat view of globalization see it as a marvelous contribution of Western civilization to the world. There is a nicely stylized history in which the great developments happened in Europe: First came the Renaissance, then *the Enlightenment and the Industrial Revolution, and these led to a massive increase in living standards in the West. And now the great achievements of the West are spreading to the world. In this view, globalization is not only good, it is also a gift from the West to the world. The champions of (1)this reading of history tend to feel upset not just because this great *benefaction is seen as a curse but also because it is undervalued and condemned by an ungrateful world.

From the opposite perspective, Western dominance — sometimes seen as a continuation of Western imperialism — is (2)the devil of the piece. In this view, contemporary capitalism, driven and led by greedy Western countries in Europe and North America, has established rules of trade and business relations that do not serve the interests of the poorer people in the world. The celebration of various non-Western identities — defined by religion (as in Islamic fundamentalism), region (as in the championing of Asian values), or culture (as in the glorification of *Confucian ethics) — can add fuel to fire of confrontation with the West.

Is globalization really a new Western curse? It is, in fact, (3). Over thousands of years, globalization has contributed to the progress of the world through travel, trade, migration, spread of cultural influences, and diffusion of knowledge and understanding (including that of science and technology). These global interrelations have often been very productive in the advancement of different countries. They have not necessarily taken the form of increased Western influence. Indeed, the active agents of globalization have often been located far from the West.

To illustrate, consider the world at the beginning of the last millennium rather than at its end. Around 1000 A.D., the global reach of science, technology, and mathematics was changing the nature of the old world, but the diffusion then was, to a great extent, (4)[of / in / we / what / see / direction / today / the opposite]. The high technology in the world of 1000 A.D. included paper, the printing press, the *crossbow, gunpowder, the iron-chain suspension bridge, the kite, the magnetic compass, the *wheelbarrow, and the rotary fan. A millennium ago, these items were used extensively in China — and were practically unknown elsewhere. Globalization spread them across the world, including Europe.

(5)Indeed, Europe would have been a lot poorer — economically, culturally, and scientifically — had it resisted the globalization of mathematics, science, and technology at that time. And today, the same principle applies, though in the reverse direction (from West to East). To reject the globalization of science and technology because it represents Western influence and imperialism would not only amount to overlooking global contributions — drawn from many different parts of the world — that lie solidly behind so-called Western science and technology, but would also be quite a silly practical decision, given the extent to which the whole world can benefit from the process.

The misdiagnosis that globalization of ideas and practices has to be resisted because it entails dreaded Westernization has played quite a *regressive part in the colonial and postcolonial world. This assumption encourages *parochial tendencies and undermines the possibility of objectivity in science and knowledge. It is not only counterproductive in itself; given the global interactions throughout history, (6)it can also cause non-Western societies to shoot themselves in the foot — even in their precious cultural foot.

To see globalization as merely Western imperialism of ideas and beliefs would be a serious and costly error, in the same way that any European resistance to Eastern influence would have been at the beginning of the last millennium. Of course, there are issues related to globalization that do connect with imperialism (the history of conquests, colonialism, and alien rule remains relevant today in many ways), and a postcolonial understanding of the world has its merits. But it would be a great mistake to see globalization primarily as a feature of imperialism. (7)It is much bigger — much greater — than that.

(8)The issue of the distribution of economic gains and losses from globalization remains an entirely separate question, and it must be addressed as a further — and extremely relevant — issue. There is extensive evidence that the global economy has brought prosperity to many different areas of the globe. Pervasive poverty dominated the world a few centuries ago; there were only a few rare pockets of affluence. In overcoming that poverty, extensive economic interrelations and modern technology have been and remain influential. What has happened in Europe, America, Japan, and East Asia has important messages for all other regions, and we cannot go very far into understanding the nature of globalization today without first acknowledging the positive fruits of global economic contacts.

Indeed, we cannot reverse the economic *predicament of the poor across the world by withholding from them the great advantages of contemporary technology, the well-established efficiency of international trade and exchange, and the social as well as economic merits of living in an open society. Rather, the main issue is how to make good use of the remarkable benefits of economic intercourse and technological progress in a way that pays adequate attention to the interests of the deprived and the weak. That is, I would argue, the constructive question that emerges from the so-called antiglobalization movements.

(注) the Enlightenment：啓蒙運動(18世紀ヨーロッパに起こった理性主義的思想に基づく運動)
benefaction：施し物　　Confucian：儒教の　　crossbow：石弓　　wheelbarrow：手押し車
regressive：後退的な　　parochial：偏狭な　　predicament：逆境

(Amartya Sen, How to Judge Globalism, *The American Prospect*, January 5, 2002)

（金沢大）

問1　下線部(1)の内容を80字以内の日本語で述べなさい。
問2　下線部(2)の意味として最も適当なものを，次のア～エから1つ選びなさい。
　　ア．generated by an evil force
　　イ．regarded as a defeat of the East
　　ウ．the cause of all the trouble
　　エ．an urgent issue at present
問3　空所(　3　)に入れるのに最も適当なものを，次のア～エから1つ選びなさい。
　　ア．both new and often Western; but it is not a curse
　　イ．neither new nor necessarily Western; but it is a blessing
　　ウ．both new and often Western; and it is a blessing
　　エ．neither new nor necessarily Western; and it is not a curse

問4　下線部(4)の語(句)を文意が通るように並べ換えなさい。

問5　下線部(5)を日本語に訳しなさい。

問6　下線部(6)の内容を50字以内の日本語で述べなさい。

問7　下線部(7)を It と that の内容を明らかにして日本語に訳しなさい。

問8　下線部(8)に関して，筆者は何が主要な問題であると考えているか。本文に即して70字以内の日本語で述べなさい。

次の英文を読んで，設問に答えなさい。

If you grow up under one particular system or culture, it is actually very difficult to imagine what life might really have been like before it, or is like outside it. It is almost impossible for urban teenagers, for example, to imagine life before the car or the telephone (or before the cell phone for that matter). In the same way it is hard for citizens of the Western world to get an accurate impression of what life was like before the era of scientific medicine.

Yet (1)[is / however / it / to / healing in past eras / difficult / visualize], if we could go back a century or two we would see that what we now call conventional medicine was not always the established (and conventional) school. Furthermore, what we now call *alternative medicine was not the alternative to it. In the fairly recent past, the two schools were virtually indistinguishable.

Looking at today's conventional doctors equipped with their white coats, diplomas and, stethoscopes, and comparing them and their *appurtenances with the wide range of dress, fashion, thought, speech and techniques employed by complementary *practitioners it is hard for us now to imagine that the two schools ever had anything in common. But (2)they did. In fact it's conventional medicine that is the recent upstart, the brash new kid on the block.

What we now call conventional medicine has only recently graduated as a scientific (or partly scientific) discipline embracing a central corps of accepted philosophy, rules and regulations. Before that comparatively recent era, the ancestors of our modern conventional doctors were an ill-assorted group, comprising a few scientists, a few skillful and observant bedside physicians, and a larger collection of hopefuls, fakes and frauds, all of whom can trace their ancestry back beyond alchemists, herbalists, priests, and nuns, to tribal shamans and magicians.

Painful though it is for patients and healers to admit, the true origins of healing go back further than a few centuries of clever clinicians and experiential herbalists. The true pre-history of medicine is (3).

The earliest origins of human healing activities pre-date any form of man-made recorded history, so that most of what follows is necessarily conjecture (a polite word for guesswork). However, healing seems to be mentioned in the very earliest known physical records of mankind's activities — so some form of it must have been in existence by the time (4).

In the earliest days of human society, the local Wise Man was probably the one who had the answers to everything. He (or sometimes she) was the one who had the answers to the birth of the universe, the origins of mankind, the purpose of life and the remedy for disease. All these activities would almost certainly have been linked by a theory or legend unifying the forces of life, the purposes of the gods and nature, and the place of human beings in the universe. (5)There would have been, presumably, a sense of continuity between mankind and the other inhabitants of the planet, and a sense of overall satisfaction with the way the universe operated.

When things seemed to go wrong — such as storms, *predation by vicious animals or occasional infections — the Wise Man would offer some explanations and some *incantation or specific action to remedy the problem. If the problem was self-limiting (such as a solar eclipse), then the action (such as the South Sea Islanders' custom of banging drums and blowing trumpets to make the moon *disgorge the sun) would be seen to be effective and would be repeated each time the problem arose.

Precisely what the Wise Man said, we shall never know. But what the Wise Man did, we can guess at. He bashed holes in his patients' skulls. *Trephining (the technical term for the therapeutic ventilation of a fellow human's skull) is offered by archaeologists as evidence of the earliest medical intervention. Skulls as old as 10,000 years have been found with unambiguous evidence that they have been trephined.

The Incas of Peru were masters of the art of trephining, but (6)the idea seems to have occurred to many different societies, with little likelihood of them learning from each other. If we are looking for evidence of the first doctor-patient relationship, this seems to be what we are seeking. And, like most doctor-patient relationships since, it caused greater pain to the patient than to the doctor.

The holes in the skulls are neat and accurate, and there is usually fresh growth of bone around them, suggesting first, that someone other than the owner of the skull did the trephining, and the second, that the patient survived. So what was the purpose of the surgery? There are some clues. The holes are usually found near a preexisting crack in the skull, indicating an attempt to relieve the effect of a fracture.

Presumably the trephiner must have had some special skills — or at least a lack of *squeamishness — and his professional qualifications would probably have been inferred by potential patients from the survival of a few of his earlier clients. One skull in Sardinia dating from about 1400 BC shows that its late owner had had three operations before *succumbing to a fourth.

Here, then, is the first evidence of treatment for headache, perhaps pre-dating the discovery of aspirin (originally extracted from willow-bark) by five millennia or more. Whether or not the pre-historic healers ever said, 'Make two holes in his head and call me in the morning' we shall never know, but at least we are certain that, at the dawn of mankind's social organization, somebody seemed to be trying to do something to (7) somebody else.

(注)　alternative medicine：代替医学(西洋医学に対して鍼療法などをいう)

　　　appurtenance：道具　　practitioner：医者　　predation：捕食　　incantation：呪文

　　　disgorge：吐き出す　　trephining〈trephine：頭蓋骨に穴を開けて治療する

　　　squeamishness：気の弱さ　　succumb：死ぬ

(Reproduced from *MAGIC OR MEDICINE* by Robert Buckman, published by Prometheus. Copyright © 1995 Robert Buckman and Karl Sabbagh, reproduced by arrangement with Globe Pequot.)

(慶應義塾大)

問1　下線部(1)の語(句)を文意が通るように並べ換えなさい。

問2　下線部(2)の内容を60字以内の日本語で述べなさい。

問3　空所(3)に入れるのに最も適当なものを，次のア～エから1つ選びなさい。

　　ア．art　　　　　　イ．magic　　　　　ウ．inspiration　　　エ．nature

問4　空所(4)に入れるのに最も適当なものを，次のア～エから1つ選びなさい。

　　ア．oral tradition began to die out

　　イ．human beings started to cultivate a wide variety of crops

　　ウ．man began to evolve symbolic language

　　エ．the field of medicine was established

問5　下線部(5)を日本語に訳しなさい。

問6　下線部(6)を the idea の内容を明らかにして日本語に訳しなさい。

問7　空所(　7　)に入れるのに最も適当なものを，次のア〜エから１つ選びなさい。

　　ア．console　　　　イ．injure　　　　ウ．heal　　　　エ．frighten

問8　the Wise Man とはどのような人で，何をしたのか。本文に即して100字以内の日本語で述べなさい。

次の英文を読んで，設問に答えなさい。

Languages have played a crucial role in human communities for hundreds of thousands of years, and naturally the typical language community has changed in that time. The presumption is that before the discovery and expansion of agriculture, human communities were small bands, just as the remaining groupings of hunter-gatherers are to this day. These groups all have languages, and ancient lore and stories which the old retail to the young. The density of the human population, wherever people were living, would have been far less than it is today.

From the language point of view, the present population of the world is not eight billion, but something over six thousand. There are between six and seven thousand communities in the world today identified by the first language that they speak. They are not of equal weight. They range in size from Mandarin Chinese with some 1.1 billion speakers, alone accounting for more than one eighth of all the people in the world, followed by English and Spanish with approximately 300 million apiece, to a long tail of tiny communities: over half the languages in the world, for example, have fewer than five thousand speakers, and over a thousand languages have under a dozen. This is a dangerous time for languages.

In considering human history, the language community is a very natural unit. Languages, by their nature as means of communication, divide humanity into groups: only through a common (1)[in / group / people / can / act / a / concert / of / language], and therefore have a common history. Moreover, language that a group shares is precisely the medium in which memories of their joint history can be shared. Languages make possible both the living of a common history and also the telling of it.

And every language possesses another feature that makes it the readiest medium for preserving a group's history — every language is learnt by the young from the old, so that every living language is the embodiment of a tradition. That tradition is in principle immortal. (2)Languages change, as they pass from the lips of one generation to the next, but there is nothing about this process of transmission which makes for decay or extinction. Like life itself, each new generation can receive the gift of its language afresh. And so it is that languages, unlike any of the people who speak them, need never grow weak, or die.

Every language has a chance of immortality, but this is not to say that it will survive forever. Genes too, and the species they encode, are immortal; but extinctions are a commonplace of paleontology. Likewise, the actual lifespans of language communities vary enormously. The annals of language history are full of languages that have died out, traditions that have come to an end, leaving no speakers at all.

The language point of view on history can be contrasted with the genetic approach to human history, which is currently revolutionizing our view of our distant past. Like membership in a biological species and a matrilineal lineage, membership in a language community is based on (3)<u>a clear relation</u>. An individual is a member of a species if it can have offspring with other members of the species, and of a matrilineal lineage if its mother is in that lineage. Likewise, at the most basic level, you are a member of a language community if you can use its language.

The advantage of (4)<u>this linguistically defined unit</u> is that it necessarily defines a community that is important to us as human beings. The species unit is interesting, in defining our prehistoric relations with related groups such as *Homo erectus* and the Neanderthals, but after the rise of *Homo sapiens* its usefulness yields to the evident fact that, species-wise, we are all in this together. The lineage unit too has its points, clearly marked down the ages as it is by mitochondrial DNA and Y-chromosomes, and can yield interesting evidence on the origin of populations if some lineage clearly present today in the population is missing in one of the candidate groups put forward as ancestors. So it has been inferred that Polynesians could not have come from South America, that most of the European population have parentage away from the Near Eastern sources of agriculture, and that the ancestry of most of the population of the English Midlands is from Friesland. (5)<u>But knowing that many people's mothers, or fathers, are unaccounted for does not put a bound on a group as a whole in the way that language does.</u>

Contrast a unit such as a race. Its boundaries are defined by nothing more than a chosen set of properties, whether by superficial resemblances such as skin color or skull proportions, or by sequences of DNA. Likewise, there are insurmountable problems in defining its cultural analogue, the nation, which entail the further *imponderables of a consciousness of shared history, and perhaps shared language too. Given that so many of the properties get shuffled on to different individuals in different generations, it remains doubtful as to what to make of any set of characteristics for a race or a nation. But use of a given language is an undeniable functioning reality everywhere; (6)<u>above all, it is characteristic of every human group known and persistent over generations.</u> It provides a universal key for dividing human history into meaningful groups.

Admittedly, a language community is a more scattered and variable unit than a species or a lineage: a language changes much faster than a DNA sequence, and one cannot even be sure that it will always be transmitted from one generation to the next. Language communities are not always easy to count, or to distinguish reliably. But they are undeniably real features of the human condition.

(注) imponderables：はっきりと評価できないもの

(Reprinted by permission of HarperCollins Publishers Ltd. © 2005 Nicholas Ostler)

（東工大）

問 1　下線部(1)の語を文意が通るように並べ換えなさい。

問 2　下線部(2)を日本語に訳しなさい。

問 3　下線部(3)に関して，clear と言えるのはなぜか，40字以内の日本語で述べなさい。

問 4　下線部(4)の短所は何か，100字以内の日本語で述べなさい。

問 5　下線部(5)とほぼ同じ内容を表すものを，次のア～エから1つ選びなさい。

 ア．But the lineage unit is more helpful in distinguishing populations than the language unit is.

 イ．But the lineage unit is no more helpful in distinguishing populations than the language unit is.

 ウ．But the lineage unit is not so helpful in distinguishing populations as the language unit is.

 エ．But the lineage unit is as helpful in distinguishing populations as the language unit is.

問6　下線部(6)を it の内容を明らかにして，日本語に訳しなさい。

問7　本文の内容と一致するものを，次のア～エから1つ選びなさい。

　ア．Quite a few languages are spoken by fewer than twelve people.

　イ．A language may be considered immortal if it has a writing system.

　ウ．The species unit, the lineage unit, and the linguistic unit are crucial concepts in the study of language.

　エ．Rapid genetic mutations make it hard to trace a group's biological history accurately.

次の英文を読んで，設問に答えなさい。

Nobody designs truly great cities. They just spring up. As if by magic, they develop distinct districts that endure from century to century. Think of the silk quarter in Florence, or Savile Row in London. A city seems to *pulsate with its own rhythm, as if it is a living, breathing organism.

Steven Johnson would argue that, in some senses, (1)it is. He would say that the superorganism of the city mirrors the superorganism of the ant colony, in which a collection of individually stupid insects somehow becomes a fascinating, organized whole. Both are examples of emergence, a phenomenon where the whole is much greater than the sum of its parts. Another commonly given example of emergence is consciousness, which appears to arise spontaneously from the fact that billions of nerve cells (neurons) in the brain are firing off signals to each other.

In a new book, called *Emergence*, Johnson, an American author best known for arguing that computer graphics are as culturally important as books or films, aims to *coax the topic out of science laboratories and into the mainstream. Just as chaos was a scientific buzzword of the past century, Johnson hopes that emergence will enter the *lexicon of this century.

So many things in life look different when viewed through the lens of emergence, Johnson, 32, explains. Cities can be thought of as complex, self-organizing phenomena. Take New York City, where I live. There is a tendency to think of social systems as top-down, as driven by leaders. But what has happened here in the wake of the *awful attack is the opposite. The city has come back to life thanks largely to mass interactions by ordinary people, not because they were told by the mayor.

(2)Ant colonies are remarkably similar to cities. When watching thousands of ants marching to and from a nest, laden with food, it is easy to believe that there must be a choreographer, a leader ant who can see the bigger picture and direct the colony to act in a particular way. But scientists know better: contrary to popular belief, the queen ant does not command the colony.

They attribute ant behavior to something unclear called *swarm logic. Put 10,000 dumb ants together, and they become smart. They will calculate the shortest routes to food supplies. In fact, scientists studying the traveling salesman *conundrum of how to visit a large number of cities using the shortest routes, have studied how ants do it. (3)Get rid of one food source, and the colony will soon turn its attention to another. Ant colonies give the illusion of being intelligent, even though individual ants lack advanced brains. How do they do it? Worker ants don't communicate with each other much. They have a vocabulary of up to 20 signs, most mediated by pheromones. But ants do follow a few simple rules. They are good at sniffing out pheromone signals from other ants, which contain clues about how far away food is. By adapting their behavior to these clues, ants learn the shortest route to food. From the isolated, small-scale activities of individual ants, a global behavior jumps out.

Similarly, a few simple rules can turn an urban settlement into a thriving neighborhood. For example, cities grow because of low-level interactions of people on the street. There's a flow of information between strangers, he says. You go down a street, see a store that you never knew was there. You go in, do business, and perhaps tell your friends about it. They go there, more stores open and suddenly there's this new area that's full of funky clothes stores. That kind of vitality is more likely to be found in maze-like cities with lots of streets and lots of routes from A to B. If a city is dominated by a few large avenues, the back streets tend to be (4).

Johnson explains: Near Times Square, every block has a bar, a restaurant and a boutique. The streets are filled at all times of the day, and they're never too crowded. Go down a broad avenue and take a turn, and the streets feel totally different. They are (4).

(5)This local information flow is the lifeblood of cities. Which is why urban planners who destroy neighborhoods and replace them with tower blocks often turn districts into no-go areas without realizing what they have done.

Johnson can see that there is something unsatisfactory about saying that stupid ants can build apparently intelligent colonies. Where's the crucial step? What's the missing piece of the puzzle that turns low-level actions into high-level order? But he insists that there's no hole in the explanation. Just as its name suggests, emergent phenomena simply emerge.

Our collection of brain cells give rise to something quite magnificent and so far inexplicable self-awareness. Is it possible that the digital networks we are creating, such as the Web, may cease to be our microprocessing servants and acquire some kind of macro-intelligence? Johnson (6) this, saying that while the Web shows connectedness, it is utterly disorganized. If the Web were a city and each document a building, he says, it would be more *anarchic than any real-world city on the planet, and therefore no higher level of complexity can emerge. However, if the Web had been built in a different way, perhaps something greater than the sum of its parts would emerge.

Not that we would necessarily recognize it. (7)Machines may evolve a higher intelligence rather than having it engineered, but that doesn't mean it would look like human intelligence, he warns. It wouldn't be a robot that acted like a little boy, but a machine so smart that we wouldn't recognize it. It would be like the film *The Matrix*, where there were no *paranoid androids but a bizarre faceless regime. Now that's scary.

(注) pulsate：鼓動する　　coax：を引き出す，導く　　lexicon：語彙

awful attack：2001年9月にニューヨークで起きた同時多発テロのこと

swarm logic：群れの論理　　conundrum：難問　　anarchic：無秩序の

paranoid：偏執狂の

（東京外国語大）

問1　下線部(1)の内容を具体的に30字以内の日本語で述べなさい。

問2　下線部(2)に関して，どのような点でそう言えるのか，本文に即して50字以内の日本語で述べなさい。

問3　下線部(3)のように言えるのはなぜか，本文に即して70字以内の日本語で述べなさい。

問4　空所(4)に共通して入る最も適当なものを，次のア～エから1つ選びなさい。

　　　ア．busy　　　　　イ．crowded　　　　ウ．lively　　　　エ．deserted

問5　下線部(5)とほぼ同じ内容を表すものを，次のア～エから1つ選びなさい。

　　　ア．more detailed information about local economy

　　　イ．reliable sources of information about new stores

　　　ウ．the exchange of information among the public

　　　エ．useful information obtained on the Internet

問6　空所(　6　)に入れるのに最も適当なものを，次のア〜エから1つ選びなさい。

　　　ア．appreciates　　　イ．dismisses　　　ウ．proves　　　エ．unites

問7　下線部(7)を日本語に訳しなさい。

次の英文を読んで，設問に答えなさい。

Immigration controls are a relatively recent policy which became common only in the twentieth century. Although immigration laws may seem like common sense, an unavoidable reality, in most countries they are in fact less than 100 years old.

International migration, on the other hand, has always existed. (1)Twice as many people migrated from Europe to the rest of the world as have come in the opposite direction. And since the current theory is that human beings originated in East Africa, every other part of the world is the product of immigration. All of us are either immigrants or descended from immigrants.

Freedom of movement should be the new common sense. It is hard to see why people should *not* be allowed to move around the world in search of work or safety or both.

Within the European Union there are growing attempts to secure the principle of freedom for its citizens to live and work in any member country. In the U.S. there are no restrictions on the movement of people between states. It would be considered an *outrage if the inhabitants of a country were not free to travel to another part of that country to get a job there, or if they were not allowed to leave it. Indeed, it was considered an outrage when (2)this happened in the former U.S.S.R.

The 1948 *Universal Declaration of Human Rights asserts these rights. Yet the Declaration is strangely (3) on the question of the right to enter another country. Governments cling to what seems to be one of their last remaining rights: the right to keep people out of their territories. Few people question the morality, legality, or practicality of this right.

Nation-states are the agents and enforcers of immigration controls and country boundaries. Most were themselves not fully established until the nineteenth century. Now nation-states are supposed to be on the decline. International institutions such as the United Nations, *the International Monetary Fund, the World Bank, and the World Trade Organization attempt to control the actions of national governments. Economic power is concentrated in fewer and bigger corporations. These put pressure on governments to allow goods and capital to move freely around the world, unaffected by considerations of national sovereignty. (4)Sometimes they also press governments to allow the free movement of people, in order to secure the labour they need for expansion. Yet by the 1970s many countries, especially in Europe but not in North America, had more or less ended the right of people to enter and work.

Even if it were morally acceptable for the rich nations of the world to use immigration controls to preserve their disproportionate wealth, it is doubtful whether they achieve this purpose. There is a mass of evidence to show that immigrants actually make a big contribution to the wealth and prosperity of the countries they go to. Economists have also suggested that the abolition of immigration controls would cause a doubling of world incomes.

Immigration is not just good for business. It also improves both the job prospects and the wages and conditions of workers. (5)Without immigration, some sectors of industry would collapse or move abroad, which would result in the loss of many other jobs connected to those industries. The U.S. economy, especially its agriculture, building trades, and services, is heavily dependent on immigrants, including those who have no legal permission to work.

Many industrialized countries — especially in Europe — have declining and ageing populations. Unless immigration is increased, there will not be enough young workers to pay taxes, keep the public sector and industry functioning, and look after old people. It has also been shown that on average immigrants contribute more in taxes than they receive in public services.

Those who defend immigration controls often refer to the need to 'preserve national identity'. National identity is hard to define, however. More or less every country in the world is the product of successive waves of immigration. While immigrants sometimes acquire the negative image of being unable to assimilate, prone to disease and crime, and so on, most of the migrants and refugees who make it to the rich countries are in fact exceptional people who have to have some money and a great deal of courage and enterprise. They come because there are jobs, or because they are in desperate danger.

A precedent for the opening of borders exists in the European Union. Those who worked for the abolition of European internal frontiers were inspired not only by the interests of big business and free trade, but by an idealistic view of the future of Europe. Contrary to (6)predictions, the introduction of free internal movement within Europe did not lead to mass migration from poor areas to richer areas; on the contrary the authorities would like to have more rather than less labour mobility in the European Union.

The ability of governments to enforce immigration controls is becoming increasingly unsustainable. The costs and suffering caused by these controls are increasing. (7)Clearly it would not make much sense to campaign for immigration controls to be ended only in one country. Their abolition would need to be by agreement among the governments of the world.

Abolition of borders implies complete freedom of movement for all, and the right to settle and work in a place of the person's choice, just as people can now do within countries. In a more just world order, movements of capital would be democratically controlled to meet people's needs and to reduce inequalities. But people are not goods or capital — and they should be free to move. The attempt to limit this basic freedom leads to some of the worst abuses of human rights which exist in the world today. (8)The abolition of immigration controls would mean a vast increase in freedom and prosperity for all of us.

(注)　outrage：人権侵害　　Universal Declaration of Human Rights：世界人権宣言
　　　the International Monetary Fund：国際通貨基金

(Reprinted by kind permission of New Internationalist. Copyright New Internationalist. www. newint.org)

（青山学院大）

問1　下線部(1)を the opposite direction の内容を明らかにして日本語に訳しなさい。

問2　下線部(2)の内容を50字以内の日本語で述べなさい。

問3　空所(　3　)に入れるのに最も適当なものを，次のア～エから1つ選びなさい。

　　　ア．acceptable　　　イ．affirmative　　　ウ．decisive　　　エ．silent

問4　下線部(4)を they の内容を明らかにして日本語に訳しなさい。

問5　下線部(5)を日本語に訳しなさい。

問6　下線部(6)の内容を60字以内の日本語で述べなさい。

問7　下線部(7)を日本語に訳しなさい。

問8　下線部(8)の理由を，本文に即して170字以内の日本語で述べなさい。

次の英文を読んで，設問に答えなさい。

If a young man committed a serious crime in ancient China his parents were liable to be executed with him, on the grounds that they were also to blame. This logic is reappearing in contemporary social policy: parents are responsible for shaping their children's behaviour; the crime rate among young people is rising; parents must be doing something wrong. If a few were made an example of, the rest might mend their ways and bring up their children properly. But do even the best of parents have that much control?

More and more psychological researchers seem to be suggesting one unexpected theory: (1) parents do not have nearly as much influence over their children as we both hope and fear they have. A decade of research by the geneticist Robert Plomin and others suggest that about half of our adult personality is the result of our genes. Surprisingly, many parents' actions, which you would imagine must make a difference, apparently do not.

For example, eating: what could be more obvious than the idea that children whose parents both overeat will grow up to do the same? (2) But this is not the case. Adopted children, who do not share the overeating parents' genes, do not copy their behaviour. The same applies to watching television. Adopted children in a household which watches a lot of television will *not* sit glued to the box, unless watching television is something their biological parents also like to do. Even attitudes to, say, the death penalty or jazz, apparently prime candidates for parental influence, turn out to have a strong genetic component.

(3) Public debates about the effect on children of physical punishment, divorce or violence on television, scarcely mention a fact which every parent of more than one child knows — that different children respond differently to the same broad influences. This is because developmental psychology has resolutely ignored genetics for the past 50 years.

There are many reasons why the genetic element in the study of personality has been unpopular — from liberal commitment to equal opportunity based on merit, to the shadow of *Nazi eugenics. Most educators and social commentators have placed responsibility for a child's development on his or her environment, especially on the parents. Mountains of books and articles describe how authoritarian and over-protective parents can make a child timid, while a more tolerant approach produces anxious children.

Such views, however, now seem rather old-fashioned as genetic influence becomes more accepted among doctors. Until the 1970s, for instance, *psychoanalysts claimed that *autistic children were the result of mothers who were so emotionally distant that their children never learned to form close relationships. Now *autism is generally accepted to have a strong genetic basis. Similarly, hardly anyone now believes that the reason why some children have speech problems is that their parents failed to talk to them enough. The development of language is acknowledged to have a large genetic component. $_{(4)}$It is also not very useful to report that children of parents who have bad eating habits or suffer from depression tend to do the same, because when the genetic element is removed, as in adoption studies, the link usually disappears.

Genes, however, are not the only deciding factor; they rather provide the raw material which a child's environment then forms into different finished material. What is it, then, that shapes the child's environment if it is not the parents? Recently, a new attempt to answer this question has been made by the American psychologist Judith Harris. In the journal *Psychological Review*, she suggests that adult character is not shaped by a family drama played out between ourselves and our parents, but by how we get along with other children in the neighborhood.

Combining evidence from areas of psychological research not usually considered in child development debates, Harris makes a powerful case for $_{(5)}$group socialisation (GS) theory. She starts from the fact that we learn a particular behaviour in a specific context. The home is just one of several environments in which children have to learn how to behave, and although you can affect children's behaviour in the way they behave at home, this is not necessarily the case in other situations. "This makes evolutionary sense," says Harris. "The parental home is not where children are likely to spend their future. They are already genetically similar to their parents. Adopting all their habits as well would give them (6) flexibility for adapting to changing conditions in the outside world."

Humans are social animals. Over millions of years of evolution we have developed mechanisms for getting on with others in the group, as well as competing for status and mates. Those who subscribe to nurture theory concentrate on relationships between two people, typically mother and baby. But learning how to behave with one person does not tell you much about how to behave with someone else quite different — your father, for instance. Far more powerful in shaping behaviour, according to GS theory, is the effect of the group.

Take gender roles. From the nurture viewpoint, gender roles are a key area where parents have an influence — the distant father, the critical mother and a variety of other parenting styles can, it is claimed, significantly affect the development of a child's sexual identity. But evidence to the contrary is strong.

John Archer of the University of Central Lancashire has been studying how gender differences develop. "We have now had about 20 years of a serious attempt by a generation of parents to raise boys and girls in much the same way," he says. "Yet, as every school and every parent knows, boys and girls automatically split themselves into single sex groups from an early age." Once in these groups, they develop quite distinct patterns of behaviour. (7)It is these, rather than their parents', which children pick up. Gender roles seem to be under the control of the group.

Children do share their parents' beliefs — not because of the parents' careful upbringing, but because of the way that the parents' group affects the children's group. You can see the effect clearly when the parents of a child do *not* share the values of the parents of the rest of the children in the group. This often occurs with immigrants: GS theory predicts that the children will follow the values of the group, not those of the parents.

There is nothing new in the idea that peer pressure influences children. What is original about GS theory is its claim that the long-term influence of the group is much greater than that of the home and that it starts much earlier than has generally been acknowledged. GS theory does not deny that the way parents behave towards their kids affects the way they behave at home. But learned behaviour is tied to the situation it was learned in. The fact that your kids complain and quarrel at home does not mean that they will do so in the playground: the standards of acceptable behaviour, as well as the punishments and rewards, are quite different. Parents are often surprised when they talk to their child's teacher: "Is she talking about my child?"

These findings could lead to a less anxious approach to childraising and a greater appreciation of the role played by schools and seem to suggest that blaming individual parents is (　8　).

(注)　Nazi eugenics：ナチズムの優生学　　psychoanalyst：精神分析学者

autistic：自閉症の　　autism：自閉症

(Jerome Burne, The Roots of Personality, Prospect)

（東京医科歯科大）

問1　下線部(1)の理由を，本文に即して60字以内の日本語で述べなさい。

問2　下線部(2)を this の内容を明らかにして日本語に訳しなさい。

問3　下線部(3)を日本語に訳しなさい。

問4　下線部(4)を日本語に訳しなさい。

問5　下線部(5)の独創的な点を，本文に即して70字以内の日本語で述べなさい。

問6　空所(　6　)に入れるのに最も適当なものを，次のア～エから1つ選びなさい。

　　ア．far more　　　イ．much less　　　ウ．the same　　　エ．all the more

問7　下線部(7)を these の内容を明らかにして日本語に訳しなさい。

問8　空所(　8　)に入れるのに最も適当なものを，次のア～エから1つ選びなさい。

　　ア．avoided in the media　　　イ．appropriate social policy

　　ウ．grounded on facts　　　　　エ．a waste of time

次の英文を読んで，設問に答えなさい。

Humans had been counting things for many thousands of years before the first number system was developed. Early counting was typically carried out by scratching _(1a)tally marks on a stick, stone, or bone. The oldest known example, consisting of twenty-nine distinct notches deliberately cut into the leg bone of a monkey, was discovered in the Lebombo Mountains of Eswatini and dated to approximately 35,000 B.C. It has been suggested that women used such notched bones to keep track of their monthly fertility cycles. Other examples of notched bones discovered in Africa and elsewhere may also have been early attempts to quantify time. The Ishango bone, found in 1960 near the headwaters of the Nile in north-eastern Congo and perhaps twenty thousand years old, bears a series of tally marks carved in three columns running the length of the bone. A common interpretation is that the Ishango bone served as a (　2　).

With tally marks, a vertical scratch or line is made to record each item in a collection: |, ||, |||, ||||, |||||, ||||||, and so on. However, tally marks become hard to read once you have more than four or five items to count. A common way to reduce the complexity is to group the tally marks in fives, often by drawing a diagonal line across each group. _(1b)The Roman numeral system, found throughout the Roman Empire and still used today in certain specialized functions, such as the numbering of the early pages of printed books, was a more sophisticated version of this simple idea involving a few additional symbols: V for five, X for ten, L for fifty, C for a hundred, and M for a thousand. For example, using this system, the number one thousand two hundred and seventy eight can be written as MCCLXXVIII (1,000 + 100 + 100 + 50 + 10 + 10 + 5 + 1 + 1 + 1 = 1,278).

Addition in the Roman system is fairly easy, since you simply group all like symbols. For example, to add MCCXXIII to MCXII you simply collect together all the M's, all the C's, all the X's, and all the I's, like this: MCCXXIII (1,223) + MCXII (1,112) = MMCCCXXXIIIII (2,335). Occasionally, you might have to convert one group of symbols to a higher symbol. In this example, the five I's could be replaced by V, to write the answer as (3). Subtraction, too, is relatively easy. But the only tolerable way to do multiplication and division is by repeated addition and repeated subtraction respectively. For example, V times MCLIII can be computed by adding the second number to itself four times. This method only works in practice when one of the two numbers being multiplied is small, of course.

The impracticality of the Roman system for doing multiplication or division meant it was inadequate for many important applications that arose in commerce and trade, such as currency conversion or determining a commission fee for a transaction. And there is no way Roman numerals could form the basis for any scientific or technical work. Societies that wrote numbers in Roman numerals had to use elaborate systems of finger arithmetic or mechanical devices like the counting board and the abacus to perform the actual calculations, using the numerals simply to record the answers. Although systems of finger arithmetic could manage calculations involving numbers up to 10,000, and it was possible to carry out a computation on an abacus almost as fast as a person today using a calculator, these required both (4) and mental skills of a high order. Moreover, since there was no record of the calculation, the answer had to be taken on trust.

The number system we use today — the Hindu-Arabic system — was developed in India. It seems to have been completed before 700 A.D., though it did not become generally known in Europe until at least five hundred years later. (5) Indian mathematicians made advances in what would today be described as arithmetic, algebra, and geometry, much of their work being motivated by an interest in astronomy. The system is based on three key ideas: simple symbols for the numerals, place value, and zero. The choice of ten basic number symbols — that is, the Hindus' choice of the base 10 for counting and doing arithmetic — is presumably a direct consequence of using fingers to count. When we reach ten on our fingers, we have to find some way of starting again, while retaining the calculation already made. The role played by finger counting in the development of early number systems would explain why we use the word "digit" for the basic numerals, deriving from the Latin word *digitus* for finger.

The introduction of zero was a decisive step in the development of Hindu arithmetic and came after the other numerals. The major advantage of the Hindu number system is that it is positional — the place of each numeral matters. This allows for addition, subtraction, multiplication, and even division using fairly straightforward and easily learned rules for manipulating symbols. But for an efficient place-value number system, you need to be able to show when a particular (6) has no entry. For example, without a zero symbol, the expression " 1 3 " could mean thirteen (13), or a hundred and three (103), or a hundred and thirty (130), or maybe a thousand and thirty (1,030). One can put spaces between the numerals to show that a particular column has no entry, but unless one is writing on a surface marked off into columns, one can never be sure whether a particular space indicates a zero entry or is merely the gap separating the symbols. Everything becomes much clearer when there is a special symbol to mark a space with no value.

The concept of zero took a long time to develop. The number symbols were viewed as numbers themselves — things you used to count the number of objects in a collection — but 0 would be the number of objects in a collection having no members, which makes no sense. Other societies were never able to make the zero breakthrough. For instance, long before the Indians developed their system, (7) the Babylonians had a positional number system, based on 60. Today, when we measure time, aspects of their system remain: 60 seconds equal one minute, and 60 minutes one hour. But the Babylonians did not have a symbol denoting zero, a limitation to their system they were never able to overcome.

The Hindus got to zero in two stages. First they overcame the problem of indicating empty spaces by drawing a circle around the space where there was a "missing" entry. This much the Babylonians had done. The circle gave rise to the present-day symbol 0 for zero. The second step was to regard that extra symbol just like the other nine. This meant developing the rules for doing arithmetic using this additional symbol along with all the others. This second step — changing the underlying concept so that the rules of arithmetic operated not on the numbers themselves (which excluded 0) but on symbols for numbers (which included 0) — was the key. Over time it led to a change in the idea of numbers to a more abstract one that includes 0.

The zero breakthrough was made by a brilliant mathematician called Brahmagupta, who was born in 598 A.D. in Bhinmal in northwest India, and went on to become the head of the astronomical observatory at Ujjain, then the foremost mathematical center of ancient India. As early as 628 A.D., when he was only thirty years old, Brahmagupta wrote a lengthy text in Sanskrit called *Brahmasphutasiddhanta*, which can be translated as "The Opening of the Universe." In that work, written entirely in verse, Brahmagupta introduced the number zero, (8)[as / defining / it / obtained / result / the / you / when] subtract a number from itself. At the same time, he worked out some basic properties that zero must have. These included the recognition that, when zero is either added to a number or subtracted from a number, the number remains unchanged, and that a number multiplied by zero becomes zero.

(©Keith Devlin, 2011, *The Man of Numbers: Fibonacci's Arithmetic Revolution*, Bloomsbury Publishing Inc.)

（早稲田大）

問1　下線部(1a)(1b)の短所として述べられているものを，次のア～エからそれぞれ 1つずつ選びなさい。
　　ア．You find it troublesome to do multiplication and division.
　　イ．You have to remember sixty different symbols representing numbers.
　　ウ．You cannot perform simple arithmetic with your fingers.
　　エ．You have trouble reading when there are more than four or five items in a collection.
問2　空所(　2　)に入れるのに最も適当なものを，次のア～エから1つ選びなさい。
　　ア．calendar　　　イ．hammer　　　ウ．compass　　　エ．ruler
問3　空所(　3　)に入れるのに最も適当なローマ数字を書きなさい。
問4　空所(　4　)に入れるのに最も適当なものを，次のア～エから1つ選びなさい。
　　ア．artistic　　　イ．manual　　　ウ．mathematical　　エ．verbal
問5　下線部(5)を日本語に訳しなさい。
問6　空所(　6　)に入れるのに最も適当なものを，次のア～エから1つ選びなさい。
　　ア．number　　　イ．symbol　　　ウ．position　　　エ．rule
問7　下線部(7)が0を発見できなかった理由を，本文に即して50字以内の日本語で述べなさい。
問8　下線部(8)の語を文意が通るように並べ換えなさい。

次の英文を読んで，設問に答えなさい。

Fundamentally, there are just two major food illnesses in our society: eating too much and eating too little.　The former is more prevalent, but both have steadily increased over the past few decades, and (1)both are important because, when pushed to their extremes, they are killers.　People who are very overweight may have various health problems, the most deadly of which begins with high blood pressure and can end in death from heart disease.　At the other extreme, the rejection of food begins with dieting, can progress to more serious eating disorders, and can end in death from self-starvation.　This is not to say that there are no other medical problems centered on food.　However, it should be kept in mind that these eating disorders are important not only because they are a problem for many people but also because they reveal the complex social and psychological factors that can distort food behaviors.

The most general approach to the mysteries of being overweight has been formulated by the food and diet expert David Booth in the question "Why do we now not like being fat?"　The question should not be dismissed as mere rhetoric. It points to a recent and profoundly significant change in the social and emotional meanings of food and our ideas about our bodies.　Up through the end of the 19th and the early years of the 20th century, we did like being fat.　Fat had obvious survival value as protection against the effects of starvation in a world where local food shortages and widespread famines were not unusual.　And it still does in parts of Africa, Asia, and the former Soviet Union.　In almost all human societies, being fat was also a conspicuous sign of material success and high social status for both men and women.　Yet today in North America and most of Europe, fat means just the opposite.　It is (2a) who are most likely to be fat, and (2b), particularly women, who live out the doctrine "You can never be too rich or too thin." (3)How did this reversal happen?　Why is possessing a well-padded body or indulging in the joy of eating to the limit no longer desirable in modern societies?

The politically correct response today would simply be "health."　But the widespread prejudice, in many cases disgust, against being fat in our society today is not mainly due to the medical risks that have become common knowledge over the past thirty years. It is much more a matter of aesthetics and, perhaps even more importantly, a psychological effect of the new industrial and urban environments that emerged most dramatically in North America and Western Europe early in the 20th century. Most discussions of this topic only note that changes in aesthetic values and fashion styles are responsible for the trend away from the bulky, heavier bodies admired during the 19th century and earlier. They give little attention to the question of why this trend occurred. But closer examination suggests that the answer involves a combination of biological, social, and psychological adaptations to modern industrial life. With the dawn of the machine age and all the technological changes associated with it, including new food processing, distribution, and consumption patterns, heavy bodies became as out-of-date as the manual and physical activities that once justified them.

A well-fleshed, bulky body with substantial fat reserves is clearly very desirable if you are working outdoors in all sorts of weather or shoveling coal for a living. But if you are in a protected indoor environment working at tasks that require little physical effort, such a heavy body is essentially useless. And from the standpoint of prevalent social class values, it is also a mark of social status, in the same way that rough work boots and overalls reveal or define a person as low-end working class. On the other hand, to have a thin body is to be marked as frail: unfit for the heavy outdoor work or frequent childbearing reserved for "the masses," but well adapted to office work and driving cars with automatic transmissions. In short, with the rise of modern industrial society, the body begins to lose its "use value" while gaining "exchange value." It takes on a symbolic meaning revealing social class status and becomes valued less for its survival uses against heavy work or harsh weather than for its decorative or aesthetic functions.

(4) Essential to this transformation of the body from an object geared to the harsh demands of nature to one defined by its fit to the modern world is a new, culturally driven view of the body. The body is now not simply a natural "given" but a form of personal property, an object one owns and is responsible for maintaining and developing. Nor are such maintenance and development merely a matter of individual choice. There is (5) a clear, if unspoken, underlying concept

of the contemporary body that is directly in line with the values represented in all the other creations of modern times.

The industrial age idealized efficiency and rationality. The efficiency of any machine is defined by its energy input to output ratio and its power to weight ratio. This ideal can be achieved only through applying rationality, in the form of mechanical engineering. Like the ideal machine, the efficiency of the modern body requires excess weight to be removed, and the means to accomplish this are provided by the rationality of diet and food science. (6)And so it is no mere change of fashion that creates a lean, lightweight human body as the modern ideal but, rather, a blend of the fundamental values associated with modern culture. Nothing, however, is more opposed to those values than excess body weight. Living in a culture dedicated almost everywhere to the achievement of light, slim, energy-efficient design, how could we not apply these criteria to ourselves?

But having applied them, we encounter one of the paradoxes of modern life. The same conditions of relative wealth and freedom from the dangers of nature that technology provides for us also make it very difficult for us to avoid becoming fat. It is all too obvious that, while many of our objects (telephones, televisions, computers, and so on) have steadily grown slimmer, our bodies have not. On the one hand, surrounded on all sides by energy-saving devices, we lack the everyday, fat-burning activities that once helped prevent excessive weight. On the other hand, surrounded by an ever-growing variety of foods and drinks from all over the world, many of which have been carefully designed and marketed to stimulate our appetites, we are more and more easily led into eating too much. The way out of (7)this paradox that began to emerge in North America during the 1920s and is still with us is dieting.

By way of conclusion, perhaps the most appropriate thing to emphasize about the food disorders and unhealthy eating behaviors discussed here is that they are a growing problem in our society precisely at a time when, by all objective accounts, we have the safest and most varied food supplies in history. The irony is evident and speaks directly to the fact that psychological meanings of food often have little or no connection with food science or other "objective" facts. Instead, it seems that the very availability of food in our society is what stimulates the growth of the major disorders and the various minor eating problems.

A convincing explanation for this state of affairs can be drawn from the discussion of the contrast between the "use value" of any object and its "exchange value." As it applies to food, this suggests that, since it is readily available in our society, food's (8a) value for the satisfaction of hunger and biological needs is easily taken for granted and overlooked, whereas its symbolic or (8b) value becomes increasingly prominent. More concretely, the mere satisfaction of hunger becomes secondary to the functions that food can serve as a status symbol or a sign of good taste, aesthetic sensitivity, love and affection, or ethnic, religious, or even political convictions. The social-psychological significance of caviar, for example, is far out of proportion to its ability to satisfy hunger. This fact suggests that the prevalence of eating problems in our wealthy society is closely connected to the increasing importance we have placed on the social and emotional exchange value of food.

(*How We Eat: Appetite, Culture and the Psychology of Food* by Leon Rappoport, published by ECW Press Ltd., 2003, 9781550225631)

（東京大）

問1　下線部(1)の理由として本文に<u>述べられていない</u>ものを，次のア～エから1つ選びなさい。

ア．More and more people have been suffering from them in the past decades.

イ．They can deprive people of their lives in extreme cases.

ウ．They are the only problems concerning food in the world today.

エ．They are related to how we feel about the body and food in our industrial society.

問2　空所(2a)(2b)に入れるのに最も適当な組み合わせを，次のア～エから1つ選びなさい。

ア．the rich and famous — the poor

イ．the poor — the rich and famous

ウ．people in Europe — people in North America

エ．people in North America — people in Europe

問3　下線部(3)の問いに対する主要な答えとして本文に述べられているものを，次の
　　ア～エから1つ選びなさい。
　　ア．It has been proved by decades of medical research that being overweight
　　　　increases the risk of heart attack.
　　イ．A sudden change in aesthetic values has taken place and being fat has
　　　　gone out of fashion.
　　ウ．Slim bodies regarded as ideal in Western Europe during the 19th
　　　　century and earlier have come to be admired all over the world.
　　エ．In our industrial environment the necessity of manual labor has been
　　　　reduced and heavy bodies have come to be considered unattractive.
問4　下線部(4)を日本語に訳しなさい。
問5　下線部(5)の内容として最も適当なものを，次のア～エから1つ選びなさい。
　　ア．You can gain an ideal body when excess weight is removed through
　　　　rational approaches.
　　イ．You have to maintain and develop your body carefully, since it is a gift
　　　　from God.
　　ウ．You should make efficient use of the energy of your body as well as
　　　　energy-saving devices.
　　エ．You must go on a scientifically based diet in order to enjoy a healthy
　　　　and long life.
問6　下線部(6)を日本語に訳しなさい。
問7　下線部(7)の内容を90字以内の日本語で述べなさい。
問8　空所(8a)(8b)に入れるのに最も適当な組み合わせを，次のア～エから
　　1つ選びなさい。
　　ア．nutrition — market　　　　　　イ．market — nutrition
　　ウ．use — exchange　　　　　　　　エ．exchange — use

50 min.
1574 words

次の英文を読んで，設問に答えなさい。

Picture two cartoon characters, one round and the other spiky. Which would you name Bouba, and which one Kiki? And which do you then think is more outgoing? Perhaps surprisingly, most of you will probably attribute the same name and characteristics to each of the shapes. A growing body of research suggests that people tend to make a range of judgments based on nothing but the sound of a word or name.

At its most basic, this is known as the *bouba-kiki* effect, or *maluma-takete* effect, because of how our minds link certain sounds and shapes. (1)Across many different languages, people tend to associate the sounds "b", "m", "l", and "o" (as in the made-up words *bouba* and *maluma*) with round shapes. The sounds "k", "t", "p", and "i", as in the nonsense words *kiki* and *takete*, are commonly seen as spiky. These associations may be partly rooted in the physical experience of saying and hearing sounds, with some feeling more effortful and rough than others.

Surprisingly, the *bouba-kiki* effect even extends into human relationships, and how we imagine the personalities of people we've never met. Cognitive psychologist David Sidhu at University College London and psycholinguist Penny Pexman at the University of Calgary have found that people perceive certain personal names such as Bob and Molly as (2a), and others such as Kirk and Kate as (2b). In French, they showed the same effect with the "(2c)" Benoit versus the "(2d)" Eric. In a separate study, participants pictured people with those names as having rounded or spiky personalities. "The basic thing we find is that if you compare these very smooth, soft-sounding names like Molly to these harsher-sounding names like Kate, the smoother-sounding names like Molly get associated with things like being more agreeable, more emotional, more responsible, whereas the harsher, spikier-sounding names are thought of as being more extroverted," says Sidhu.

These widespread associations may originate in how these sounds feel in our mouth, according to Sidhu. "If you think about pronouncing an 'm' versus a 't', for example, that 'm'-sound feels much smoother, and that symbolically captures the smoothness of the rounded shape versus the spiky shape." Sounds like "t" and "k" may feel more energetic, capturing an extroverted, cheerful, lively quality.

And this mouthfeel of the words we use can influence how we experience the world. At any given moment we use a series of subtle cues to pull together information from all our senses, and make judgments and predictions about our environment. "There's something about how (3)<u>humans are fundamentally associative</u>," Pexman says. "We want to see patterns in things, we want to find connections between things, and we'll find them even between sounds and the things those sounds stand for in the world."

The research adds to a growing body of evidence that challenges a long-held view in linguistics: that sounds are arbitrary and have no inherent meaning. (4)<u>Instead, certain sounds have been found to bring to mind consistent associations not just with shapes and sizes, but even with flavours and textures.</u> Milk chocolate, *brie cheese, and still water tend to be perceived as *bouba/maluma*, while crisps, bitter chocolate, mint chocolate, and sparkling water are more likely to be experienced as *kiki/takete.*

Such associations can help us with important real-life tasks, such as language-learning and guessing the meaning of unfamiliar words. In English, words for round things are often round-sounding, as in blob, balloon, ball, marble. Words like prickly, spiny, sting, and perky are spiky both in sound and meaning. Sounds can also indicate size. An "i"-sound is linked to smallness, while an "o"-sound indicates largeness. Some of these links exist across thousands of languages, with the "i"-sound excessively popping up in words for "small" around the world.

For people learning new words, whether babies, young children, or adults, these patterns can be very helpful. Young children and even babies already match round sounds with round shapes. Parents tend to use sound-shape associations to emphasise the meaning of certain words, such as "teeny tiny." Adults benefit from associations when they learn a new language, finding it easier to guess or remember foreign words when their sound matches their meaning.

Some argue that these instinctive connections between sounds and meaning may even be a leftover from humanity's earliest stages of language evolution and that human language itself started as a string of such expressive, readily guessable sounds.

When it comes to people's personalities, however, sound is not a reliable guide at all. Sidhu, Pexman, and their collaborators tested whether there was a link between a person's name and their personality, perhaps because the round or spiky sound of the name became attached to the wearer. They found no such association. "People worry when choosing baby names. That's because they assume that the label matters so much," Pexman says. "Our data would suggest that (5) although that's what we think, if you call a kid Bob, he's not any more likely to end up with one set of personality characteristics than another."

Instead, our reaction to a name probably reveals more about our own prejudices. "It does suggest that we're prepared to read a lot into somebody's name that probably isn't a cue to what that person is actually like," says Pexman.

Results from an ongoing study by Sidhu, Pexman, and their collaborators suggest that the sound of a name has (6a) of an impact as we find out (6b) about people. When participants were shown videos of people with supposedly round or spiky names, the names made no difference to their judgment of them. "When all you know is the name, like in these studies when you're just shown a name and asked about the personality, then maybe these sounds will play a role," Sidhu says. "But as you start getting more information about the person, then that actual information about the personality is probably going to cancel these biases."

As widespread as the *bouba-kiki* effect is, it can be changed or cancelled out by different factors, such as the sounds commonly used in our own native language. Suzy Styles and her PhD student Nan Shang tested the *bouba-kiki* effect with *Mandarin Chinese. Mandarin is a *tonal language, where the meaning of a word can completely change depending on the tone in which it is said. In English, tone can carry some meaning, for example by signalling a question, but not to the extent it does in Mandarin. The researchers presented English- and Mandarin-speakers with two Mandarin Chinese tones, one high and one falling. The English-speaking participants in the experiment perceived the high tone as spiky, and the falling one as rounded. But Mandarin speakers drew the opposite conclusion, picturing the high tone as rounded, and the falling tone as spiky.

One possible explanation is that if we are unfamiliar with tones in a language, as English-speakers are, then we may mainly hear them as high or low, and form associations based on pitch. But if we are familiar with tones, as Chinese speakers are, we may be able to distinguish finer nuances. In the experiment, the Mandarin speakers heard the high tone as smooth, drawn-out, and steady, and therefore, rounded. The falling tone was experienced as sudden because it dropped quickly, making it spiky.

Other studies also found variations in the *bouba-kiki* pattern. The Himba, a remote community in Northern Namibia who speak the Otjiherero language, judged *bouba* to be round and *kiki* to be spiky, in line with the general trend. But they found milk chocolate to be spiky-tasting, suggesting that our associations with regard to our senses are not universal.

When Styles and the linguist Lauren Gawne tested the *bouba-kiki* effect on speakers of Syuba, a language in the Himalayas in Nepal, they found no consistent response either way. The Syuba speakers seemed confused by the made-up words, possibly because they did not sound like any actual Syuba words. This made it hard to form any meaningful associations. An analogy would be to say the made-up word "ngf" to an English speaker, and ask if it is round or spiky. It would probably be difficult to make a meaningful choice. "When we hear words that don't follow the word-pattern of our native language, it's often hard to do things with that word," Styles says. "We can't hold it in our short-term memory long enough to make decisions about it."

Cultural factors are also likely to affect our reactions to the sound of personal names. In English, the sounds "k" and "oo" are perceived as inherently humorous. English female names are more likely to contain sounds that are perceived as small, such as the "i"-sound in Emily, and also feature more soft sounds than male names. But in other languages, names can follow a completely different sound pattern. Sidhu hasn't yet tested the name-personality association across different languages, but expects that it would vary.

Uncovering these hidden associations holds one important real-life lesson.
 7 "I think that makes a lot of sense," he says. "When someone is being judged, taking away all of these extra things that could bias the judgment is always a good idea."

(注)　brie cheese：ブリーチーズ(フランス産チーズの一種)

　　　Mandarin Chinese：標準中国語(Mandarin)　　tonal language：声調言語

(Content provided by BBC Studios Learning)

(一橋大)

問1 下線部(1)のような傾向はなぜ生じるのか，m 音の場合を例にして，本文に即して50字以内の日本語で述べなさい。

問2 空所(2a)〜(2d)のそれぞれに，文意が通るように round か spiky のいずれかを入れなさい。

問3 下線部(3)の内容を40字以内の日本語で具体的に述べなさい。

問4 下線部(4)を日本語に訳しなさい。

問5 下線部(5)を that の指す内容を明らかにして日本語に訳しなさい。

問6 空所(6a)と(6b)に入れるのに最も適当な組み合わせを，次のア〜エから1つ選びなさい。

　　　ア．less — less　　　　　　　　イ．less — more
　　　ウ．more — less　　　　　　　　エ．more — more

問7 ┌─ 7 ─┐ に入るア〜エの文を，文脈に適した順に並べ換えなさい。

　　　ア．Sidhu supports the idea.

　　　イ．We probably read too much into other people's names.

　　　ウ．After all, Sidhu and Pexman found no evidence that Bobs are actually friendlier, or Kirks more extroverted.

　　　エ．Their findings may add weight to calls to remove names from important documents such as scientific papers under review, to prevent unconscious bias.

問8 外国語学習における the *bouba-kiki* effect の利点を，本文に即して60字以内の日本語で述べなさい。

問9 the *bouba-kiki* effect が生じない要因として本文で述べられていないものを，次のア〜エから1つ選びなさい。

　　　ア．Differences in the sound systems of our native languages.

　　　イ．Inherent associations between sounds and letters.

　　　ウ．The use of sounds not used in our native languages.

　　　エ．The name-personality association across different languages.

河合塾
SERIES

改訂版

やっておきたい

英語長文

1000

[解答・解説編]

河合塾講師

杉山 俊一
塚越 友幸
山下 博子
［共著］

河合出版

はじめに

　大学の入試問題では、読解問題が最も大きな割合を占めていますし、その割合はますます高くなっています。読解問題を解けるようにすることは、受験を突破するうえで避けては通ることができません。それでは、読解問題を解くためには、どのような力が必要なのでしょうか。語い力に加えて、一文一文の構造を正確に捉え、内容を把握する力が必要です。さらに、複数の文が集まって文章が構成されている以上、文と文のつながり、すなわち文脈を読み取る力も必要です。また、今日的な話題が出題されることが増えています。そうした話題について知っておくことも、内容を理解するためには大切です。

　こうした力をつけるためには、何よりも良い英文を読み、良い問題を解くことです。そこで、これまでに出題された問題の中から、英文の長さと難易度を基準に繰り返し読むに値する英文を選び、4冊の問題集にまとめました。設問は、ある文章に対して問うべきこと—内容の理解と英語の理解—という観点から、ほぼ全面的に作り変えてあります。

　やっておきたい英語長文1000は、**900語から1600語**程度のやや難から難レベルの英文10題で構成されています。英文が長くなることで、論旨の展開上重要な情報や問いに関る情報を素速く確実に読み取ることが求められることになります。そうした読み方ができているかを確認できるように、論旨展開上重要な情報を **Outline** としてまとめてあります。

	words 0　200　400　600　800　1000　1600	level 易　　　標準　　　難
やっておきたい英語長文300		
やっておきたい英語長文500		
やっておきたい英語長文700		
やっておきたい英語長文1000		

　本書が皆さんの想いの実現に向けて、役に立つことを願ってやみません。それでは、問題1にトライしてみましょう。

　最後に、本書を改訂するにあたり、Kathryn A. Craft 先生に英文校閲を行っていただきました。この場を借りて御礼申し上げます。

著者記す

本書の使い方

1　問題には語数と標準解答時間を示してあります。標準解答時間を目標に問題を解いてください。

2　解説には，解答と設問解説，要約，構文・語句解説があります。設問解説を読み，解答を確認してください。設問解説中の「第1段落第5文」といった表記は，構文・語句解説の番号に対応しています。

3　構文・語句解説では，訳例と設問解説で触れなかった，構文および語句の解説がしてあります。設問以外の箇所で理解できなかった部分を確認してください。

4　構文・語句解説では，問題文から下線を省き空所を埋めた形で英文を再録してあります。英文を繰り返し読んでもらいたいからです。こうすることが，速読の練習にもなりますし，語いの定着にもつながります。また，このときは，英文の構造よりも，内容・論旨を追うことを心がけてください。また，確認のために要約を活用してください。

5　英文を読む際には，音読とリスニングを組み合わせることで，リスニング力も強化できます。英語のネイティブ・スピーカーが読み上げた音声が用意されていますので，利用してください。

　　音声は，パソコンやスマートフォンから下記の URL にアクセスして聴くことができます。QR コードからもアクセスできます。

https://www.kawai-publishing.jp/onsei/01/index.html

・ファイルは MP4形式の音声です。再生するには，最新版の OS をご利用ください。

また，パソコンから URL にアクセスしていただくことで，音声データのダウンロードも可能です。

※ホームページより直接スマートフォンへのダウンロードはできません。パソコンにダウンロードしていただいた上で，スマートフォンへお取り込みいただきますよう，お願いいたします。
・ファイルは ZIP 形式で圧縮されていますので，解凍ソフトが必要です。
・ファイルは MP3形式の音声です。再生するには，Windows Media Player や iTunes などの再生ソフトが必要です。
・Y101〜Y110の全10ファイル構成となっています。

＜音声データに関する注意＞
・当サイトに掲載されている音声ファイルのデータは著作権法で保護されています。本データあるいはそれを加工したものを複製・譲渡・配信・販売することはできません。また，データを使用できるのは，本教材の購入者がリスニングの学習を目的とする場合に限られます。
・お客様のパソコンやネット環境により音声を再生できない場合，当社は責任を負いかねます。ご理解とご了承をいただきますよう，お願いいたします。
・ダウンロードや配信サイトから聴くことができるのは，本書を改訂するまでの期間です。

本書で用いた記号

- ( ) は省略可能な語句を表す。
- [ ] は直前の語句と書き換え可能な語句を表す。
- S は主語，O は目的語，C は補語を表す。
- A, B は名詞を表す。
- X, Y は文の中で同じ働きをするものを表す。
- *do* は動詞の原形を表す。
- to *do* は不定詞を表す。
- *doing* は動名詞または現在分詞を表す。
- *done* は過去分詞を表す。
- *one's* は主語と同じ所有格を表す。
- A's は主語と同じになるとは限らない所有格を表す。
- 「自動詞＋前置詞」型の熟語は，account for A のように表す。
- 「他動詞＋副詞」型の熟語は，put A off のように表す。
- 他動詞は，solve「を解く」のように表す。
- ¶ は段落を表す。

目　次

動物の感情

▶▶▶ 設問解説 ◀◀◀

問1　下線部(1)を含む文は「動物が感情を持つという考えは、依然として多くの科学者の間で賛否両論がある」という意味である。第2段落以降で「動物が感情を持つという考え」に関して、賛否それぞれの立場が展開されているが、第11段落第1文で「最も説得力のある論拠は進化論から出てくるのかもしれない」と述べられ、続く第2文で神経科学者シヴィーの言葉を引用して、その具体的内容が述べられている。したがって、この内容を制限字数内でまとめればよい。

問2　全体の文構造は、Even those ... animal passion(S)、agree(V)、that many ... and grief(O) である。S には those who ...「…する人々」が用いられている。that節内の構造は、many creatures(S)、experience(V)、fear(O)である。ダッシュ(——)以下は fear を修飾する関係代名詞節であるが、ここでは fear について補足的に説明を加えており、非制限用法の関係詞節と同様に前から訳出すればよい。なお、that contrasts with secondary emotions such as love and grief は、a primary emotion を修飾する関係代名詞節である。

□ believe in A「Aの存在を信じる，Aを正しいと信じる」　　□ passion「感情」

□ agree that節「…であることに同意する」　　□ creature「生物」

□ experience「を経験する」　　□ define O as C「OをCと定義する」

□ primary「一次的な」　　□ contrast with A「Aと対照をなす」

□ secondary「二次的な」　　□ A such as B「たとえばBのようなA」

□ grief「悲しみ」

問3　filter は「〈水・ガスなど〉を濾過する，濾してきれいにする」という意味である。したがって，filter their feelings「感情を濾過する」とは「本当の感情を隠して表に見せない」という意味。the way we do は the way S V ...「…するように」の表現で，do は代動詞で，ここでは filter our feelings の代用。よって，下線部は「動物は人間がするように感情を隠すことはない」という意味になる。

　　ア.「動物は人間と同じように感情を修正する」

　　イ.「動物は人間と同じように効果的に感情を隠す」

　　ウ.「動物は人間よりも容易に感情を制御する」

　　エ.「動物は人間よりも直接的に感情を表現する」

問4　(4a)空所を含む文は「最も明白な動物の感情の1つは（　4a　）である」という意味。続く第5段落第2文 animals often appear to be happy および第3文 Beastly joy seems particularly apparent から判断する。

　　(4b)空所を含む文の後半部分 particularly following the death of a mate, parent, offspring, or even close companion および同段落第2文 loses its partner, the bird's head and body droop disappointedly, 第3文 a young chimpanzee starve after his mother died の部分から判断する。

　　(4c)空所を含む文は「さらに彼は（　4c　）以外に，証拠はそれほど明らかではないが，扁桃体は他の感情とも関係がある，と述べている」という意味。したがって，(4c)には「扁桃体と関係のある」感情が入ることがわかる。第8段落第2文には「扁桃体のある場所を刺激すると強い恐怖の状態が引き起こされる」ことが述べられ，続く第3・4文にも「人間とラット」の例を挙げて「扁桃体と恐怖との関係」について述べている。よって(4c)には「恐怖」が入ることがわかる。

　　□ despair「絶望」　　□ fear「恐怖」　　□ anger「怒り」　　□ pleasure「喜び」

問5　文構造は，emotions(S) seem to arise(V) である。ポイントは ancient parts of the brain と regions 以下が同格の関係であることを見抜くこと。なお，that have ... throughout evolution は regions を修飾する関係代名詞節である。また，文頭の In animals studied so far において studied so far は animals を

修飾する過去分詞句。

□ so far「これまで，今までのところ」　　□ including A「Aを含めて」

□ arise from A「Aから起こる，生じる」　　□ ancient「非常に古い／古代の」

□ save「を保存する」　　□ across A「Aを越えて」　　□ species「(生物の)種」

□ throughout A「Aを通してずっと」　　□ evolution「進化」

問6　warrant は「を正当であるとする／保証する」という意味。また，it は下線部
　　の前にある to be afraid の内容を指している。したがって，下線部は「状況が
　　恐れることを正当であるとする」が逐語訳で，「状況から恐れるのが当然であ
　　る」ということ。

　　ア.「損傷が十分深刻である」

　　イ.「神経科学者が状況を分析できない」

　　ウ.「恐怖を感じるのが適切である」

　　エ.「人が喜びの感情を表す」

　　□ situation「状況」

問7　If節内の do は動詞強調の助動詞である。ポイントは it が If節の内容を受けて
　　いること。主節の it が if / when などで始まる副詞節の内容を受ける場合があ
　　ることに注意。

　　例　It'll be a pity if the book is never published.
　　　　「その本が出版されないとなると残念だ」

　　how humans ... the future は have implications for A「Aに対する影響を持
　　つ」の A に当たる名詞節である。

　　□ a wide range of A「広範囲のA」　　□ profound「重大な」

　　□ humans「人間」　　□ interact「互いに影響しあう」

Outline

¶ 1	主題	動物における感情の存在には賛否両論あるが，存在を示す証拠が増えている
¶ 2		動物は恐怖を体験するという点では，意見の一致が見られる
¶ 3-4	展開1	動物の行動を観察することで動物の感情がわかると考える科学者もいる
¶ 5	例1	動物は喜びを表す
¶ 6	例2	動物は悲しみを表す
¶ 7	展開2	人間と動物の脳の類似点による科学的証拠もある
¶ 8	例1	扁桃体と恐怖との関係
¶ 9	例2	ドーパミンと喜びや興奮との関係
¶ 10	反論	動物に感情があるとしても，動物がそれを意識しているのかは疑問である
¶ 11-12	結論	進化論からすれば，動物にも感情は存在することになり，その解明は人間と

要 約

　動物は感情を持つという考えに関しては，依然として賛否両論があるが，近年，野外観察による結果と，人間と動物の脳の類似点に着目し，動物は感情を持つということが科学的にも証明されつつある。進化論からすれば，動物にも感情は存在することになり，その解明は人間と動物の相互関係に大きな影響を与える。(143字)

▶▶▶ **構文・語句解説** ◀◀◀

―― 第１段落 ――

¹The idea that animals feel emotions remains controversial among many scientists. ²Researchers' doubt is fueled in part by the very nonscientific tendency to attribute human qualities to nonhumans. ³Many scientists also say that standard scientific methods cannot prove the existence of emotions in animals. ⁴Today, however, with mounting evidence to the contrary, "the tide is turning radically and rapidly," says biologist Marc Bekoff, who is at the forefront of this movement.

　¹動物が感情を持つという考えは，依然として多くの科学者の間で賛否両論がある。²研究者の疑念は，１つには，人間の持つ性質を人間以外のものにもあると考えるまったく非科学的な傾向によって強まっている。³多くの科学者はまた，標準的な科学的方法では動物における感情の存在を証明できないと言う。⁴しかし，今日，それとは反対の証拠が増えてきており，「形勢は根本的に急速に変わりつつある」と，この動向の先頭に立つ生物学者マルク・ベコフは言う。

1 □ remain C「Cのままである」　□ controversial「賛否両論のある，議論を引き起こす」

2 □ researcher「研究者」　□ doubt「疑い」　□ fuel「(感情などを)あおり立てる」

　□ in part「１つには」　□ the very A「まさにそのA」　□ nonscientific「非科学的な」

　□ tendency to *do*「…する傾向」

　□ attribute A to B「A〈性質・特徴など〉がB〈人・物〉にあると考える」　□ quality「性質」

　□ nonhumans「人間以外のもの」

3 □ standard「標準的な」　□ method「方法」　□ prove「を証明する」

　□ existence「存在」

4 □ mounting「ますます増える」　□ evidence「証拠」

　□ A to the contrary「それと反対のA，そうではないとするA」

―― 第2段落 ――

[1]Even those who do not believe in animal passion agree that many creatures experience fear — which some scientists define as a primary emotion that contrasts with secondary emotions such as love and grief. [2]Unlike these more complex feelings, fear is instinctive, they say, and requires no conscious thought.

　[1]動物が感情を持つことを信じない人でさえ，多くの生物が恐怖を体験することを認めている。そしてこの恐怖を，愛や悲しみのような二次的な感情とは対照的な一次的な感情とみなす科学者もいる。[2]これらのより複雑な感情とは違って，恐怖は本能的なものであり，意識的思考を要しない，と彼らは言う。

2 Unlike these ... conscious thought = They say (that) unlike these ... conscious thought
and は is instinctive と requires no conscious thought を結んでいる。
□ complex「複雑な」　　□ instinctive「本能的な」　　□ require「を必要とする」
□ conscious「意識的な」

―― 第3段落 ――

[1]But beyond such instinctive emotions, the possibility of more complex animal feelings is difficult to demonstrate. [2]"I can't even prove that another human being is feeling happy or sad," says Bekoff, "but I can deduce how they're feeling through body language and facial expression." [3]As a scientist who has conducted field studies of coyotes and foxes for the past three decades, Bekoff also believes he can accurately tell what these animals are feeling by observing their behavior. [4]He adds that animal emotions may actually be more knowable than those of humans, because they don't filter their feelings the way we do.

　[1]しかし，そのような本能的な感情以外に，もっと複雑な感情を動物が持っている可能性を実証することは難しい。[2]「他人がうれしいのか悲しいのかさえ証明することはできない。しかし，身振り言語や表情から人がどう感じているかを推測することはできる」とベコフは言う。[3]過去30年間コヨーテやキツネの野外研究を行ってきた科学者として，ベコフはまた，これらの動物がどう感じているのか，その行動を観察することで正確にわかると信じている。[4]さらに彼

は，動物は人間のように感情を隠さないので，動物の感情は実際には人間の感情よりもわかりやすいかもしれないと言う。

1 the possibility ... is difficult to demonstrate = it is difficult to demonstrate the possibility ...

　□ beyond A「A以外に」　　□ demonstrate「を実証する」

2 through body language and facial expression は can deduce を修飾する副詞句。

　□ deduce「を推測する」　　□ body language「身振り言語」

　□ facial expression「(顔の)表情」

3 by observing their behavior は can tell を修飾する副詞句。

　□ conduct「を行う」　　□ field studies「野外研究」　　□ coyote「コヨーテ」

　□ decade「10年」　　□ can tell wh節「…かがわかる」　　□ accurately「正確に」

　□ observe「を観察する」

4 those of humans = the emotions of humans

　□ add that節「…と付け加える」　　□ actually「実際に」　　□ knowable「理解できる」

第4段落

¹Yet because feelings are intangible and difficult to study scientifically, "most researchers don't even want to talk about animal emotions," says neuroscientist Jaak Panksepp. ²Within his field, Panksepp is a rare exception. ³Focusing on similarities between the brains of humans and those of other animals, he suggests that at least some creatures have true feelings. ⁴"Imagine where we'd be in physics if we hadn't guessed what's inside the atom," says Panksepp. ⁵"Most of what goes on in nature is invisible, yet we don't deny that it exists." ⁶The new case for animal emotions comes in part from the growing acceptability of field observations. ⁷The latest contribution to this body of knowledge is a book, *The Smile of a Dolphin*, which presents personal reports from more than 50 researchers who have spent their careers studying animals — from cats, dogs, bears and chimpanzees to birds, iguanas, and fish. ⁸Edited by Bekoff, the volume already has caught scientific attention.

---

¹しかし，感情は触れることができず科学的に研究しにくいので，「ほとんどの研究者は動物の感情について話したいとさえ思わない」と神経科学者のヤーク・パンクセップは言う。²彼の専門領域では，パンクセップはきわめて例外的な存在である。³彼は人間の脳と他の動物の脳の類似点に焦点を当てて，少なくとも動物の中には真の意味での感情を持つものがいると述べている。⁴「我々が原子の内部に何があるのか考えなかったとすれば，我々の物理学はどうなって

いるのかを想像してみてください」とパンクセップは言う。⁵「自然の中で起こることの大半は目に見えないが，我々はそれが存在していることは否定しないのです」⁶動物が感情を持つというこの新たな主張は，１つには野外観察がますます受け入れられつつあることからきている。⁷この一連の知識に最新の寄与を行ったのが「イルカの微笑」という本である。そこには自分の生涯を動物—ネコ，犬，クマ，チンパンジーから鳥，イグアナ，魚に至るまで—を研究するのに費やした50人以上の研究者が１人１人書いた報告書が掲載されている。⁸その本はベコフによって編集されたもので，すでに科学者の関心を引いている。

1 and は intangible と difficult to study scientifically を結んでいる。

　□ yet「しかし」　　　□ scientifically「科学的に」

2 □ field「(研究などの)分野」　　　□ rare「まれな」　　　□ exception「例外」

3 Focusing on ... of other animals は付帯状況を表す分詞構文。

　those of other animals ＝ the brains of other animals

　□ focus on A「Aに焦点を当てる」　　　□ similarity「類似点」

　□ suggest that節「…だと示唆する」

4 we'd be ... if we hadn't guessed ... は条件節が仮定法過去完了，帰結節が仮定法過去の形。

　□ physics「物理学」　　　□ guess「を推測する」　　　□ atom「原子」

5 it ＝ Most of what goes on in nature

　□ go on「起こる」　　　□ invisible「目に見えない」

　□ deny that節「…ということを否定する」

6 □ case「主張，論拠」　　　□ growing「増大する」　　　□ acceptability「受容性」

　□ field observation「野外観察」

7 which presents ... and fish は a book を修飾する非制限用法の関係代名詞節で，who have ... and fish は more than 50 researchers を修飾する関係代名詞節。

　□ the latest A「最新のA」　　　□ contribution to A「Aへの貢献」

　□ a body of A「大量のA」　　　□ present「を示す」　　　□ personal「個人の」

　□ career「生涯／経歴」

8 Edited by Bekoff は分詞構文。

　□ edit「を編集する」　　　□ volume「書籍，本」

．．

─ 第5段落 ─

¹One of the most obvious animal emotions is pleasure. ²Anyone who has ever been greeted by a bounding, barking, tail-wagging dog knows that animals often appear to be happy. ³Beastly joy seems particularly apparent when the animals are playing with one another or sometimes, in the case of pets, with people.

¹最も明白な動物の感情の1つは喜びである。²飛び跳ね，吠え，尻尾を振っている犬に迎えられたことのある人なら誰でも，動物もしばしばうれしそうに見えることがあることを知っている。³動物の喜びは動物同士で遊ぶときや，ときにはペットの場合，人と遊ぶときにとりわけはっきりと現れるようである。

1 □ obvious「明白な」

2 Anyone は肯定文で用いられているので「誰でも」の意味。

　　□ greet「を出迎える」　　　□ bound「飛び跳ねる」　　　□ bark「吠える」

　　□ tail-wagging「尻尾を振っている」

3 or は with one another と with people を結んでいる。

　　□ beastly「獣のような」　　　□ apparent「明白な」　　　□ in the case of A「Aの場合」

― 第6段落 ―

¹Grief also seems to be common in the wild, particularly following the death of a mate, parent, offspring, or even close companion. ²When a goose, which mates for life, loses its partner, the bird's head and body droop disappointedly. ³Jane Goodall, who has studied chimpanzees in Tanzania for four decades, saw a young chimpanzee starve after his mother died. ⁴Goodall maintains that the animal died of grief.

¹悲しみもまた野生ではよく見られるようで，特につがいの一方，親，子孫，さらには親しい仲間の死後によく見られる。²一生をつがいで過ごすガチョウが相手を失うと，この鳥の頭と体は落胆したようにうなだれる。³40年間タンザニアでチンパンジーを研究してきたジェイン・グドールは，ある若いチンパンジーが母親の死後，餓死するのを見た。⁴チンパンジーは悲しみで死んだのだとグドールは主張している。

1 particularly following ... close companion は分詞構文。

　　□ the wild「自然の状態」　　　□ follow「に続いて起こる」

　　□ mate「(鳥・動物の)つがいの一方／配偶者」　　　□ offspring「子孫」

　　□ companion「仲間」

2 □ goose「ガチョウ」　　　□ mate「〈鳥・動物が〉つがう」　　　□ for life「死ぬまで，一生」

　　□ droop「うなだれる」　　　□ disappointedly「がっかりしたように」

3 □ starve「餓死する」

4 □ maintain that 節「…だと主張する」　　　□ die of A「Aで死ぬ」

¹There is hard scientific evidence for animal feelings as well. ²Scientists who study the biology of emotions, a field still in its infancy, are discovering many similarities between the brains of humans and those of other animals. ³In animals studied so far, including humans, emotions seem to arise from ancient parts of the brain, regions that have been saved across many species throughout evolution.

¹動物には感情があることを示す確固とした科学的証拠もある。²まだ生まれて間もない分野である，感情の生物学を研究する科学者は，人間の脳と他の動物の脳の間に多くの類似点があることを発見している。³人間を含むこれまでに研究されてきた動物において，感情は進化を通じて多くの動物種の間で保持されてきた領域である，脳の非常に古い部分から生じるようである。

1 □ hard「厳然たる」　　□ as well「…も」

2 the biology of emotions と a field still in its infancy は同格の関係で，still in its infancy は a field を修飾する前置詞句。

those of other animals = the brains of other animals

□ biology「生物学」　　□ in A's infancy「A の (発達の) 初期段階に」

¹The most important emotional site identified so far is the amygdala, an almond-shaped structure in the center of the brain. ²Working with rats, neuroscientists have discovered that stimulating a certain part of the amygdala induces a state of intense fear. ³In humans, brain-imaging studies show that when people experience fear, their amygdalas, too, are made active. ⁴And just like the rats, people whose amygdalas are damaged by accident or disease seem unable to be afraid when the situation warrants it. ⁵In humans and rats, at least, amygdalas are "basically wired the same way," says neuroscientist Joseph LeDoux. ⁶He adds that, beyond fear, the evidence is less clear, but the amygdala has a connection with other emotions as well.

¹これまでに特定された，感情に関する最も重要な場所は，脳の中央にあるアーモンドの形をした組織である扁桃体である。²神経科学者はラットを使って研究を行い，扁桃体のある場所を

刺激すると強い恐怖の状態が引き起こされることを発見した。³人間では，恐怖を感じたときには扁桃体も活動することが，脳の画像研究によりわかっている。⁴また，ラットと同様に，事故や病気で扁桃体が損傷を受けた人は，恐怖を感じて当然の状況でも恐れることができなくなるようである。⁵少なくとも人間とラットの場合には，扁桃体は「基本的に同じような神経経路と接続している」と神経科学者のジョセフ・ルドウは言う。⁶さらに彼は恐怖以外に，証拠はそれほど明らかではないが，扁桃体は他の感情とも関係がある，と述べている。

1 □ site「場所」　　□ identify「と特定する」　　□ structure「組織，構造」
2 Working with rats は分詞構文。
　□ rat「ラット，ネズミ」　　□ stimulate「を刺激する」　　□ certain A「ある A」
　□ induce「を引き起こす」　　□ state「状態」　　□ intense「激しい」
3 □ brain-imaging studies「脳の画像による研究」　　□ active「活発な」
4 □ damage「に損傷を与える」
5 wire は「に電線をつなぐ，配線を行う」という意味だが，ここでは「神経経路が接続している」という意味合いで用いられている。
　□ basically「基本的に」
6 □ have a connection with A「A と関係がある」

―― 第9段落 ――

¹The case for animal emotions is also supported by recent studies of brain chemistry. ²Steven Siviy has found that when rats play, their brains release large amounts of dopamine, a chemical that is associated with pleasure and excitement in humans.

¹動物は感情を持つという主張は最近の脳の化学的性質の研究によっても裏付けられている。²スティーブン・シビーは，ラットが遊ぶときに，人間では喜びと興奮に関係がある化学物質ドーパミンがラットの脳から大量に放出されることを発見した。

1 □ support「を立証する／を支持する」　　□ chemistry「化学的性質」
2 dopamine と a chemical ... in humans は同格の関係で，that is ... in humans は a chemical を修飾する関係代名詞節。
　□ release「を放出する」　　□ large amounts of A「大量の A」
　□ associate A with B「A を B と結びつける，A で B を連想する」

[1]Doubtful scientists remain unconvinced. [2]"A whale may behave as if it's in love, but you can't prove what it's feeling, if anything," says LeDoux. [3]He maintains that the question of feelings boils down to whether or not animals are conscious. [4]And though animals "may have snapshots of self-awareness," he says, "the movie we call consciousness is not there."

[1]懐疑的な科学者は依然として納得していない。[2]「クジラはあたかも恋しているかのような振る舞いをするかもしれないが，何かを感じているにしても，何を感じているか証明することはできない」とルドウは言う。[3]彼は，感情の問題は結局，動物が意識しているかどうかということになると主張している。[4]そして，動物は「スナップ写真のような自己認識は持っているかもしれないが，我々が意識と呼ぶ映画のようなものは存在しないのだ」と彼は言う。

1 □ doubtful「懐疑的な」　　□ unconvinced「納得していない」
2 □ as if ...「まるで…のように」　　□ be in love「恋している」
　 □ if anything「もしあるとしても」
3 □ boil down to A「〈状況・問題などが〉つまるところAになる」
4 □ snapshot「スナップ写真」　　□ self-awareness「自意識，自己認識」

[1]The most convincing argument, perhaps, comes from the theory of evolution, widely accepted by biologists of all types. [2]Citing similarities in the brain structure and chemistry of humans and other animals, neuroscientist Siviy asks: "If you believe in evolution by natural selection, how can you believe that feelings suddenly appeared, out of the blue, with human beings?" [3]Goodall says it is illogical for scientists to use animals to study the human brain and then deny that animals have feelings.

[1]最も説得力のある論拠は，あらゆるタイプの生物学者が広く受け入れている進化論から出てくるのかもしれない。[2]人間と他の動物の脳の仕組みや化学的性質の類似点を挙げて，神経科学者のシヴィーは次のように問う。「自然淘汰による進化を信じるのであれば，感情が何もないところから，人間において突然に出現したとどうして信じられるだろうか」[3]グドールは科学者が人間の脳を研究するために動物を使い，その上，動物が感情を持つことを否定するのは筋が通らないと言う。

1 widely accepted by biologists of all types は the theory of evolution を修飾する過去分詞句。

☐ convincing「納得のいく，説得力のある」　　☐ argument「論拠」

☐ the theory of evolution「進化論」

2 Citing similarities ... other animals は分詞構文。

of humans and other animals は the brain structure and chemistry を修飾している。

how can ... human beings? は修辞疑問文。

☐ cite「を（例として）挙げる，を引き合いに出す」　　☐ natural selection「自然淘汰」

☐ out of the blue「だしぬけに，思いがけなく」

3 ☐ illogical「非論理的な」

- -

第12段落

[1]In the end, what difference does it really make? [2]According to many scientists, resolving the debate over animal emotions could turn out to be much more than an intellectual exercise. [3]If animals do indeed experience a wide range of feelings, it has profound implications for how humans and animals interact in the future. [4]Bekoff hopes that greater understanding of what animals are feeling will spur more strict rules on how animals should be treated, everywhere from zoos and circuses to farms and backyards.

[1]結局のところ，実際にどのような違いがあるのだろうか。[2]多くの科学者によれば，動物の感情についての議論を解決することは単なる知的行為というよりもはるかに大きなものになる可能性があるということである。[3]もし動物が広範囲にわたる感情を実際に経験しているとすれば，それは人間と動物が将来どのように関り合っていくのかについて深い意味を持つ。[4]ベコフは，動物が何を感じているかについての理解が進むことによって，動物園やサーカスから農場や裏庭に至るすべてのところで，動物の扱い方に関するより厳格な規則を作るきっかけになることを期待している。

1 ☐ in the end「結局」　　☐ make difference「違いを生じる」

2 ☐ resolve「を解決する」　　☐ turn out to be C「結局Cになる」

☐ much＋比較級「ずっと…，はるかに…」　　☐ intellectual exercise「知的行為」

4 ☐ spur「に拍車をかける，を促進する」　　☐ strict「厳しい」

☐ everywhere from A to B「AからBに至るすべてのところ」　　☐ circus「サーカス」

☐ backyard「裏庭」

グローバル化の恩恵

問1　ヨーロッパでまずルネサンスが起き，続いて啓蒙運動と産業革命が起き，西洋における生活水準の向上につながり，今ではこの偉大な業績が世界に広まっているという歴史観。(79字)

問2　ウ. the cause of all the trouble

問3　エ. neither new nor necessarily Western; and it is not a curse

問4　in the opposite direction of what we see today

問5　実際，ヨーロッパが当時の数学と科学と技術のグローバル化に抵抗していたのであれば，経済的にも文化的にも科学的にも，はるかに貧しかったであろう。

問6　懸念される西洋化を伴うものであるため，思想や慣習のグローバル化には抵抗せねばならないという想定。(48字)

問7　グローバル化は帝国主義の特徴である以上に，はるかに大きなもので，はるかにすばらしいものである。

問8　貧しい人々や敗者の利益に十分注意を払うようなやり方で，経済的交流と技術の進歩の目覚しい恩恵をいかにして有効に活用するかということ。(65字)

▶▶▶　**設問解説**　◀◀◀

問1　下線部(1)は「このような歴史の解釈」という意味。第1段落第4文に「ヨーロッパにおいて大きな進歩が生まれたという見事に型にはまった歴史の記述」とあり，その具体的内容がコロン以下と，続く第5文に「ヨーロッパでまずルネサンスが起き，続いて啓蒙運動と産業革命が起き，これらが西洋における生活水準の向上につながった。そして，今では西洋の偉大な業績が世界に広まっている」と述べられている。したがって，この内容をまとめる。

　　□ reading「解釈」

問2　下線部(2)を含む文の the opposite perspective とは，第1段落で述べられた「グローバル化に対する肯定的な捉え方」とは正反対の立場，すなわち「グローバル化に対する否定的な捉え方」のこと。また，直後の第2段落第2文で「この見解では，現代の資本主義は，ヨーロッパと北アメリカの貪欲な西洋諸国に

よって後押しされ，導かれており，世界のより貧しい人々の利益にはならない貿易や取引関係の規則を定めたのである」と具体的内容が述べられている。したがって，下線部(2)を含む文は「西洋による支配が，ときに西洋の帝国主義が続いているとみなされることもあり，問題の原因なのである」という意味であると推測できる。

ア.「邪悪な力によって生まれる」

イ.「東洋の敗北であるとみなされる」

ウ.「すべての問題の原因」

エ.「現在急を要する問題」

問3　空所(3)を含む文は，直前の文の「果たしてグローバル化は本当に新たな西洋による災いなのであろうか」という問いに対する答えを述べた文。It は globalization の代用である。続く第3段落第3・4文では，「数千年にわたって，グローバル化は，移動や貿易，移住，文化的影響の伝播，科学や技術に関するものを含めて知識と理解の普及を通じて世界の進歩に貢献してきたのである。こうした世界規模の相互関係は，様々な国を前進させるのに大きな成果をあげることが多かった」とあり，「グローバル化が新しいものでもなく，災いでもない」ということを言っている。さらに，同段落第5・6文では「それらは必ずしも西洋の影響が増大したものとなって現れたわけではない。実際，グローバル化を推し進めた中心は，西洋から遠く離れたところであることが多かった」とあり，「グローバル化が必ずしも西洋によるものではなかった」と言っている。よって，正解はエ。

ア.「新しいものであり，しばしば西洋によるものであるが，災いではない」

イ.「新しいものでもなければ，必ずしも西洋によるものでもないが，恩恵である」

ウ.「新しいものであり，しばしば西洋によるものであり，恩恵である」

エ.「新しいものでもなければ，必ずしも西洋によるものでもないし，災いでもない」

問4　下線部(4)を含む第4段落は，第3段落第6文で述べた「グローバル化を推し進めた中心は，西洋から遠く離れたところであることが多かった」ことの具体例として，紀元1000年頃の状況について論じている。下線部の後ろの第4段落第3～5文では「当時中国がグローバル化を推し進めた中心であった」と言っている。また，第5段落第2文では，今日の状況について「西洋から東洋という逆方向であるが」と述べている。よって，下線部(4)を含む文が「紀元1000年頃，科学と技術，数学が世界規模に勢力を広げたことで旧世界の性質が変わろうとしていたが，その普及は当時，かなりの部分が，今日私たちが目にしてい

るものとは<u>逆方向</u>であった」という意味なると考えられる。正解は in the opposite direction of what we see today となる。

　　□ in the direction of A「Aの方向に」　　□ opposite「反対の」

問5　ポイントは，had it resisted 以下が，仮定法過去完了の条件節が倒置の語順になったものであること。if it had resisted ... と書き換えられる。前置詞 of に続く名詞が and で結ばれた mathematics と science と technology で，全体として the globalization を修飾していることに注意。

　　□ a lot + 比較級「ずっと…，はるかに…」　　□ resist「に抵抗する」

問6　下線部(6)を含む文は「それ自体望ましくない結果を生むだけではない。歴史を通じた世界規模での交流を考えると，非西洋社会は自ら墓穴を，貴重な文化という面でも墓穴を掘ることになりかねない」という意味。it が指すものは「それ自体望ましくない結果を生むだけではなく，非西洋社会が自ら墓穴を掘ることにもなりかねない」ことである。前の文には「このような想定は偏狭な傾向を助長し，科学と知識の客観性の可能性をむしばむ」とあることから，下線部の it は，This assumption を指している。This assumption とはさらに前の文に述べられた「思想と慣習のグローバル化には，懸念される西洋化を伴うという理由で抵抗しなければならないという誤った判断」ということである。

問7　下線部(7)の直前の文で，「グローバル化を何にもまして帝国主義の特徴であるとみなすとしたら大きな間違いであろう」と述べていることから，that よりもはるかに大きなもので，はるかにすばらしいものである It とは globalization のことであり，それより劣る that とは a feature of imperialism のことである。ダッシュ内の much greater は直前の much bigger を言い換えたもの。

　　□ much + 比較級「ずっと…，はるかに…」

問8　下線部(8)を含む文は「グローバル化による経済的な利益と損失の分配という論点は，まったく別の問題であることに変わりなく，さらに進んだ，そして極めて実際的意味のある論点として，取り組まなければならない」という意味。「グローバル化による利益と損失の分配という論点」については，第9段落第2文に「大きな問題は，貧しい人々や弱者の利益に十分注意を払うようなやり方で，経済的交流と技術の進歩の目覚しい恩恵をいかにして有効に活用するかということである」と述べられている。

　　□ issue「問題，論点」　　□ distribution「分配」　　□ gain「利益」　　□ loss「損失」

> ## Outline
>
> ¶ 1　　**導入**　賛成派は，グローバル化を西洋文明による世界に対する貢献であるとみなす
>
> ¶ 2　　　　　　反対派は，グローバル化を西洋による支配であるとみなす

要 約

　グローバル化の賛成派も反対派も西洋化であるとみなす点は一致しているが，グローバル化は古くからあるもので，必ずしも西洋によるものではなく，世界の進歩に貢献してきた。グローバル化による恩恵を認めた上で，いかに公平に分配し有効に活用するかが問題である。(123字)

▶▶ 構文・語句解説 ◀◀

─ 第1段落 ─

　[1]Globalization is often seen as global Westernization. [2]On this point, there is substantial agreement among many proponents and opponents. [3]Those who take an upbeat view of globalization see it as a marvelous contribution of Western civilization to the world. [4]There is a nicely stylized history in which the great developments happened in Europe: First came the Renaissance, then the Enlightenment and the Industrial Revolution, and these led to a massive increase in living standards in the West. [5]And now the great achievements of the West are spreading to the world. [6]In this view, globalization is not only good, it is also a gift from the West to the world. [7]The champions of this reading of history tend to feel upset not just because this great benefaction is seen as a curse but also because it is undervalued and condemned by an ungrateful world.

　[1]グローバル化は世界規模での西洋化であるとみなされることが多い。[2]この点では，多くの賛成派と反対派の間で実質的に意見は一致している。[3]グローバル化を楽観的に捉える者は，グローバル化とは西洋文明による世界に対するすばらしい貢献であるとみなしている。[4]ヨーロッパにおいて大きな進歩が生まれたという見事に型にはまった歴史の記述がある。つまり，ルネサンスが起き，続いて啓蒙運動と産業革命が起き，これらが西洋における生活水準の大幅な向上につながった。[5]そして，今では西洋の偉大な業績が世界に広まっているというものである。[6]この見解では，グローバル化とは良いものであるというだけではなく，西洋から世界への贈り物でもある。[7]このような歴史の解釈を支持する者が腹を立てがちなのは，このようなすば

らしい施し物が災いの元であるとみなされているからだけではなく，恩知らずな世界に過小評価され，非難されているからでもある。

1 □ globalization「グローバル化」　　□ see O as C「OがCであるとみなす」
　□ global「全世界の，世界的な」　　□ Westernization「西洋化」

2 □ substantial「実質上の／かなりの，相当な」　　□ agreement「同意，（意見の）一致」
　□ proponent「支持者」　　□ opponent「反対者」

3 □ those who ...「…する人々」　　□ take a ... view of A「Aを…に考える」
　□ upbeat「楽天的な」　　□ marvelous「すばらしい」
　□ contribution of A to B「AのBに対する貢献」

4 First came the Renaissance は副詞＋Ｖ Ｓ の語順。
　□ stylized「型にはまった」　　□ the Renaissance「ルネサンス」
　□ the Industrial Revolution「産業革命」　　□ lead to A「Aにつながる」
　□ massive「大きな」　　□ living standard「生活水準」

5 □ achievement「業績，達成」　　□ spread「拡大する／拡大」

6 globalization is not only good, it is also a gift ... は not only X but also Y「XだけでなくYも」の but が省略されたもの。

7 not just because ... but also because ～ は not just X but also Y「XだけでなくYも」の X，Y に because節がきたもの。
　□ champion「擁護者／を擁護する」　　□ feel upset「腹を立てる」　　□ curse「災い」
　□ undervalue「を過小評価する」　　□ condemn「を非難する」　　□ ungrateful「恩知らずの」

第２段落

¹From the opposite perspective, Western dominance — sometimes seen as a continuation of Western imperialism — is the devil of the piece. ²In this view, contemporary capitalism, driven and led by greedy Western countries in Europe and North America, has established rules of trade and business relations that do not serve the interests of the poorer people in the world. ³The celebration of various non-Western identities — defined by religion (as in Islamic fundamentalism), region (as in the championing of Asian values), or culture (as in the glorification of Confucian ethics) — can add fuel to fire of confrontation with the West.

¹反対の立場からは，西洋による支配が，ときに西洋の帝国主義が続いているものであるとみなされることもあり，諸悪の根源なのである。²この見解では，現代の資本主義は，ヨーロッパと北アメリカの貪欲な西洋諸国によって後押しされ，導かれており，世界のより貧しい人々の

利益にはならない貿易や取引関係の規則を定めたのである。³様々な非西洋的な独自性を賞賛することは，イスラム原理主義のような宗教によって規定されるものであれ，アジア的価値観の支持のような地域によって規定されるものであれ，儒教倫理の賛美のような文化によって規定されるものであれ，西洋との対立に油を注ぐことになりかねない。

1 sometimes seen ... Western imperialism は，Western dominance を補足説明する過去分詞句。

☐ perspective「大局的な見方」　　☐ dominance「支配」　　☐ continuation「継続」

☐ imperialism「帝国主義」

2 driven and led by ... North America は contemporary capitalism を補足説明する過去分詞句で，by 以下は driven と led に共通して続いている。

that 以下は rules of trade and business relations を修飾する関係代名詞節。

☐ contemporary「現代の」　　☐ capitalism「資本主義」　　☐ drive「を動かす」

☐ lead「を導く」　　☐ greedy「貪欲な」　　☐ business relation「取引関係」

☐ serve「に役立つ」　　☐ interest「利益／関心」

3 defined by ... Confucian ethics) は The celebration of various non-Western identities を補足説明する過去分詞句。

☐ celebration「賞賛」　　☐ identity「独自性，アイデンティティー」

☐ define「を規定する，定義する」　　☐ religion「宗教」

☐ Islamic fundamentalism「イスラム原理主義」　　☐ region「地域」　　☐ values「価値観」

☐ glorification「賛美」　　☐ ethics「倫理」

☐ add fuel to A「Aに油を注ぐ，Aをあおり立てる」　　☐ confrontation「対立」

───── 第3段落 ─────

¹Is globalization really a new Western curse? ²It is, in fact, neither new nor necessarily Western; and it is not a curse. ³Over thousands of years, globalization has contributed to the progress of the world through travel, trade, migration, spread of cultural influences, and diffusion of knowledge and understanding (including that of science and technology). ⁴These global interrelations have often been very productive in the advancement of different countries. ⁵They have not necessarily taken the form of increased Western influence. ⁶Indeed, the active agents of globalization have often been located far from the West.

　¹果たしてグローバル化は本当に新たな西洋による災いなのであろうか。²実際は，新しいものでもなければ，必ずしも西洋によるものでもないし，災いでもない。³数千年にわたって，グローバル化は，移動や貿易，移住，文化的影響の伝播，科学や技術に関するものを含めて知識

と理解の普及を通じて世界の進歩に貢献してきたのである。⁴こうした世界規模の相互関係は、様々な国を前進させるのに大きな成果をあげることが多かった。⁵それらは必ずしも西洋の影響が増大したものとなって現れたわけではない。⁶実際、グローバル化を推し進めた中心は、西洋から遠く離れたところであることが多かった。

3 that of science and technology = the diffusion of knowledge and understanding of science and technology

□ contribute to A「Aに貢献する」　　□ migration「移住」　　□ diffusion「普及」
□ including A「Aを含めて」
4 □ interrelation「相互関係」　　□ productive「成果の上がる、生産的な」
□ advancement「促進、前進」
5 □ take the form of A「Aとなって現れる、Aの形をとる」
6 □ agent「動因、主体」　　□ be located「位置する」

- -

第4段落

¹To illustrate, consider the world at the beginning of the last millennium rather than at its end. ²Around 1000 A.D., the global reach of science, technology, and mathematics was changing the nature of the old world, but the diffusion then was, to a great extent, in the opposite direction of what we see today. ³The high technology in the world of 1000 A.D. included paper, the printing press, the crossbow, gunpowder, the iron-chain suspension bridge, the kite, the magnetic compass, the wheelbarrow, and the rotary fan. ⁴A millennium ago, these items were used extensively in China — and were practically unknown elsewhere. ⁵Globalization spread them across the world, including Europe.

¹具体例として、先の千年紀の終わりというよりは、始まりの頃の世界を考えてみよう。²紀元1000年頃、科学と技術、数学が世界規模に勢力を広げたことで旧世界の性質が変わろうとしていたが、その普及は当時、かなりの部分、今日私たちが目にしているものとは逆方向であった。³紀元1000年の世界の先端技術には、紙や印刷機、石弓、火薬、鉄製のつり橋、凧、磁気羅針盤、手押し車、扇風機が含まれていた。⁴1000年前に、こうしたものは中国で大規模に使われていたのであり、それ以外のところではほとんど知られていなかった。⁵グローバル化が、これらをヨーロッパを含む世界中に広めたのである。

1 □ to illustrate「例を挙げて説明すると、たとえば」　　□ millennium「千年紀、千年間」
□ X rather than Y「YよりむしろX」

2 □ reach「範囲，勢力範囲」　　□ the nature of A「Aの性質」

　□ to a great extent「大部分は，大いに」

3 □ printing press「印刷機」　　□ gunpowder「火薬」　　□ iron-chain「鉄鎖」

　□ suspension bridge「つり橋」　　□ kite「凧」　　□ magnetic compass「磁気羅針盤」

　□ rotary fan「扇風機」

4 □ extensively「広範囲に，大規模に」　　□ practically「ほとんど」

　□ elsewhere「それ以外のところで」

─── 第5段落 ───

¹Indeed, Europe would have been a lot poorer — economically, culturally, and scientifically — had it resisted the globalization of mathematics, science, and technology at that time. ²And today, the same principle applies, though in the reverse direction (from West to East). ³To reject the globalization of science and technology because it represents Western influence and imperialism would not only amount to overlooking global contributions — drawn from many different parts of the world — that lie solidly behind so-called Western science and technology, but would also be quite a silly practical decision, given the extent to which the whole world can benefit from the process.

　¹実際，ヨーロッパが当時の数学と科学と技術のグローバル化に抵抗していたのであれば，経済的にも文化的にも科学的にも，はるかに貧しかったであろう。²そして，今日，同じ原理が，西洋から東洋という逆方向ではあるが，当てはまる。³西洋の影響力や帝国主義を象徴するからといって科学と技術のグローバル化を拒絶するとしたら，いわゆる西洋の科学や技術の背後にしっかりと存在する世界規模での貢献を，もとをただせば世界の様々な地域に由来するものであるが，見落とすことになるばかりか，全世界がその過程からどれほど利益を得られるのかを考えれば，まったく浅はかな実務的決定ということになるだろう。

2 □ principle「原理，原則」　　□ apply「当てはまる」　　□ reverse「逆の／を逆にする」

3 because it ... and imperialism は reject を修飾する副詞節。

not only X but also Y の X に amount to ... and technology，Y に be quite ... the process がきている。

ダッシュ内の drawn from ... the world は global contributions を補足説明しており，that lie ... and technology は global contributions を修飾する関係代名詞節。

□ reject「を拒絶する」　　□ represent「を表す」　　□ amount to A「Aに相当する，等しい」

□ overlook「を見過ごす，見落とす」　　□ solidly「しっかりと」　　□ so-called「いわゆる」

27

第6段落

¹The misdiagnosis that globalization of ideas and practices has to be resisted because it entails dreaded Westernization has played quite a regressive part in the colonial and postcolonial world. ²This assumption encourages parochial tendencies and undermines the possibility of objectivity in science and knowledge. ³It is not only counterproductive in itself; given the global interactions throughout history, it can also cause non-Western societies to shoot themselves in the foot — even in their precious cultural foot.

---

¹思想と慣習のグローバル化には，懸念される西洋化が伴うという理由で抵抗しなければならないという誤った判断は，植民地や植民地独立後の世界でかなり退行的役割を果たしてきた。²このような想定は偏狭な傾向を助長し，科学と知識の客観性の可能性をむしばむ。³それ自体望ましくない結果を生むだけではない。歴史を通じた世界規模での交流を考えると，非西洋社会は自ら墓穴を，貴重な文化という面でも墓穴を掘ることにもなりかねない。

1 that globalization ... dreaded Westernization は The misdiagnosis と同格の名詞節。

□ misdiagnosis「誤った判断，誤診」　　□ practice「慣習」　　□ entail「を（必然的に）伴う」

□ dreaded「恐ろしい」　　□ play a ... part in A「Aで…の役割を果たす」

□ colonial「植民地の」　　□ postcolonial「植民地独立後の」

2 □ assumption「想定，仮定」　　□ undermine「を徐々に衰えさせる」

□ objectivity「客観性」

3 It is not only counterproductive ... throughout history, it can also cause ～ は not only X but also Y「XだけでなくYも」の but が省略されたもの。

□ counterproductive「逆効果の」　　□ in itself「それ自体」

□ interaction「交流，相互作用」　　□ shoot *oneself* in the foot「自ら墓穴を掘る」

□ precious「貴重な」

第7段落

¹To see globalization as merely Western imperialism of ideas and beliefs would be a serious and costly error, in the same way that any European resistance to Eastern influence would have been at the beginning of the last millennium. ²Of course, there are

issues related to globalization that do connect with imperialism (the history of conquests, colonialism, and alien rule remains relevant today in many ways), and a postcolonial understanding of the world has its merits. ³But it would be a great mistake to see globalization primarily as a feature of imperialism. ⁴It is much bigger — much greater — than that.

---

¹グローバル化を思想と信念による西洋の帝国主義にすぎないとみなすとすれば，重大なそして手痛い誤りとなるであろう。先の千年紀の始まりに，東洋の影響に対してヨーロッパが抵抗していたとすればそうであったのと同じことである。²もちろん，グローバル化と関連したことには，確かに帝国主義とつながる論点があるし(征服や植民地化，外国の支配の歴史は今日なお多くの面で実際的意味がある)，また世界に対する植民地独立後の理解はそれ相応の価値がある。³しかし，グローバル化を何にもまして帝国主義の特徴であるとみなすとしたら大きな間違いであろう。⁴グローバル化は帝国主義の特徴である以上に，はるかに大きなもので，はるかにすばらしいものである。

1 □ costly「手痛い，犠牲の大きい」　　□ resistance to A「Aに対する抵抗」
2 Of course は第3文の But と呼応して，「もちろん…である。しかし〜」という意味。
　that do connect with imperialism は issues を修飾する関係代名詞節。
　do connect の do は動詞強調の助動詞。
　□ related to A「Aと関連している」　　□ connect with A「Aとつながる」
　□ conquest「征服」　　□ colonialism「植民地化，植民地主義」　　□ alien「外国の」
　□ rule「支配」　　□ remain C「Cのままである」　　□ relevant「実際的意味がある」
　□ in many ways「多くの点で」　　□ merit「価値」
3 □ primarily「主に」

- -

─── 第8段落 ───

¹The issue of the distribution of economic gains and losses from globalization remains an entirely separate question, and it must be addressed as a further — and extremely relevant — issue. ²There is extensive evidence that the global economy has brought prosperity to many different areas of the globe. ³Pervasive poverty dominated the world a few centuries ago; there were only a few rare pockets of affluence. ⁴In overcoming that poverty, extensive economic interrelations and modern technology have been and remain influential. ⁵What has happened in Europe, America, Japan, and East Asia has important messages for all other regions, and we cannot go very far into understanding the nature of globalization

today without first acknowledging the positive fruits of global economic contacts.

^{1}グローバル化による経済的な利益と損失の分配という論点は，まったく別の問題であることに変わりなく，さらに進んだ，そして極めて実際的意味のある論点として，取り組まなければならない。^{2}世界規模の経済が地球上の多くの様々な地域に繁栄をもたらしたという広範囲に及ぶ証拠がある。^{3}数世紀前には，蔓延する貧困が世界を席巻していたし，豊かなところはほんのわずかしかなかった。^{4}そうした貧困を克服する上で，広範囲に及ぶ経済的相互関係や近代技術が影響を与えてきたし，そうであることに今も変わりない。^{5}ヨーロッパやアメリカ，日本，東アジアで起こったことは，他のあらゆる地域にとって重要な意味合いがあるし，まず世界規模での経済関係の実り多い成果を認めることなくしては，今日のグローバル化の性質をあまり深く理解することはできない。

1 □ address「に取り組む，焦点を当てる」
2 that 以下は extensive evidence と同格の名詞節。
　 □ extensive「広範囲に渡る」　　□ prosperity「繁栄」　　□ different A（複数名詞）「様々な A」
3 □ pervasive「蔓延する」　　□ dominate「に著しく影響する」
　 □ pocket「〈周囲と異なる〉地域」　　□ affluence「豊かさ」
4 □ overcome「を克服する」　　□ influential「影響力がある」
5 □ acknowledge「を認める」　　□ positive「好ましい」　　□ fruit「成果」

─── 第9段落 ───

^{1}Indeed, we cannot reverse the economic predicament of the poor across the world by withholding from them the great advantages of contemporary technology, the well-established efficiency of international trade and exchange, and the social as well as economic merits of living in an open society. ^{2}Rather, the main issue is how to make good use of the remarkable benefits of economic intercourse and technological progress in a way that pays adequate attention to the interests of the deprived and the weak. ^{3}That is, I would argue, the constructive question that emerges from the so-called antiglobalization movements.

^{1}実際，現代の技術のすばらしい利点と，国際貿易や交換の定評ある効率，開放的な社会で暮らすことの経済的価値だけでなく社会的価値を世界中の貧しい人々に与えないでおくことでは，こうした人々の経済的逆境を順境に変えることはできない。^{2}むしろ，大きな問題は，貧し

い人々や弱者の利益に十分注意を払うようなやり方で，経済的交流と技術の進歩の目覚しい恩恵をいかにして有効に活用するかということである。³それこそ，いわゆる反グローバル化運動から現れる建設的な問いかけではないか，と私は言いたい。

---

1 withholding from ... open society は withhold A from B「AをBに与えずにおく」の A に当たる the great ... open society が後ろに移動している。

the social as well as economic merits ... は X as well as Y「XもYも／YだけでなくXも」の X に social，Y に economic がきており，ともに merits を修飾している。

□ well-established「定評のある，確立した」　　□ efficiency「効率」

2 □ make use of A「Aを利用する」　　□ remarkable「目覚しい，注目に値する」

□ intercourse「交流」　　□ pay attention to A「Aに注意を払う」

□ adequate「十分な，適切な」　　□ the deprived「貧しい人々」　　□ the weak「弱者」

3 That is, I would argue, the constructive ... ＝ I would argue (that) that is the constructive ...

□ constructive「建設的な」　　□ emerge from A「Aから現れる」

□ antiglobalization movement「反グローバル化運動」

医学の起源

解 答

問1 however difficult it is to visualize healing in past eras

問2 現代の通常の医療を行う医師と，通常の医療に欠けているものを補う代替医療を行う者には共通点があった，ということ。(55字)

問3 イ．magic

問4 ウ．man began to evolve symbolic language

問5 おそらく，人間と地球に住む他の生物との間には連続感があり，宇宙が作用するあり方に対して全体的な満足感があったであろう。

問6 頭蓋骨に穴を開けるという考えは，多くの様々な社会が思いついたように思われるが，その社会が互いに習得しあった可能性はほとんどない。

問7 ウ．heal

問8 人間社会の最も初期の時代に，あらゆることについて答えを知っていた人で，物事がうまくいかないときには問題を解決し，最も初期の医療の介入として，患者の頭蓋骨に穴をあけるというような手術も施した。(95字)

▶▶▶ 設問解説 ◀◀◀

問1 下線部の直後に if we … or two と副詞節があり，その後ろに we would see … と主節が続いていることから下線部は副詞節となるはずである。与えられた語(句)と第1段落最終文に「科学的医学の時代以前の生活がどのようであったかという正確な印象を得るのは難しい」と述べられていることと，下線部の直前の Yet に着目すると「過去の時代の治療を想像することがどれほど難しくても」という意味になるとわかる。したがって，however＋形容詞＋S V「たとえどれほど…しても」という譲歩の表現になる。it は形式主語で，to visualize healing in past eras が真主語。

　□ visualize「を心に思い浮かべる」　□ healing「治療」　□ era「時代」

問2 下線部の did は代動詞である。したがって，本問は they と did がそれぞれ何を指しているのか明らかにすることがポイント。直前の第3段落第1文の主節に「2つの流派にかつて共通点があったということを想像するのは難しい」と述べられている。これを受けて第2文で they did とあるので，they did は the two schools ever had anything in common の代用である。さらに，与え

られた制限字数から the two schools の内容を明示する必要があるが，これは第2段落第3文の the two schools，つまり同段落第1文の what we now call conventional medicine と第2文の what we now call alternative medicine のこと。よって，これらの内容を制限字数内でまとめる。

問3 空所を含む文は「医学はもとをただせば実は(3)なのである」という意味。直前の第5段落第1文には「治療の本当の起源は，ここ数世紀の抜け目のない臨床医と経験に頼る薬草医の時代よりもさらにさかのぼる」と述べられ，さらに第4段落第2文には「医学の先祖をさかのぼれば，部族のシャーマンや魔術師にたどりつく」とある。また，空所の後ろの第6段落以降で「医学の起源」について，「言語の発達より以前であること」および「賢者が問題解決のために呪文を唱えたり，頭蓋開口術のような手術を施したこと」が述べられている。これらの内容から，医学がもとをただすと何であったかを判断する。
ア.「芸術」イ.「魔術」ウ.「霊感」エ.「自然」

問4 空所を含む第6段落の第1文に「人間による治療行為の最も古い起源は，どのような形であれ，人間によって記録された歴史以前のものである」ことが述べられている。また，第2文前半には「治療の記録」が存在することが述べられている。したがって，「治療行為は言語に先立つもの」であることは明らか。
ア.「口承による伝承が滅び始めた」
イ.「人間が多様な作物を栽培し始めた」
ウ.「人間が記号による言語を発達させ始めた」
エ.「医学が確立した」

問5 There be S「Sがある」の表現で，would have been は過去に関する推量を表す。ポイントは2つの and が結ぶものの確定であるが，mankind と the other inhabitants of the planet が between A and B「AとBの間に」の A と B に当たる。2つ目の and は a sense of continuity と a sense of overall satisfaction を結んでいる。なお，the way the universe operated は the way S V ...「…する方法，様子」の表現。
□ presumably「おそらく，たぶん」　　□ sense of continuity「連続感」
□ mankind「人類，人間」　　□ inhabitant「住人」　　□ the planet「地球」
□ overall「全体の」　　□ satisfaction with A「Aに満足すること」
□ operate「作用する」

問6 the idea は直前の trephining を指しており，前半部では S occur to A「S〈考えなど〉がA〈人〉に思い浮かぶ」が用いられている。seem to have *done* と完了形不定詞になっているので「…したと思われる」と意味をとる。後半部は「それら（＝多くの様々な社会）がお互いから学んだ可能性はほとんどなくて」が

逐語訳。them は動名詞 learning の意味上の主語である。注意すべきは with が付帯状況の with ではないので「…しながら」などと訳さないこと。ここでは前半部に対して補足説明をしているので，前から訳出すればよい。

　　□ different A（複数名詞）「様々なA」　　□ likelihood「可能性」

問7 空所を含む第13段落の第1文では，第9〜12段落の内容を受けて，「ここには頭痛の治療の最初の証拠がある」と述べている。つまり，「人間社会の初期の時代に，誰かが自分以外の人間を治療しようと試みていた」ことがわかる。

　　ア.「を慰める」　イ.「を傷つける」　ウ.「を治療する」　エ.「をぞっとさせる」

問8 第7段落第1文には「人間社会の最も初期に，あらゆることに対する答えを知っていた」ことが述べられ，第8段落第1文には「物事がうまくいかないときには問題を解決した」ことが述べられている。また，第9段落第2〜4文に「最も初期の医療的介入として，患者の頭蓋骨に穴を開けるというような手術をした」ことが述べられている。これらの内容を制限字数内でまとめる。

Outline

¶ 1	導入	科学的医学の時代以前のことを想像するのは難しい
¶2-3	主題	通常の医学と代替医学には共通点が多い
¶4-5	展開	医学の起源は呪術である
¶ 6		医療行為は言語以前のものである
¶7-12	例	賢者が問題解決をしたり，頭蓋開口術のような手術を施した
¶ 13	結論	人間社会の最も初期の時代に医療行為が存在していた

要　約

　通常の医学と代替医学は一昔前まで区別できないものであり，医学の起源は呪術にあり，頭蓋開口術のような医療行為が行われていた証拠もある。人間社会の最も初期の時代に医療行為が存在していた。(91字)

▶▶▶ 構文・語句解説 ◀◀◀

─ 第1段落 ─

　[1]If you grow up under one particular system or culture, it is actually very difficult to imagine what life might really have been like before it, or is like outside it.　[2]It is almost impossible for urban teenagers, for example, to imagine life before the car or the telephone (or before the cell phone for that matter).　[3]In the same way it is hard for citizens of the Western world to get an accurate impression of what life was like before the era of scientific medicine.

¹ある特定の体制あるいは文化の中で育つと，その体制や文化が存在する前の生活は実際どのようであったのかとか，その体制や文化の外ではどのようなのか，ということを想像するのは，実のところ大変難しい。²たとえば，都会の十代の若者が，車や電話が登場する前（さらに言うなら，携帯電話が登場する前）の生活を想像することはほとんど不可能である。³同様に，西洋諸国の国民が，科学的医学の時代以前の生活がどのようであったかという正確な印象を得るのは難しい。

1 or は have been like before it と is like outside it を結んでいる。
　□ grow up「成長する，大人になる」　　□ particular「特定の」　　□ system「制度」
　□ actually「実際に」　　□ what A is like「Aはどのようなものか」
2 before the car ... that matter は life を修飾する前置詞句。
　□ urban「都会の」　　□ for that matter「それをさらに言うと」
3 □ citizen「国民／市民」　　□ accurate「正確な」　　□ impression of A「Aの印象」
　□ medicine「医学，医療」

━━━ 第2段落 ━━━

¹Yet however difficult it is to visualize healing in past eras, if we could go back a century or two we would see that what we now call conventional medicine was not always the established (and conventional) school. ²Furthermore, what we now call alternative medicine was not the alternative to it. ³In the fairly recent past, the two schools were virtually indistinguishable.

¹しかし，過去の時代の治療を想像することがどれほど難しくても，1，2世紀戻ることができれば，通常の医学と現在呼ばれているものが，必ずしも確立された（そして通常の）流派ではなかったことがわかるだろう。²さらに，代替医学と現在呼ばれているものは，通常の医学に対する代替物ではなかったのである。³ほんの一昔前はこの2つの流派はほとんど区別ができなかった。

1 if we ...., we would see ... は仮定法過去。
　□ see that節「…だとわかる」　　□ what we call A「いわゆるA」
　□ conventional「通常の，従来の」　　□ not always「必ずしも…とは限らない」
　□ established「確立された」　　□ school「（学問・芸術の）流派，学派」
2 □ furthermore「さらに」　　□ alternative to A「Aの代わり（となるもの）」

3 □ fairly「かなり」　　□ virtually「ほとんど」

　□ indistinguishable「区別することができない」

. . . .

┌─ 第3段落 ────────────────────────────

　[1]Looking at today's conventional doctors equipped with their white coats, diplomas and, stethoscopes, and comparing them and their appurtenances with the wide range of dress, fashion, thought, speech and techniques employed by complementary practitioners it is hard for us now to imagine that the two schools ever had anything in common.　[2]But they did. [3]In fact it's conventional medicine that is the recent upstart, the brash new kid on the block.

└──────────────────────────────────────

　[1]白衣と医師免状と聴診器を身につけた今日の通常の医師を見て，彼らと彼らの道具を，補助的な治療を行う者が使っている多様な衣服，流儀，思想，言葉遣い，技術と比較すれば，今の我々がこれら2つの流派にかつて共通点があったということを想像するのは難しい。[2]しかし，共通点はあった。[3]実際，通常の医学こそ，最近の成り上がり者であり，生意気な新参者なのである。

1 Looking at ... complementary practioners は分詞構文。and は Looking ... と comparing で始まる2つの分詞構文を結んでいる。

equipped with ... and, stethoscopes は doctors を修飾する過去分詞句。

employed by complementary practitioners は the wide ... and techniques を修飾する過去分詞句。

　□ equip A with B「A〈人・建物など〉にB〈必要な道具など〉を備え付ける」

　□ diploma「資格免許／卒業証書」　　□ stethoscope「聴診器」

　□ compare A with B「AをBと比較する」　　□ a range of A「多種多様なA」

　□ fashion「やり方，流儀」　　□ speech「言葉遣い」　　□ employ「を使用する」

　□ complementary「補足的な」　　□ have A in common「Aを共有している」

3 it's conventional medicine that ... の it is ... that 〜 は強調構文。is の主語である conventional medicine が強調されている。

　□ in fact「実際に」　　□ upstart「成り上がり者」

　□ brash「生意気な」　　□ new kid on the block「(素性・実力の不明な)新入り」

. . . .

[1]What we now call conventional medicine has only recently graduated as a scientific (or partly scientific) discipline embracing a central corps of accepted philosophy, rules and regulations. [2]Before that comparatively recent era, the ancestors of our modern conventional doctors were an ill-assorted group, comprising a few scientists, a few skillful and observant bedside physicians, and a larger collection of hopefuls, fakes and frauds, all of whom can trace their ancestry back beyond alchemists, herbalists, priests, and nuns, to tribal shamans and magicians.

[1]現在，我々が通常の医学と呼んでいるものは，一連の広く認められている哲学，規則，規制を含む科学的な（あるいは部分的に科学的な）学問として，ごく最近独り立ちした。[2]この比較的新しい時代を迎える以前には，現代の通常の医学に携わる者の祖先は，雑多な者の集まりで，少数の科学者と少数の腕が良く観察の鋭い臨床医と，成功を期する人，詐欺師やぺてん師といった大勢の集団から構成されていたのであり，その全員が自分の先祖をさかのぼれば，錬金術師，薬草医，聖職者や修道女を経て，部族のシャーマンや魔術師にたどりつくことができる。

1 □ graduate「独り立ちする／卒業する」　　□ partly「部分的に」　　□ discipline「学問（分野）」
□ embrace「を包含する」　　□ corps「集団，団体」　　□ accepted「受け入れられている」
□ philosophy「哲学」　　□ regulation「規制，規定」

2 comprising a ... bedside physicians は an ill-assorted group を補足説明する分詞句。
all of whom ... 以下は a few scientists, ... and frauds を修飾する非制限用法の関係代名詞節。
□ comparatively「比較的」　　□ ancestor「祖先」
□ ill-assorted「ばらばらな／不釣り合いな」　　□ comprise「を構成する」
□ observant「観察の鋭い」　　□ physician「医者，内科医」
□ hopeful「希望を持っている人」　　□ fake「詐欺師」　　□ fraud「ぺてん師」
□ trace A back to B「A〈出所・起源など〉をBまでさかのぼって探る，たどる」
□ ancestry「先祖」　　□ alchemist「錬金術師」　　□ herbalist「薬草医」
□ priest「聖職者」　　□ nun「修道女」　　□ tribal「部族の」
□ shaman「シャーマン」北米・アジアなどの部族の宗教における霊能者。
□ magician「魔術師」

[1]Painful though it is for patients and healers to admit, the true origins of healing go back further than a few centuries of clever clinicians and experiential herbalists. [2]The true

pre-history of medicine is magic.

　¹患者にとっても治療する者にとっても認めるのはつらいことではあるが，治療の本当の起源は，ここ数世紀の抜け目のない臨床医と経験に頼る薬草医の時代よりもさらにさかのぼる。²医学はもとをただせば実は呪術なのである。

1 Painful though it is ... は形容詞＋though＋S V「Sは…だけれども」の譲歩の表現で，it は形式主語で，to admit が真主語。

□ painful「つらい，苦しい」　　□ healer「治療する人」　　□ origin「起源」

□ further than A「Aよりさらに昔に」　　□ clinician「臨床医」

2 □ pre-history「前段階」

第6段落

　¹The earliest origins of human healing activities pre-date any form of man-made recorded history, so that most of what follows is necessarily conjecture (a polite word for guesswork). ²However, healing seems to be mentioned in the very earliest known physical records of mankind's activities — so some form of it must have been in existence by the time man began to evolve symbolic language.

　¹人間による治療行為の最も古い起源は，どのような形であれ，人間によって記録された歴史以前のものである。それで，これから述べることの大部分はどうしても推測(当てずっぽうを丁寧に言い換えた語)になってしまう。²しかし治療は，現在知られている最も古い，人間の活動についての有形の記録の中で記述されているようである。したがって，人間が記号による言語を発達させ始めるより前に，何らかの形での治療が存在していたに違いない。

1 so that は「結果」を表し「それで…，その結果…」という意味。

□ pre-date「に先行する」　　□ follow「次に来る，続く」　　□ necessarily「必然的に」

□ conjecture「推測」　　□ polite「丁寧な」　　□ guesswork「当てずっぽう」

2 some＋単数名詞で「何らかの…，ある…」という意味。

some form of it の it は healing を指す。

□ mention「に触れる，言及する」　　□ physical「有形の，物質の」　　□ record「記録」

□ must have *done*「…したに違いない」　　□ in existence「存在して」

¹In the earliest days of human society, the local Wise Man was probably the one who had the answers to everything. ²He (or sometimes she) was the one who had the answers to the birth of the universe, the origins of mankind, the purpose of life and the remedy for disease. ³All these activities would almost certainly have been linked by a theory or legend unifying the forces of life, the purposes of the gods and nature, and the place of human beings in the universe. ⁴There would have been, presumably, a sense of continuity between mankind and the other inhabitants of the planet, and a sense of overall satisfaction with the way the universe operated.

¹人間社会の最も初期には，その土地の賢者がおそらく，あらゆることに対する答えを知る人間だっただろう。²彼（ときには彼女）は，宇宙の誕生，人類の起源，人生の目的，病気の治療法に対する答えを知っている人間だった。³これらの活動のすべては，ほとんど間違いなく，この世の様々な力や神と自然の目的，そして宇宙における人間の位置を統合する理論あるいは伝説に結びつけられていたであろう。⁴おそらく，人間と地球に住む他の生物との間には連続感があり，宇宙が作用するあり方に対して全体的な満足感があったであろう。

1 □ local「その土地の」

2 answer to A「Aへの答え」の A に当たるものが，and で結ばれた the birth of the universe, the origins of mankind, the purpose of life, the remedy for disease である。

　□ universe「宇宙」　　□ remedy「治療法／を治療する」

3 would have *done* は過去に関する推量を表し「…しただろう」という意味。

unifying 以下は a theory or legend を修飾する現在分詞句。

the forces of life と the purposes of the gods and nature と the place of human beings in the universe を and が結んでいる。

　□ almost certainly「〈文修飾で〉ほとんど間違いなく」　　□ link「を結びつける」
　□ theory「理論，学説」　　□ legend「伝説」

¹When things seemed to go wrong — such as storms, predation by vicious animals or occasional infections — the Wise Man would offer some explanations and some incantation or specific action to remedy the problem. ²If the problem was self-limiting (such as a solar eclipse), then the action (such as the South Sea Islanders' custom of banging drums and blowing trumpets to make the moon disgorge the sun) would be seen to be effective

and would be repeated each time the problem arose.

---

　¹物事がうまくいかないように見えるとき，たとえば嵐や，凶暴な動物に食べられたときや，ときおり発生する伝染病のときには，賢者が説明をしたり，その問題を取り除くために呪文を唱えたり特定の行為をしたりした。²その問題が自ずと解決するようなもの（たとえば日食）であったなら，その行為（たとえば太鼓を叩いたりラッパを吹いたりして，月に太陽を吐き出させるという南洋諸島の住人の慣習）は効き目があるとみなされ，その問題が生じるたびに繰り返された。

---

1 ダッシュ（——）以下は things の具体例。A such as B「たとえばBのようなA」の形である。

some explanations と some incantation or specific action を and が結んでおり，to remedy the problem は some incantation or specific action を修飾する形容詞用法の不定詞句。

　□ go wrong「うまくいかない」　　□ vicious「凶暴な」　　□ occasional「時折の」

　□ infection「伝染病」　　□ would *do*「…したものだ」

　□ offer O₁ O₂「O₁〈人〉に O₂〈物・事〉を提供する」　　□ specific「特定の」

2 then は If と呼応して「もし…なら，それなら〜」という意味。

each time the problem arose は would be repeated を修飾する副詞節。

　□ self-limiting「自ずと解決する／自ら制限する」　　□ solar eclipse「日食」

　□ South Sea Islander「南洋諸島の住人」　　□ custom「習慣」　　□ bang「を叩く」

　□ drum「太鼓」　　□ blow「を吹く」　　□ effective「効果的な」

　□ each time S V「…するたびに」　　□ arose＜arise「起こる，生じる」の過去形

- -

第9段落

　¹Precisely what the Wise Man said, we shall never know. ²But what the Wise Man did, we can guess at. ³He bashed holes in his patients' skulls. ⁴Trephining (the technical term for the therapeutic ventilation of a fellow human's skull) is offered by archaeologists as evidence of the earliest medical intervention. ⁵Skulls as old as 10,000 years have been found with unambiguous evidence that they have been trephined.

---

　¹正確には賢者がどんなことを言ったのか，我々には知る由もない。²しかし賢者が何をしたかは推測できる。³患者の頭蓋骨を叩いて穴を開けたのである。⁴頭蓋開口術（人間の頭蓋骨に治療上の通気穴を開けることを指す専門用語）は，考古学者たちが，最古の医療介入の証拠として提示している。⁵頭蓋開口術を受けたことがあるという紛れもない証拠のある，１万年も昔の頭

蓋骨が発見されている。

1 precisely what the Wise Man said は know の目的語である名詞節が主語の前に移動した形。

　　□ precisely「正確に」

2 what the Wise Man did は guess at A「Aを推測する」の A が主語の前に移動したもの。

3 □ bash「を強打する，へこます」　　□ skull「頭蓋骨」

4 □ technical term「専門用語」　　□ therapeutic「治療法の」　　□ ventilation「換気(装置)」

　　□ fellow human「人」　　□ archaeologist「考古学者」　　□ evidence「証拠」

　　□ intervention「介入」

5 as old as 10,000 years は Skulls を修飾する形容詞句。なお，with 以下も Skulls を修飾している。

　　□ unambiguous「紛れもない」

- -

――― 第10段落 ―――

[1]The Incas of Peru were masters of the art of trephining, but the idea seems to have occurred to many different societies, with little likelihood of them learning from each other. [2]If we are looking for evidence of the first doctor-patient relationship, this seems to be what we are seeking. [3]And, like most doctor-patient relationships since, it caused greater pain to the patient than to the doctor.

[1]ペルーのインカ族は頭蓋開口術を習得していたが，その考えは，多くの様々な社会が思いついたように思われるが，その社会が互いに習得しあった可能性はほとんどない。[2]もし我々が最初の医者と患者との関係を示す証拠を捜しているのなら，これこそが求めているもののようである。[3]そして，それ以降の医者と患者のほとんどの関係と同様に，この頭蓋開口術は医者よりも患者に大きな苦痛を与えた。

1 □ the Incas「インカ族」　　□ master of A「Aに精通した人」　　□ art「技術」

2 □ relationship「関係」　　□ seek「を捜し求める」

3 □ cause A to B「B〈人〉にA〈苦痛・損害など〉をもたらす，与える」　　□ pain「苦痛」

- -

――― 第11段落 ―――

[1]The holes in the skulls are neat and accurate, and there is usually fresh growth of bone around them, suggesting first, that someone other than the owner of the skull did the trephining, and the second, that the patient survived. [2]So what was the purpose of the

surgery? ³There are some clues. ⁴The holes are usually found near a preexisting crack in the skull, indicating an attempt to relieve the effect of a fracture.

¹頭蓋骨に開いた穴は整っていて正確であり，たいていその周囲に新たな骨の成長が見られる。このことが示唆するのは，第一に，この頭蓋骨の主以外の何者かが頭蓋開口術を施したということ，第二に患者がその後も生存していたことである。²それではこの外科手術の目的は何だったのか。³手がかりがいくつかある。⁴穴はたいてい，頭蓋骨のすでにひび割れていた箇所の近くに見つかっており，頭蓋骨折の影響を軽減しようとしたことを示している。

1 suggesting 以下は The holes ... around them の内容を追加説明する分詞句。

　suggesting の目的語である 2 つの that節を and が結んでいる。

　□ neat「きちんとした」　　□ A other than B「B以外のA」　　□ owner「所有者」

　□ survive「生き残る」

2 □ surgery「外科手術」

3 □ clue「手がかり」

4 indicating 以下は The holes ... the skull の内容を補足説明する分詞句。

　□ preexisting「すでに存在している」　　□ crack「裂け目，ひび」

　□ attempt to *do*「…する試み」　　□ relieve「を軽減する」　　□ effect of A「Aの影響」

　□ fracture「骨折」

- 第12段落 -

¹Presumably the trephiner must have had some special skills — or at least a lack of squeamishness — and his professional qualifications would probably have been inferred by potential patients from the survival of a few of his earlier clients. ²One skull in Sardinia dating from about 1400 BC shows that its late owner had had three operations before succumbing to a fourth.

¹たぶん，頭蓋開口術を行う者は特別な技術を持っていたか，あるいは少なくとも気が弱いということはなかったに違いない。そしてその人物の職業適性はおそらく，彼の患者となる可能性のある者によって，彼のそれまでの患者の数人が生き延びたということから推測されたことだろう。²サルジニアで見つかった紀元前1400年頃の頭蓋骨からは，今は亡きその持ち主が4度目の手術で死ぬまでに，3回の手術を受けていたことがわかっている。

1 would have *done* は過去に関する推量を表す。

☐ skill「技術」　　☐ a lack of A「Aの不足」　　☐ professional qualification「職業適性」

☐ infer「を推測する」　　☐ potential「潜在的な」　　☐ survival「生存」　　☐ client「依頼人」

2 in Sardinia と dating from about 1400 BC は共に One skull を修飾している。

☐ date from A「Aから始まる，Aにさかのぼる」　　☐ late A「故A，亡きA」

☐ operation「手術」

....

─── 第13段落 ───

^{1}Here, then, is the first evidence of treatment for headache, perhaps pre-dating the discovery of aspirin (originally extracted from willow-bark) by five millennia or more. ^{2}Whether or not the pre-historic healers ever said, 'Make two holes in his head and call me in the morning' we shall never know, but at least we are certain that, at the dawn of mankind's social organization, somebody seemed to be trying to do something to heal somebody else.

^{1}そうすると，ここには頭痛の治療の最初の証拠があり，おそらく（もともと柳の樹皮から抽出された）アスピリンの発見に5千年かそれ以上先行していることになるだろう。^{2}先史時代の治療者が「彼の頭に穴を2つ開けて，朝になったら私を呼びに来なさい」と言ったかどうか知る由もないが，少なくとも次のことは確かである。人類の社会的な組織体が生まれようとしていた頃，誰かが自分以外の人間を治療するために何かしようと試みていたようなのだ。

1 perhaps pre-dating 以下は the first evidence を補足説明する現在分詞句。

☐ Here is S「ここにSがある」　　☐ then「そうすると」　　☐ treatment「治療」

☐ aspirin「アスピリン」　　☐ originally「もともと」

☐ extract A from B「BからAを抽出する」　　☐ willow-bark「柳の樹皮」

☐ by A「Aだけ，Aの分」差を表す。　　☐ millennia＜millennium「1000年間」の複数形

2 Whether or ... the morning' は know の目的語である名詞節が主語の前に移動した形。

☐ pre-historic「先史時代の」　　☐ be certain that節「…だと確信している」

☐ the dawn「(事の)始まり，誕生，幕開け」　　☐ organization「組織」

4 言語の役割

問1 language can a group of people act in concert
問2 言語がある世代から次の世代へ口頭で伝わると，その言語は変化するが，この伝承過程には衰退や破滅に向かうものは何もない。
問3 ある言語を使用するなら，その人がその言語共同体に属することを意味するから。(37字)
問4 言語は種や血統と比べて拡散し変わりやすく，ある世代から次の世代へと必ず継承されるという確信を持つことさえできないので，言語共同体を数えたり確実に区別したりするのは必ずしも容易ではない，ということ。(98字)
問5 ウ
問6 とりわけ，ある特定の言語を使うということは，すべての既知の人間集団が持つ特徴であり，何世代にもわたって継続していくものである。
問7 ア

▶▶▶ 設問解説 ◀◀◀

問1 下線部(1)を含む第3段落第2文には「言語は人類を集団に分ける」ことが述べられ，下線部の直後には「それゆえに共通の歴史を持つことができる」と述べられている。したがって，「共通の言語を通して，ある集団の人々は協調できる」という意味の文を作る。下線部の直前に only を伴った副詞句が文頭に来ているので，倒置が起きることに注意。なお，in concert は「協同で，協力して」という意味。

問2 Languages change, ... the next と there is ... or extinction の2つの節をbut が結んでいる。前半部の as は「…するにつれて，…すると」という意味の接続詞。the next は the next generation のこと。後半部の which 以下は this process of transmission ではなく，nothing を修飾する関係代名詞節。下線部の前後に「言語は伝統を具現化したものであり，その伝統は不滅で，言語は衰退したり絶滅したりすることはない」と述べられていることから判断する。or は decay と extinction を結んでいる。
□ pass from A to B「AからBに伝わる」　　□ generation「世代」
□ process「過程」　　□ transmission「伝承」　　□ make for A「Aに向かう，進む」

44

□ decay「衰退」　　□ extinction「破滅」

問3　下線文(3)を含む文は「生物学的種および母系血統の一員であるかどうかと同様に，ある言語共同体の一員であるかどうかは明確な関係性に基づいている」という意味。直後の第6段落第3文には「生物学的種および母系血統の一員」であることが述べられており，第4文は Likewise「同様に」で始まり，「言語共同体の一員」であることが述べられている。したがって，この内容をまとめる。

□ relation「関係，関連」

問4　下線部(4)は「この言語的に定義された構成単位」という意味。つまり，直前の第6段落最終文の「言語共同体」を指す。したがって，言語共同体の短所が解答となるわけであるが，下線部を含む第7段落及び続く第8段落には，言語共同体の長所が述べられており，最終段落である第9段落に「言語共同体は種や血統と比べて拡散し変わりやすいので，数えたり確実に区別したりするのは必ずしも容易ではない」ことが述べられている。この内容を制限字数に留意してまとめればよい。

問5　下線部(5)は「しかし，多くの人々の母親，または父親の起源がわからないと知ったところで，言語のように，全体として集団ごとに境界線が引けるわけではない」という意味。つまり「血統は人口集団を区別するのに言語ほど役に立つものではない」という内容のものを選ぶ。したがって，正解はウ。なお，下線部の最後にある in the way that language does の does は puts a bound on a group as a whole の代用。

ア.「しかし，血統という単位は言語単位より人口集団を区別するのに役立つ」

イ.「しかし，血統という単位は言語単位と同様に人口集団を区別するのに役立たない」

ウ.「しかし，血統という単位は言語単位ほど人口集団を区別するのに役立たない」

エ.「しかし，血統という単位は言語単位と同じくらい人口集団を区別するのに役立つ」

□ be unaccounted for A「Aに対する理由の説明ができない」　　□ bound「境界(線)」
□ as a whole「全体として(の)」

問6　it は直前の名詞句 an undeniable functioning reality ではなく，下線部(6)を含む文の先頭の use (of a given language) を指す。and は characteristic of every human group known と persistent over generations を結んでいる。known は every human group を修飾する過去分詞。なお，given A は「一定のA，定められたA」という意味。

☐ above all「とりわけ，何よりも」　　☐ be characteristic of A「Aの特徴を示している」

☐ persistent「継続している，長続きしている」

☐ over generations「何世代にもわたって」

問7　ア.「かなり多くの言語が12人にも満たない人によって話されている」第2段落第4文の内容と一致。

イ.「言語は文字体系を持つなら不滅だとみなされるかもしれない」本文中に該当する記述がないので不一致。

ウ.「種という単位，血統という単位，そして言語的単位は言語の研究において極めて重要な概念である」第7段落の内容に関連するが，「言語の研究において極めて重要な概念である」とは述べられていないので不一致。

エ.「急速な遺伝的突然変異により，ある集団の生物学的歴史を正確にたどるのは難しくなる」本文中に該当する記述がないので不一致。

Outline

¶ 1　　導入　　人間は共通の言語を話す集団を形成してきた

¶ 2　　　　　　今日，世界には言語共同体が6000から7000あるが，半数は話者数が5000人を下回る

¶3-4　展開1　人間は共通言語によって協力して行動し，歴史と伝統を保持することができる

¶ 5　　補足　　言語は変化し消滅することもある

¶6-8　展開2　種，血統と同様，言語共同体はその一員であることが明確であるが，種，血統，人種，国家よりも人間として重要な共同体を定義するのに役立つ

¶ 9　　結論　　言語共同体は人間が置かれた状況を現実に特徴づける

要約

　今日の世界には，言語共同体が6000から7000あり，共通言語によって協力して行動し，歴史と伝統を保持することができる。言語は変化し消滅することもあるが，種，血統，人種，国家よりも言語共同体は人間が置かれた状況を現実に特徴づけるものである。(116字)

▶▶▶ 構文・語句解説 ◀◀◀

── 第1段落 ──

¹Languages have played a crucial role in human communities for hundreds of thousands of years, and naturally the typical language community has changed in that time. ²The presumption is that before the discovery and expansion of agriculture, human communities were small bands, just as the remaining groupings of hunter-gatherers are to this

day. ³These groups all have languages, and ancient lore and stories which the old retail to the young. ⁴The density of the human population, wherever people were living, would have been far less than it is today.

¹言語は何十万年も人間の共同体で極めて重要な役割を果たしているが，当然ながら典型的な言語共同体はその間に変わっている。²農業の発見と拡大以前には，いまだに残っている狩猟採集者の集団が今日までそうであるのとまったく同様に，人間の共同体は小さな集団であったと推定される。³これらの集団にはすべて言語があり，年長者が若者に話し伝える大昔の伝承や物語がある。⁴人口密度は，人がどこに住んでいようと，今日と比べてはるかに低かったであろう。

1 and は Languages have ... of years と the typical language community has changed in that time の 2 つの節を結んでいる。

□ play a ... role in A「Aで…な役割を果たす」　　□ crucial「極めて重要な」
□ human「人間の」　　□ community「(地域)共同体」
□ hundreds of thousands of A「何十万ものA」　　□ naturally「当然のことながら」
□ typical「典型的な」

2 as は「様態」を表し「…と同様に」という意味。are の後ろには small bands が省略されている。

□ presumption「推定，想定」　　□ discovery「発見」　　□ expansion「拡大」
□ agriculture「農業」　　□ band「一団」　　□ remaining「残っている」
□ grouping「グループ，分類」　　□ hunter-gatherer「狩猟採集者」
□ to this day「今日まで」

3 1 つめの and は languages と ancient lore and stories を結んでいる。which 以下は ancient lore and stories を修飾する関係代名詞節。

□ ancient「大昔の，古代の」　　□ lore「伝承」　　□ retail「を言いふらす」

4 wherever people were living は譲歩を表す副詞節。

□ density「密度」　　□ population「人口」　　□ far＋比較級「はるかに…」

— 第 2 段落 —

¹From the language point of view, the present population of the world is not eight billion, but something over six thousand. ²There are between six and seven thousand communities in the world today identified by the first language that they speak. ³They are not of equal weight. ⁴They range in size from Mandarin Chinese with some 1.1

billion speakers, alone accounting for more than one eighth of all the people in the world, followed by English and Spanish with approximately 300 million apiece, to a long tail of tiny communities: over half the languages in the world, for example, have fewer than five thousand speakers, and over a thousand languages have under a dozen. ⁵This is a dangerous time for languages.

¹言語の観点から見ると，現在の世界の人口は80億ではなく，6000を少し超えるくらいである。²今日の世界には，話されている第一言語によって識別できる共同体が6000から7000ある。³それらは同じような重要性を持つわけではない。⁴規模的には，話者が約11億人で，それだけで世界の全人口の8分の1以上を占める標準中国語，それに続くそれぞれおよそ3億人の話者のいる英語とスペイン語から末端の非常に小さな共同体まである。たとえば，世界の半分以上の言語は，話者が5000人を下回り，話者が12人に満たない言語は1000を超えている。⁵今は言語にとって危険な時代である。

1 □ point of view「観点」　　□ the present A「現在のA」　　□ billion「10億」
　 □ something over ＋数詞「…を少し超えるくらいの数量」
2 that they speak は the first language を修飾する関係代名詞節。
　 □ identify「を識別する」
3 of equal weight が補語になっている。
　 □ weight「重大さ，勢力」
4 accounting for ... the world と followed by ... million apiece はともに分詞構文。
　 □ range in A from B to C「Aの点でBからCに及ぶ」　　□ Mandarin Chinese「標準中国語」
　 □ account for A「A（割合）を占める」　　□ follow「の後について行く」
　 □ approximately「およそ」　　□ apiece「1つにつき」　　□ tail「終わり，後部／尾」
　 □ tiny「とても小さい」　　□ dozen「12」

━━ 第3段落 ━━

¹In considering human history, the language community is a very natural unit. ²Languages, by their nature as means of communication, divide humanity into groups: only through a common language can a group of people act in concert, and therefore have a common history. ³Moreover, language that a group shares is precisely the medium in which memories of their joint history can be shared. ⁴Languages make possible both the living of a common history and also the telling of it.

¹人類の歴史を考える際に，言語共同体は非常に自然な構成単位である。²言語は，コミュニケーションの手段としての性質により，人類を集団に分ける。つまり，共通言語を通して初めて，ある集団の人々は協調して行動することができるのであり，それゆえに共通の歴史を持つことができる。³さらに，ある集団が共有している言語は，彼らの共通の歴史の記憶が共有されるまさに媒体である。⁴言語は，共通の歴史を生き，またそれを語ることを可能にしてくれるのだ。

1 □ in *doing*「…する際に」　□ unit「単位」
2 □ nature「性質」　□ means of communication「コミュニケーションの手段」
　□ divide A into B「AをBに分ける」　□ humanity「人類」　□ common「共通の」
　□ therefore「それゆえに」
3 that a group shares は language を修飾する関係代名詞節。in which 以下は the medium を修飾する関係代名詞節。
　□ moreover「さらに，そのうえ」　□ share「を共有する」　□ precisely「まさに」
　□ medium「媒体」　□ joint「共通の」
4 make possible both the ... of it は make O C「OをCにする」の O である both the ... of it が C の possible の後ろに移動した形。

────── 第4段落 ──────

¹And every language possesses another feature that makes it the readiest medium for preserving a group's history — every language is learnt by the young from the old, so that every living language is the embodiment of a tradition. ²That tradition is in principle immortal. ³Languages change, as they pass from the lips of one generation to the next, but there is nothing about this process of transmission which makes for decay or extinction. ⁴Like life itself, each new generation can receive the gift of its language afresh. ⁵And so it is that languages, unlike any of the people who speak them, need never grow weak, or die.

¹さらにすべての言語は，その言語をある集団の歴史を保存するための最も手っ取り早い媒体にするもう1つの特徴を持っている。つまり，すべての言語は年長者から年少者へと教えられるので，すべての生きた言語はある種の伝統を具現化したものである。²その伝統は原則として不滅のものである。³言語がある世代から次の世代へ口頭で伝わると，その言語は変化するが，この伝承過程には衰退や破滅に向かうものは何もない。⁴生命そのものと同じように，それぞれ

の新しい世代は言語という贈り物を新たに手にすることができる。⁵したがって，言語はそれを話す人々とは異なり，衰退したり絶滅したりすることは決してない。

1 that makes ... group's history は another feature を修飾する関係代名詞節。
- □ possess「を所有する」　　□ feature「特徴」　　□ ready「即座の，素早い」
- □ preserve「を保存する」　　□ so that S V ...「その結果…」　　□ living「生きている」
- □ embodiment「具体的に表現している物〔人〕」　　□ tradition「伝統」

2 □ in principle「原則として」　　□ immortal「不滅の」

4 □ like A「Aと同じように」　　□ receive「を受け取る」　　□ afresh「新たに」

5 who speak them は the people を修飾する関係代名詞節。
- □ it is that S V「（実は）…ということである」　　□ unlike A「Aと違って」
- □ grow C「Cになる」

第5・6段落

¹Every language has a chance of immortality, but this is not to say that it will survive forever. ²Genes too, and the species they encode, are immortal; but extinctions are a commonplace of paleontology. ³Likewise, the actual lifespans of language communities vary enormously. ⁴The annals of language history are full of languages that have died out, traditions that have come to an end, leaving no speakers at all.

⁵The language point of view on history can be contrasted with the genetic approach to human history, which is currently revolutionizing our view of our distant past. ⁶Like membership in a biological species and a matrilineal lineage, membership in a language community is based on a clear relation. ⁷An individual is a member of a species if it can have offspring with other members of the species, and of a matrilineal lineage if its mother is in that lineage. ⁸Likewise, at the most basic level, you are a member of a language community if you can use its language.

---

¹すべての言語に不朽不滅の可能性はあるが，これは言語が永遠に存続すると言っているのではない。²遺伝子もそしてそれがコード化する種も不滅のものである。しかし，絶滅は古生物学においてよくあることである。³同様に，言語共同体の実際の寿命は大きく変わる。⁴言語の歴史の年代記は消滅してしまった言語，話者がまったくいなくなり終わりを迎えた伝統であふれている。

⁵歴史に対する言語の観点は，現在，我々の遠い過去に対する見方を根本的に変えつつある，人類の歴史に対する遺伝子的アプローチと対比できる。⁶生物学的種および母系血統の一員であ

るかどうかと同様に，ある言語共同体の一員であるかどうかは明確な関係性に基づいている。⁷ある個体がその種に属する他の構成員と子孫を残せるならば，その個体はその種の一員となり，もし母親がある母系血統に属しているならば，その個体はその母系血統の一員となる。⁸それと同様に，最も基本的なレベルでは，もしその言語が使えるならば，その言語共同体の一員なのである。

1 but は Every language ... of immortality と this is ... survive forever の 2 つの節を結んでいる。

□ immortality「不死，不滅」

□ This is not to say that S V ...「だからといって…ということではない」

□ survive「生き残る」　　□ forever「永遠に」

2 and は Genes too と the species they encode を結んでいる。they encode は the species を修飾する関係代名詞節。

□ gene「遺伝子」　　□ species「(生物の)種」　　□ encode「をコード化する，符号化する」

□ commonplace「ごく普通のこと，よくあること」　　□ paleontology「古生物学」

3 □ likewise「同様に」　　□ actual「実際の」　　□ lifespan「寿命」

□ vary「異なる，様々である」　　□ enormously「非常に」

4 that have died out は languages を修飾する関係代名詞節。that have ... at all は traditions を修飾する関係代名詞節。leaving 以下は分詞構文。

□ annals「年代記，記録」　　□ die out「絶滅する，廃れる」　　□ come to an end「終わる」

5 which is 以下は the genetic approach to human history を補足説明する非制限用法の関係代名詞節。

□ contrast A with B「AをBと対比する」　　□ genetic「遺伝的な」

□ approach to A「Aへのアプローチ，取り組み」　　□ currently「現在，今は」

□ revolutionize「を根本的に変える」　　□ distant「遠い」　　□ past「過去」

6 and は a biological species と a matrilineal lineage を結んでいる。

□ membership「会員であること／構成員」　　□ biological「生物学的な」

□ matrilineal「母系の」　　□ lineage「家系」　　□ be based on A「Aに基づいている」

7 and は of a species ... the species と of a matrilineal ... that lineage を結んでいる。

□ individual「個体，個人」　　□ offspring「子孫」

─── 第 7 段落 ───

¹The advantage of this linguistically defined unit is that it necessarily defines a community that is important to us as human beings. ²The species unit is interesting, in defining our prehistoric relations with related groups such as *Homo erectus* and the

Neanderthals, but after the rise of *Homo sapiens* its usefulness yields to the evident fact that, species-wise, we are all in this together. [3]The lineage unit too has its points, clearly marked down the ages as it is by mitochondrial DNA and Y-chromosomes, and can yield interesting evidence on the origin of populations if some lineage clearly present today in the population is missing in one of the candidate groups put forward as ancestors. [4]So it has been inferred that Polynesians could not have come from South America, that most of the European population have parentage away from the Near Eastern sources of agriculture, and that the ancestry of most of the population of the English Midlands is from Friesland. [5]But knowing that many people's mothers, or fathers, are unaccounted for does not put a bound on a group as a whole in the way that language does.

---

[1]この言語的に定義された構成単位の長所は，それが必然的に人間として我々に重要な共同体を定義するということである。[2]ホモエレクトスやネアンデルタール人のような近縁種集団と我々の先史時代の関係を定義する際には，種という単位は興味深いものであるが，ホモサピエンスが台頭して以降，その有用性は，種の観点からすると，我々全員がみなそこに含まれるという明白な事実に屈服している。[3]血統による構成単位は，ミトコンドリア DNA と Y 染色体によって昔からはっきりと特徴づけられているので，やはり利点があり，人口集団の中で今日明らかに存在しているある血統が，祖先として名前を挙げられている候補群の中の１つに入っていなければ，その人口集団の起源に関する興味深い証拠を与えてくれる。[4]その結果，ポリネシア人は南アメリカから来たはずがないこと，大半のヨーロッパ人の起源ははるか近東の農耕発祥の地にあること，イギリス中部のほとんどの人の祖先はフリースラント出身であることがこれまで推測されている。[5]しかし，多くの人々の母親，または父親の起源がわからないと知ったところで，言語のように，全体として集団ごとに境界線が引けるわけではない。

1 that it … human beings は補語となる名詞節。that is important to us as human beings は a community を修飾する関係代名詞節。
- □ advantage「長所，有利な点」　　□ linguistically「言語的に」　　□ define「を定義する」
- □ necessarily「必然的に」　　□ as A「Aとして」　　□ human beings「人間」

2 but は The species unit is interesting と its usefulness yields to the evident fact の２つの節を結んでいる。that 以下は the evident fact と同格の名詞節。
- □ prehistoric「先史時代の」　　□ related「関係のある」
- □ A such as B「たとえばBのようなA」　　□ Homo erectus「ホモエレクトス，初期の人類」
- □ Neanderthal「ネアンデルタール人」　　□ Homo sapiens「ホモサピエンス，現生人類」
- □ yield to A「Aに屈する」　　□ evident「明白な」

3 marked down ... and Y-chromosomes は分詞構文。and can の and は The lineage unit の動詞句である has its points と can yield ... as ancestors を結んでいる。clearly present today は some lineage を修飾する形容詞句。put forward as ancestors は the candidate groups を修飾する過去分詞句。

□ have *one's* points「(それなりに)よいところがある」　　□ clearly「明らかに」

□ down the ages「昔から，長年にわたって」

□ mitochondrial DNA「ミトコンドリア DNA」　　□ Y-chromosome「Y 染色体」

□ yield「を生む，産出する」　　□ evidence「証拠」　　□ origin「起源」

□ present「存在している」　　□ missing「欠けている」　　□ candidate「候補(者)」

□ put A forward「Aの名前を挙げる／Aを示す」　　□ ancestor「祖先」

4 it は形式主語で that 以下が真主語。真主語となる that 節が3つ and で結ばれている。

□ infer「を推測する」　　□ Polynesian「ポリネシア人」　　□ parentage「生まれ，出身」

□ Near Eastern「近東の」　　□ Friesland「フリースラント」(オランダの地名)

―― 第 8 段落 ――

¹Contrast a unit such as a race. ²Its boundaries are defined by nothing more than a chosen set of properties, whether by superficial resemblances such as skin color or skull proportions, or by sequences of DNA. ³Likewise, there are insurmountable problems in defining its cultural analogue, the nation, which entail the further imponderables of a consciousness of shared history, and perhaps shared language too. ⁴Given that so many of the properties get shuffled on to different individuals in different generations, it remains doubtful as to what to make of any set of characteristics for a race or a nation. ⁵But use of a given language is an undeniable functioning reality everywhere; above all, it is characteristic of every human group known and persistent over generations. ⁶It provides a universal key for dividing human history into meaningful groups.

---

¹人種のような構成単位を対照として考えるとよい。²その境界線は，肌の色や頭蓋骨の大きさといった表面的な類似点によってであれ，DNA の配列によってであれ，選ばれた一連の特性によって定義されるにすぎない。³同様に，その文化的に類似するものである国家を定義する際にも，乗り越えられない問題が存在する。なぜならそこには歴史を共有しているという意識や，おそらくは言語も共有しているという意識という，さらにはっきりと評価することができないものが含まれるからである。⁴そうした特性の非常に多くが様々な世代の様々な個人に移されることを考えると，人種や国家にとっての一連の特徴が何であれ，それをどう考えるべきか

は，はっきりしない。⁵しかし，ある特定の言語を使うということは，あらゆるところで機能を果たしている否定できない現実である。とりわけ，ある特定の言語を使うということは，すべての既知の人間集団が持つ特徴であり，何世代にもわたって継続していくものである。⁶それは人類の歴史を集団として意味を持つものに分けるのに普遍的な手がかりを与えてくれる。

1 □ race「人種」

2 □ boundary「境界線」 □ nothing more than A「Aにすぎない，Aだけ」
□ a set of A「一連のA」 □ property「特性」
□ whether by A or by B「AによってであれBによってであれ」
□ superficial「表面的な」 □ resemblance「類似（点）」 □ skin color「肌の色」
□ skull「頭蓋骨」 □ proportion「割合」 □ sequence「配列」

3 the nation は its cultural analogue を同格的に言い換えたもの。which 以下は insurmountable problems を補足説明する非制限用法の関係代名詞節。and は shared history と shared language を結んでいる。
□ insurmountable「乗り越えられない」 □ analogue「類似（するもの）」
□ entail「を含む」 □ consciousness「意識」

4 □ given that 節「…ということを考慮すると」 □ shuffle「あちこちと動く」
□ remain C「依然としてCである」 □ doubtful「はっきりしない，不確かな」
□ as to A「Aについて」 □ what to make of A「Aをどう考えるべきか」
□ characteristic「特徴」 □ nation「国家」

5 □ undeniable「否定できない」 □ function「機能する」 □ reality「現実」
□ everywhere「あらゆるところで」

6 □ provide「を与える」 □ universal「普遍的な」 □ key「手がかり」
□ meaningful「意味のある」

・・・

第9段落

¹Admittedly, a language community is a more scattered and variable unit than a species or a lineage: a language changes much faster than a DNA sequence, and one cannot even be sure that it will always be transmitted from one generation to the next. ²Language communities are not always easy to count, or to distinguish reliably. ³But they are undeniably real features of the human condition.

¹明らかに，言語共同体は種や血統より拡散した変わりやすい構成単位である。すなわち，言語は DNA 配列よりもずっと速く変化し，ある世代から次の世代へと必ず継承されるという確

信を持つことさえできない。²言語共同体は，数えたり確実に区別したりするのは必ずしも容易ではない。³しかし，言語共同体が人間が置かれた状況を現実に特徴づけるものであることは否定できないのだ。

1 1つめの and は scattered と variable を結んでいる。2つめの and は a language ... DNA sequence と one cannot ... the next の2つの節を結んでいる。

　□ admittedly「明らかに，認めざるを得ないことだが」　　□ scattered「拡散した」

　□ variable「変わりやすい」　　□ transmit「を伝達する」

2 □ not always「必ずしも…とは限らない」　　□ count「を数える」

　□ distinguish「を区別する」　　□ reliably「確実に」

3 □ undeniably「〈文修飾で〉明白に」　　□ feature「特徴」　　□ condition「状況，状態」

創発

解 答

問1 都市は生きて呼吸をしている生き物であるということ。(25字)

問2 アリのコロニーも都市と同じく，トップダウン方式ではなく，個の集団的相互作用によって動いているから。(49字)

問3 食料に関する手がかりが含まれる，他のアリの出すフェロモンの合図を嗅ぎ出し，その手がかりに個々のアリが自分の行動を適応させるから。(64字)

問4 エ. deserted

問5 ウ. the exchange of information among the public

問6 イ. dismisses

問7 機械は高度な知性を設計してもらうというよりも，むしろ高度な知性を進化させるであろうが，だからといって，それが人間の知性のように見えることにはならないだろう，と彼は警告する。

▶▶▶ **設問解説** ◀◀◀

問1 is の後ろの省略がポイント。補語が繰り返しを避けるために省略されているので，補語を含む文を探せばよい。第1段落第5文に「都市はまるで生きて呼吸をしている生き物のように，独自のリズムで鼓動しているように思われる」と述べられている。これを受けて，下線部を含む文で「スティーヴン・ジョンソンは，いくつかの意味でその通りだと主張するだろう」とあるので，is の後ろに a living, breathing organism が省略されていることがわかる。なお，it は as if の節内の it と同じで a city のこと。

問2 下線部は「アリのコロニーは都市に著しく似ている」という意味。前の第4段落に，ニューヨークを例に挙げて「都市はトップダウン方式ではなく，普通の人々の集団的相互作用によって動いている」と述べられている。下線部を含む第5段落には「アリの場合も女王アリによるトップダウン方式ではない」ことが述べられている。また，第6段落第1文には「アリの行動の原因が群れの論理と呼ばれるものにある」とあることから，アリのコロニーも都市も共に「トップダウン方式ではない」ことと「集団によって動かされる」ことがわかる。この内容を制限字数内でまとめればよい。

□ ant colony「アリのコロニー」　　□ remarkably「著しく」

56

問3 下線部は「ある食料供給源を取り除くと，コロニーはすぐに関心を別のところに向けるだろう」という意味。第6段落第7文で How do they do it?「彼らはどうやってそれをするのだろうか」と問いかけて，その答えが第11・12文に述べられている。したがって，この内容を制限字数内でまとめればよい。

　□ get rid of A「Aを取り除く」　　□ source「供給源」
　□ turn A to B「AをBに向ける」　□ attention「関心，注意」

問4 第7段落第2〜7文に「都市の居住地区がどのように繁華街に変化する」のかが述べられている。この内容から「都市の主役が2，3の大通りである場合」，裏通りがどのようになるのか判断する。また，第8段落では「タイムズスクエア周辺」を例に挙げ，具体的に説明されているが，第2・3文の内容から空所には crowded「混み合った」の反意語が入ることがわかる。

　ア.「賑やかな」イ.「混み合った」ウ.「活気のある」エ.「さびれた」

問5 下線部は「この局所的な情報の流れ」という意味。これは第7段落第2〜5文で具体的に述べられた「都市が発展する一因である，普通の人々の低レベルの相互作用」のこと。したがって，正解はウ。

　□ local「局所的な」　　□ flow「流れ」
　ア.「地元の経済についてのより詳細な情報」
　イ.「新しい店についての信頼できる情報源」
　ウ.「大衆の間での情報交換」
　エ.「インターネットで得られる役立つ情報」

問6 空所の直後の this は直前の疑問文 Is it ... of macro-intelligence？を指している。空所の後ろの saying 以下に「ウェブは連結性を示すが，まったく組織化されていない」と述べられている。また，第4文にも「高レベルの複雑さは出現しえない」と述べられていることから判断する。

　ア.「を正しく理解する」イ.「を退ける」ウ.「を証明する」エ.「を結びつける」

問7 前半は X rather than Y「YよりむしろX」の表現で，X，Y に動詞句がくるときに Y が *doing* という形になることがある。なお，Y は have O *done*「Oを…してもらう」の使役動詞の表現である。後半部の that は直前の文内容を指しており，that means (that) S V で「…ということになる」と意味をとればよい。that節内は S look like A「SはAのように見える」の表現である。なお，it は2つとも a higher intelligence のこと。文末の he warns は，本来は主節に相当する節が挿入された形。後ろに that節を従える動詞に起こり，挿入された場合には that は必ず省略される。

例　His explanation, I suppose, was a little unsatisfactory.

＝I suppose (that) his explanation was a little unsatisfactory.

　　「彼の説明は少し不満足であったと思う」

□ evolve「を進化させる」　　□ intelligence「知性」　　□ engineer「を設計する」

□ warn that節「…だと警告する」

Outline

¶ 1	導入	都市は突然現れ，生物に似ている
¶ 2–3	展開	ある作家は，全体が個々の部分の総和よりもはるかに大きい現象である「創発」を提唱している
¶ 4	例 1	テロ後のニューヨークの復興
¶ 5–6	例 2	アリのコロニー
¶ 7–9	例 3	都市の発展
¶ 10	結論	「創発」は個々の情報交換によって起きる自然発生的なものである
¶ 11–12	補足	機械が進化しても巨大な知性は生まれない

要　約

　全体が個々の部分の総和よりもはるかに大きい現象が「創発」であり，都市もアリのコロニーもその具体例である。「創発」は個々の情報交換によって起きる自然発生的なものである。機械が「創発」によって人間の知性のようなものになることは現状では考えられない。(122字)

▶▶▶ 構文・語句解説 ◀◀◀

第 1 段落

　[1]Nobody designs truly great cities. [2]They just spring up. [3]As if by magic, they develop distinct districts that endure from century to century. [4]Think of the silk quarter in Florence, or Savile Row in London. [5]A city seems to pulsate with its own rhythm, as if it is a living, breathing organism.

　[1]真の大都市は誰が設計するものでもない。[2]大都市はただ突然現れる。[3]まるで魔法のように，大都市は世紀を越えて持ちこたえる独特の地区を発達させる。[4]フィレンツェのシルク地区あるいはロンドンのサヴィルローを考えてみるとよい。[5]都市はまるで生きて呼吸をしている生き物のように，独自のリズムで鼓動しているように思われる。

1 □ design「を設計する」　　□ truly「本当に」

2 □ spring up「突然現れる」

3 □ as if ...「まるで…のように」　　□ by magic「魔法によって」

　□ distinct「独特の，異なる」　　□ district「地域，地区」

　□ endure「持ちこたえる，存続する」　　□ from century to century「世紀を越えて」

4 □ quarter「地区，街」　　□ Florence「フィレンツェ」イタリア中部の都市。

5 □ rhythm「リズム」　　□ living「生きている」　　□ breathing「呼吸している」

　□ organism「生物，有機体」

───── 第2段落 ─────

[1]Steven Johnson would argue that, in some senses, it is. [2]He would say that the superorganism of the city mirrors the superorganism of the ant colony, in which a collection of individually stupid insects somehow becomes a fascinating, organized whole. [3]Both are examples of emergence, a phenomenon where the whole is much greater than the sum of its parts. [4]Another commonly given example of emergence is consciousness, which appears to arise spontaneously from the fact that billions of nerve cells (neurons) in the brain are firing off signals to each other.

　[1]スティーヴン・ジョンソンは，いくつかの意味でその通りだと主張するだろう。[2]彼に言わせると，都市という超個体はアリのコロニーという超個体を反映しており，アリのコロニーでは，個々に見れば愚かな昆虫が集まると，どういうわけか魅惑的な組織化された統一体となる。[3]両者とも創発，つまり全体が個々の部分の総和よりもはるかに大きい現象の実例である。[4]一般的に挙げられる創発のもう1つの例は意識である。意識は何十億という脳内の神経細胞（ニューロン）が互いに信号を送っているという事実から自然発生的に生じているように思われる。

1 □ argue that節「…だと主張する」　　□ sense「意味」

2 □ superorganism「超個体」　　□ mirror「を反映する」　　□ collection「集積」

　□ individually「個々に」　　□ stupid「愚かな」　　□ insect「昆虫」

　□ somehow「どういうわけか」　　□ fascinating「魅力的な」

　□ organized「組織（化）された」　　□ whole「統一体」

3 a phenomenon ... its parts は emergence と同格の関係で，where 以下は a phenomenon を修飾する関係副詞節。

　□ emergence「創発」　　□ phenomenon「現象」

　□ much＋比較級「ずっと…，はるかに…」　　□ the sum of A「Aの合計，総計」

4 which 以下は consciousness を補足説明する非制限用法の関係代名詞節。

that billions ... each other は the fact と同格の名詞節。

□ commonly「一般的に」　　□ consciousness「意識」

□ arise from A「Aから起こる，生じる」　　□ spontaneously「自然発生的に，自発的に」

□ billions of A「何十億ものA」　　□ nerve cell「神経細胞」　　□ brain「脳」

□ fire A off「A〈弾丸など〉を発射する」　　□ signal「合図」

第3段落

¹In a new book, called *Emergence*, Johnson, an American author best known for arguing that computer graphics are as culturally important as books or films, aims to coax the topic out of science laboratories and into the mainstream. ²Just as chaos was a scientific buzzword of the past century, Johnson hopes that emergence will enter the lexicon of this century.

---

　¹コンピュータグラフィックスは本や映画と同じくらい文化的に重要だ，と主張していることで最もよく知られているアメリカ人著述家のジョンソンは，「創発」という新しい本の中で，その話題を科学の研究室から引き出して一般に流布させることを目指している。²ちょうど，カオスが前世紀，科学の流行語であったように，ジョンソンは創発が今世紀の語彙に入ることを願っている。

---

1 called *Emergence* は a new book を補足説明する過去分詞句。

Johnson と an American author は同格の関係。なお，best known ... or films は an American author を修飾する形容詞句。

out of science laboratories と into the mainstream を and が結んでいる。

□ computer graphics「コンピュータグラフィックス」　　□ culturally「文化的に」

□ aim to *do*「…することを目指す」　　□ topic「話題」

□ science laboratory「科学の研究室」　　□ the mainstream「主流」

2 □ (just) as S V「(ちょうど)…するように」　　□ chaos「カオス，無秩序」

□ buzzword「(素人を感心させるために使うもったいぶった)専門語，宣伝文句」

□ the past century「前世紀／過去100年間」　　□ enter「に入る」

第4段落

¹So many things in life look different when viewed through the lens of emergence, Johnson, 32, explains. ²Cities can be thought of as complex, self-organizing phenomena. ³Take New York City, where I live. ⁴There is a tendency to think of social systems as

top-down, as driven by leaders. [5]But what has happened here in the wake of the awful attack is the opposite. [6]The city has come back to life thanks largely to mass interactions by ordinary people, not because they were told by the mayor.

[1]生活の中の非常に多くの事柄は，創発というレンズを通して見ると異なって見える，と32歳のジョンソンは説明する。[2]都市は複雑で自己組織的な現象と考えることができる。[3]私が住んでいるニューヨークを例に取ってみよう。[4]社会制度とはトップダウン方式つまり指導者によって動かされるものであるとみなされる傾向がある。[5]しかし，あの恐ろしい攻撃の後にここで起こったことはその正反対なのだ。[6]この都市は主に普通の人々による集団的相互作用のおかげで蘇った。彼らが市長に命令されたからではないのである。

1 So many ... Johnson, 32, explains＝Johnson, 32, explains (that) so many ... of emergence
  when viewed＝when they are viewed
  □ lens「レンズ」
2 □ think of O as C「OをCとみなす」　　□ complex「複雑な」
  □ self-organizing「自己組織的な」　　□ phenomena＜phenomenon「現象」の複数形
3 □ take「を(例として)取り上げる」
4 as driven by leaders は as top-down を説明的に言い換えたもの。
  □ tendency to do「…する傾向」　　□ social system「社会制度」
  □ top-down「上意下達式の，トップダウン方式の」　　□ drive「を動かす」
5 □ in the wake of A「Aのすぐ後に続いて」　　□ awful「恐ろしい」　　□ attack「攻撃」
  □ the opposite「正反対のこと」
6 thanks largely ..., not because ... は X, not Y「YではなくX」の表現で，X に thanks to から始まる副詞句が，Y に because から始まる副詞節がきている。
  □ come back to life「生き返る」　　□ thanks to A「Aのおかげで」　　□ largely「大いに」
  □ mass「大規模な／大衆の」　　□ interaction「交流，相互作用」　　□ ordinary「普通の」
  □ mayor「市長」

― 第5段落 ―

[1]Ant colonies are remarkably similar to cities. [2]When watching thousands of ants marching to and from a nest, laden with food, it is easy to believe that there must be a choreographer, a leader ant who can see the bigger picture and direct the colony to act in a particular way. [3]But scientists know better: contrary to popular belief, the queen ant does not command the colony.

¹アリのコロニーは都市に著しく似ている。²何千匹ものアリが食べ物を担ぎ，並んで巣を出入りしているのを観察するとき，振り付け師，つまりより広く状況を見て，コロニーを特定の方法で行動するように導くことができるリーダーのアリがいるに違いないと考えやすい。³しかし，科学者はそれほど無分別ではない。一般に思い込まれているのとは反対に，女王アリはコロニーを指揮してはいないのである。

2 When watching ＝ When you are watching

watching thousands of ants marching は知覚動詞＋O＋*doing* の表現。なお，and は to と from を結び，a nest が共通して続いている。

laden with food は marching を修飾する分詞構文。

a choreographer と a leader ant は同格の関係。who can ... particular way は a leader ant を修飾する関係代名詞節。節内では see the bigger picture と direct the colony を and が結んでいる。

☐ thousands of A「何千ものA」　　☐ march「行進する」

☐ lade A with B「A〈車など〉にBを積む」　　☐ choreographer「振り付け師」

☐ picture「状況，事態」　　☐ direct O to *do*「Oに…するよう指図する」

☐ particular「特定の」

3 ☐ know better「分別がある」　　☐ contrary to A「Aに反して」

☐ popular belief「一般に思い込まれていること」　　☐ queen ant「女王アリ」

☐ command「を指揮する，率いる」

━━ 第6段落 ━━

¹They attribute ant behavior to something unclear called swarm logic. ²Put 10,000 dumb ants together, and they become smart. ³They will calculate the shortest routes to food supplies. ⁴In fact, scientists studying the traveling salesman conundrum of how to visit a large number of cities using the shortest routes, have studied how ants do it. ⁵Get rid of one food source, and the colony will soon turn its attention to another. ⁶Ant colonies give the illusion of being intelligent, even though individual ants lack advanced brains. ⁷How do they do it? ⁸Worker ants don't communicate with each other much. ⁹They have a vocabulary of up to 20 signs, most mediated by pheromones. ¹⁰But ants do follow a few simple rules. ¹¹They are good at sniffing out pheromone signals from other ants, which contain clues about how far away food is. ¹²By adapting their behavior to these clues, ants learn the shortest route to food. ¹³From the isolated, small-scale activities of individual ants, a global behavior jumps out.

¹彼らはアリの行動が群れの論理と呼ばれる何かはっきりしないもので説明できると考える。²1万匹の愚鈍なアリを1ヶ所に集めれば，彼らは利口になるのだ。³アリは食料供給源への最短経路を計算するだろう。⁴実際，数多くの都市をいかにして最短経路で回るかという外回りのセールスマンの難問を研究している科学者は，アリがどうやっているのかを調べた。⁵ある食料供給源を取り除くと，コロニーはすぐに関心を別のところに向けるだろう。⁶個々のアリには発達した脳がないにもかかわらず，アリのコロニーは知性を持っているような錯覚を与える。⁷彼らはどうやってそれをするのだろうか。⁸働きアリは互いにあまり意志疎通をしない。⁹最大20からなる合図による語彙を持ち，その大半はフェロモンによって伝えられる。¹⁰しかし，アリは実は少数の単純な規則に従っている。¹¹彼らは他のアリが出すフェロモンの合図を嗅ぎ出すのがうまいが，その合図には食料がどれだけの距離にあるかということに関する手がかりが含まれているのだ。¹²これらの手がかりに自分の行動を適応させることによって，アリは食料への最短経路を知る。¹³個々のアリの孤立した小規模な活動から全体的行動が躍り出るのだ。

1 □ attribute A to B「AをBのせいと考える」

2 Put 10,000 ... は命令文＋and S V「…しなさい，そうすれば～」の表現。

　□ put A together「Aを集める」　　□ dumb「愚鈍な／馬鹿げた」　　□ smart「利口な」

3 □ calculate「を計算する」　　□ route「経路」　　□ supply「供給」

4 studying the ... shortest routes は scientists を修飾する現在分詞句。

　using the shortest routes は visit a large number of cities を修飾する付帯状況を表す分詞構文。

　do it＝calculate the shortest routes to food supplies

　□ in fact「実際，実は」　　□ traveling salesman「外交員，外回りのセールスマン」

　□ a large number of A「多数のA」

6 □ illusion「錯覚」　　□ intelligent「知性を持った」　　□ individual「個々の」

　□ lack「が欠けている」　　□ advanced「発達した」

7 do it＝turn its attention to another

8 □ worker ant「働きアリ」　　□ communicate with A「Aと意志疎通する」

9 most 以下は分詞構文で，most（＝most signals）は mediated の意味上の主語。

　□ vocabulary「語彙」　　□ up to A「〈最高〉Aまで」　　□ sign「合図」

　□ mediate「を伝える」　　□ pheromone「フェロモン」

10 do follow の do は動詞強調の助動詞。

　□ follow「に従う」

11 □ be good at *doing*「…するのが得意だ」　　□ sniff A out「Aを嗅ぎつける，見つけだす」

　□ contain「を含む」　　□ clue「手がかり」

12 □ adapt A to B「AをBに適合させる」

13 □ isolated「孤立した」　　□ small-scale「小規模な」

　　□ global「全体的な／全世界の，世界的な」　　□ jump out「飛び出す」

── 第7段落 ──

¹Similarly, a few simple rules can turn an urban settlement into a thriving neighborhood. ²For example, cities grow because of low-level interactions of people on the street. ³There's a flow of information between strangers, he says. ⁴You go down a street, see a store that you never knew was there. ⁵You go in, do business, and perhaps tell your friends about it. ⁶They go there, more stores open and suddenly there's this new area that's full of funky clothes stores. ⁷That kind of vitality is more likely to be found in maze-like cities with lots of streets and lots of routes from A to B. ⁸If a city is dominated by a few large avenues, the back streets tend to be deserted.

---

¹同様に，少数の単純な規則によって都市の居住地区は繁華街に変化することがある。²たとえば，都市は普通の人々の低レベルの相互作用があるために発展する。³見知らぬ者同士の間に情報の流れがある，と彼は言う。⁴あなたが通りを歩くと，そこにあると知らなかった店が目に入る。⁵あなたは中に入って，用件を済ませて，ひょっとしたら友人にその店のことを話すかもしれない。⁶友人たちはそこに行き，さらに多くの店が開店すると，突然そこにはしゃれた服屋でいっぱいの新しいエリアが出現する。⁷その種の活気は，A 地点から B 地点に行くのに多くの通りと多くの経路を持つ迷路のような都市に見られることが多い。⁸都市の主役が2，3の大通りである場合，裏通りはさびれる傾向がある。

1 □ similarly「同様に」　　□ turn A into B「AをBに変える」　　□ urban「都会の」
　　□ settlement「居住地」　　□ thriving「繁栄する」　　□ neighborhood「地域」

2 on the street は people を修飾する形容詞句で，ここでは「普通の人々」という意味。
　　□ because of A「Aの理由で」　　□ low-level「低レベルの」

3 There's a ... he says = He says (that) there's a flow of information between strangers
　　□ stranger「見知らぬ人」

4 that you never knew was there は a store を修飾する連鎖関係代名詞節。

5 □ do business「用事を済ます」

6 They go there, more stores open, there's this ... clothes stores の3つの文を and が結んでいる。
　　□ be full of A「Aでいっぱいである」　　□ funky「流行の」

64

7 with lots of streets and lots of routes from A to B は maze-like cities を修飾する形容詞句。

　□ be likely to *do*「たぶん…するだろう，…する可能性が高い」　　□ maze-like「迷路のような」

8 □ dominate「を支配する」　　□ avenue「大通り」　　□ back street「裏通り」

───── 第8段落 ─────

[1]Johnson explains: Near Times Square, every block has a bar, a restaurant and a boutique. [2]The streets are filled at all times of the day, and they're never too crowded. [3]Go down a broad avenue and take a turn, and the streets feel totally different. [4]They are deserted.

　[1]ジョンソンは次のように説明している。タイムズスクエア周辺には，すべてのブロックにバーとレストランとブティックがある。[2]通りは1日中いつも人でいっぱいで，しかも混みすぎることは決してない。[3]大通りを歩いても，角を曲がれば，通りはまったく違った感じになる。[4]そこはさびれているのだ。

1 □ Times Square「タイムズスクエア(広場)」ニューヨーク市マンハッタンの繁華街。

　□ block「ブロック，区画」　　□ boutique「ブティック」

2 □ crowded「混み合った」

3 □ broad「広い」　　□ take a turn「曲がる」　　□ feel C「Cの感じがする」

　□ totally「まったく，すっかり」

───── 第9段落 ─────

[1]This local information flow is the lifeblood of cities. [2]Which is why urban planners who destroy neighborhoods and replace them with tower blocks often turn districts into no-go areas without realizing what they have done.

　[1]この局所的な情報の流れが都市の活力源である。[2]このため，地域を壊して高層ビル街に置き換える都市設計者は，気づかないうちにしばしば地区を誰も立ち入らないエリアに変えてしまう。

1 □ lifeblood「活力源」

2 Which は前文の内容を補足説明する非制限用法の関係代名詞。ここでは独立した文として用いられている。

65

□ neighborhood「地域」　　□ replace A with B「AをBに取り替える」

□ tower block「高層ビル街」　　□ no-go area「誰も立ち入らない地区」

────　第10段落　────

¹Johnson can see that there is something unsatisfactory about saying that stupid ants can build apparently intelligent colonies.　²Where's the crucial step?　³What's the missing piece of the puzzle that turns low-level actions into high-level order?　⁴But he insists that there's no hole in the explanation.　⁵Just as its name suggests, emergent phenomena simply emerge.

¹愚かなアリがいかにもに知性のありそうなコロニーを築くことができると述べることについて，何か不十分なところがある，とジョンソンは見ている。²その決定的な段階はどこにあるのだろう。³低レベルの行為を高レベルの秩序に変えるパズルの失われた断片は何なのだろうか。⁴しかし彼は説明に欠陥はないと主張する。⁵まさにその名が示唆しているように，創発的な現象とはただ出現するのだ。

1 □ see that節「…だとわかる」

　　□ there is something＋形容詞＋about A「Aにはどこか…なところがある」

　　□ unsatisfactory「不十分な」　　□ apparently「外見上は，見たところ」

2 □ crucial「決定的な」

3 □ missing「欠けている」　　□ puzzle「パズル」　　□ order「秩序」

4 □ insist that節「…だと主張する」　　□ hole「欠点，不備」　　□ explanation「説明」

5 as は関係代名詞で，後続の主節の内容を補足説明している。

　　□ suggest「を示唆する」　　□ simply「ただ」　　□ emerge「現れる」

────　第11段落　────

¹Our collection of brain cells give rise to something quite magnificent and so far inexplicable self-awareness.　²Is it possible that the digital networks we are creating, such as the Web, may cease to be our microprocessing servants and acquire some kind of macro-intelligence?　³Johnson dismisses this, saying that while the Web shows connectedness, it is utterly disorganized.　⁴If the Web were a city and each document a building, he says, it would be more anarchic than any real-world city on the planet, and therefore no higher level of complexity can emerge.　⁵However, if the Web had been built in a different way, perhaps something greater than the sum of its parts would emerge.

¹我々の脳細胞の集合体から，非常にすばらしいものと，これまでのところ説明のついていない自意識が生まれる。²ウェブのような我々が創り出しているデジタルネットワークが我々のマイクロプロセッサーを駆使する召使いであることをやめて，何らかの類のマクロな知性を獲得することはありうるだろうか。³ジョンソンはウェブは連結性を示すが，まったく組織化されていないと言って，それを退ける。⁴仮にウェブが都市で，個々のドキュメントがビルとするならば，それは地球上のいかなる現実の都市よりも無秩序になるだろうし，したがって高レベルの複雑さは出現しえない，と彼は言う。⁵しかし，もしウェブが違った方法で構築されていたならば，おそらく部分の総和よりも大きな何かが出現するであろう。

1 something quite magnificent と so far inexplicable self-awareness を and が結んでいる。

□ brain cell「脳細胞」　　□ give rise to A「Aを生じる」　　□ magnificent「すばらしい」

□ so far「これまで，今までのところ」　　□ inexplicable「説明のつかない」

□ self-awareness「自意識，自己認識」

2 cease to ... microprocessing servants と acquire some kind of macro-intelligence を and が結んでいる。

□ microprocessing　servant「マイクロプロセッサーを駆使する召使い」ここでは人間が利用する，単なるコンピュータの処理装置という意味で用いられている。

□ A, such as B「たとえばBのようなA」　　□ cease to *do*「…するのをやめる」

□ acquire「を獲得する」　　□ some kind of A「何らかの類のA」

□ macro-intelligence「マクロな知性」

3 saying は以下は分詞構文。

□ while S V「…するけれども／ところが一方…」　　□ connectedness「連結性」

□ utterly「まったく」　　□ disorganized「組織化されていない」

4 If the ... can emerge＝He says (that) if the ... can emerge

If the ..., it would ... は仮定法過去。

each document a building＝each document were a building

on the planet は any real-world city を修飾する形容詞句。

□ document「ドキュメント，コンピュータのファイル」　　□ real-world「現実の」

□ complexity「複雑さ」

5 if the Web had been ..., something greater than the sum of its parts would emerge は条件節が仮定法過去完了，帰結節が仮定法過去の形。

greater than the sum of its parts は something を修飾する形容詞句。

¹Not that we would necessarily recognize it. ²Machines may evolve a higher intelligence rather than having it engineered, but that doesn't mean it would look like human intelligence, he warns. ³It wouldn't be a robot that acted like a little boy, but a machine so smart that we wouldn't recognize it. ⁴It would be like the film *The Matrix*, where there were no paranoid androids but a bizarre faceless regime. ⁵Now that's scary.

¹だからといって我々は必ずそれを認識するようになるというわけではない。²機械は高度な知性を設計してもらうというよりも，むしろ高度な知性を進化させるであろうが，だからといって，それが人間の知性のように見えることにはならないだろう，と彼は警告する。³それは幼い少年のように行動するロボットではなく，我々が機械だとわからないほど利口な機械となるであろう。⁴偏執狂のアンドロイドはおらず，奇怪な顔のない体制が存在する映画「マトリックス」のようなものであろう。⁵こうなると，それは恐ろしいものである。

1 not that ...「だからといって…というわけではない」

would は仮定法過去で，第3および第4文の would も同じ。

☐ recognize「を認識する」

3 It は第2文の a higher intelligence を，文末の it は a machine を指している。

wouldn't be a robot that acted like a little boy, but a machine ... は not X but Y「XではなくY」の表現で，would be not a robot ..., but a machine ... の not が移動した形。

so smart that we wouldn't recognize it は a machine を修飾する形容詞句で，so ... that ～「非常に…なので～する／～するほど…」の表現になっている。

☐ act like A「Aのように行動する」

4 It は漠然と状況を表しており，日本語には訳さない it。

the film と *The Matrix* は同格の関係で，where 以下は the film *The Matrix* を修飾する関係副詞節。

☐ S be like A「SはAのようである」

☐ android「アンドロイド，人造人間」SF の本・映画などに登場する人間そっくりな姿をしたロボット。　☐ no X but Y「XではなくY」　☐ bizarre「奇怪な」

☐ faceless「顔のない」　☐ regime「（政治）体制，政府」

5 ☐ scary「恐ろしい」

移民抑制の是非

解答

問1 ヨーロッパから世界の他の地域へ移住した人の数は，これまでに世界の他の地域からヨーロッパに移住した人の数の2倍であった。

問2 住民が職を得るために自国の別の地域に自由に移動したり，自国を離れることが許されなかったこと。(46字)

問3 エ. silent

問4 ときどき少数の大企業はまた，その拡大に必要な労働力を確保するために，人々の自由な移動を認めるように政府に強く要求している。

問5 移民がなければ，産業のいくつかの部門は崩壊するか外国に移るだろうし，それは結果的にそれらの産業と関連のある多くの他の職が失われることになるだろう。

問6 ヨーロッパ内部での自由な域内移動の導入によって，貧しい地域から豊かな地域への大量移住が起こるだろうという予想。(55字)

問7 移民抑制がただ1つの国だけで終わるように運動してもあまり意味がないだろうことは明らかだ。

問8 人間は自由に移動できるべきだという基本的自由を制限することは，人権侵害になる。その上，移民は移住先の国々の富と繁栄に大きな貢献をし，職が得られる可能性を高め，労働者の賃金と条件を改善するだろうし，高齢化が進む国では，移民が増えなければ，税金を払い，公共部門や産業を維持し，高齢者の世話をする若い労働者が不足することになるから。(163字)

▶▶▶ 設問解説 ◀◀◀

問1 倍数表現を押さえることがポイント。Twice as ... as ~「~の2倍…」の形。in the opposite direction「反対方向に」とはその前で述べられた from Europe to the rest of the world「ヨーロッパから世界の他の地域へ」と「反対方向に」ということ。

　　□ migrate「移住する」　　□ the rest of A「その他のA」

問2 下線部を含む文は「実際，旧ソ連でこれが起こったとき，それは人権侵害だと考えられた」という意味。したがって，this とは「人権侵害」と考えられることだとわかる。直前の文に「もしある国の住民が職を得るためにその国の別の

地域に移動する自由がなければ，あるいは人々がその国を離れることが許されないとしたら，それは人権侵害と考えられるであろう」と述べられている。よって，this は if the ... leave it の内容を指している。この内容を制限字数内でまとめればよい。

問3　空所(3)を含む文は「しかし，その宣言は奇妙なことに他の国に入る権利についての問いには(　3　)である」という意味。Yet に着目して，直前の文を見ると「世界人権宣言はこれらの権利を主張している」とある。these rights とは第4段落で述べられている「職を得るための移動の自由」のことである。つまり，「世界人権宣言は移動の自由を声高に主張しているが，他国に入国する権利に関しては<u>沈黙を保っている</u>」という文意にすればよい。また，続く第3文には「各国政府が人々をその領土から締め出す権利に執着している」と述べられていることからも silent が入るのは明らか。
　　ア.「受け入れられる」イ.「賛成の」ウ.「決定的な」エ.「沈黙を守る」

問4　press O to *do* は「O〈人〉に…するようにしきりに勧める」という意味。they は直前の第6文の主語 These を指しており，第5文の fewer and bigger corporations のこと。they need for expansion は the labour を修飾する関係代名詞節である。
　　□ allow「を認める」　　　□ in order to *do*「…するために」　　　□ secure「を確保する」
　　□ labour「労働力」　　□ expansion「拡大」

問5　Without immigration に条件の意味が含まれた仮定法過去の文である。which は前文の内容全体を指す非制限用法の関係代名詞。connected to those industries は many other jobs を修飾する過去分詞句。
　　□ immigration「移民，移住」　　□ sector「部門」　　□ collapse「崩壊する」
　　□ result in A「Aという結果になる」　　　□ connect A to B「AをBと結びつける」

問6　下線部を含む文は「予想に反して，ヨーロッパ内部での自由な域内移動の導入は貧しい地域から豊かな地域への大量の移住につながらなかった」という意味。したがって，「予想」されていたことは「ヨーロッパ内部での自由な域内移動の導入は貧しい地域から豊かな地域への大量の移住につながるだろう」ということ。
　　□ prediction「予想」

問7　it が形式主語で to campaign 以下が真主語という構造。to be ended only in one country は目的を表す不定詞の副詞用法で，campaign を修飾している。なお，for immigration controls は，to be ended の意味上の主語である。また，Clearly は文修飾の副詞で「疑いなく，明らかに」という意味。
　　□ make sense「意味をなす，道理にかなう」　　　□ campaign「運動を起こす」

問8 下線部は「移民抑制の撤廃は我々すべてにとって自由と繁栄が大きく増えることを意味するだろう」という意味。第4段落第3文には「移動の自由がなければ人権侵害になる」ことが，第7段落第2文には「移民は移住先の国々の富と繁栄に大きな貢献をする」ことが，第8段落第2文には「移民が職が得られる可能性を高め，労働者の賃金と条件が改善される」ことが述べられている。また，第9段落第2文には「高齢化が進む国では，移民が増えなければ，税金を払い，公共部門や産業を維持し，高齢者の世話をする若い労働者が不足する」ことが述べられている。さらに，第13段落第3・4文では「人間は自由に移動できるべきだという基本的自由を制限することは，人権蹂躙につながる」と，第4段落第3文の内容を補足している。したがって，これらの内容を制限字数内でまとめる。

□ abolition「廃止，撤廃」　　□ vast「莫大な」　　□ prosperity「繁栄」

Outline

¶ 1–2	導入	移民抑制は比較的最近の政策であり，国を越えての移住は古くからあった
¶ 3	主題	移動の自由は認められるべきである
¶ 4	展開1	移動の自由の制限は人権侵害になる
¶ 5–6	展開2	国家は移民抑制を行ってきたが，移動の自由を求める要求が強まっている
¶ 7	展開3	移民は移住先の国々に多大な貢献をする
	例1	経済面での貢献
¶ 8	例2	雇用の確保
¶ 9	例3	高齢化社会における労働力
¶ 10	展開4	移民によって国家の独自性が失われることはない
¶ 11		ヨーロッパ連合内での自由な移動
¶ 12	展開5	移民問題は一国の問題ではない
¶ 13	結論	移民抑制の撤廃は自由と繁栄に寄与する

要約

　国家間の移住は昔からあったが，現在，各国には移民を抑制する動きがある。しかし，人間の自由な移動の制限は人権侵害ともなるし，移民は移住先の国に大きな富と繁栄をもたらし，高齢化の進む国においては大切な労働力となる。したがって，移民抑制は撤廃すべきである。
（125字）

─ 第1段落 ─

[1]Immigration controls are a relatively recent policy which became common only in the twentieth century. [2]Although immigration laws may seem like common sense, an unavoidable reality, in most countries they are in fact less than 100 years old.

[1]移民抑制は20世紀になって初めて一般的になった比較的最近の政策である。[2]移民法は当然のこと，つまり避けることのできない現実であるように思われるかもしれないが，ほとんどの国において実際には制定されてから100年もたっていない。

1 □ relatively「比較的，相対的に」　　□ recent「最近の」　　□ policy「政策」
2 □ seem like A「Aのように思われる」　　□ common sense「当然のこと／常識」
　 □ unavoidable「避けられない」　　□ reality「現実」　　□ in fact「実際，実は」

─ 第2段落 ─

[1]International migration, on the other hand, has always existed. [2]Twice as many people migrated from Europe to the rest of the world as have come in the opposite direction. [3]And since the current theory is that human beings originated in East Africa, every other part of the world is the product of immigration. [4]All of us are either immigrants or descended from immigrants.

[1]一方，国を越えての移住は常に行われていた。[2]ヨーロッパから世界の他の地域へ移住した人の数は，これまでに世界の他の地域からヨーロッパに移住した人の数の2倍であった。[3]そして現在の学説で人類は東アフリカで誕生したとされている以上は，世界の他のすべての地域は移住の産物なのである。[4]我々はみんな移民か移民の子孫である。

1 □ international「国家間の」　　□ migration「移住」
　 □ on the other hand「それに対して，他方で」
3 □ current「現在の」　　□ theory「理論，学説」　　□ originate「生じる，始まる」
　 □ product「産物」
4 □ either X or Y「XかYかどちらか」immigrants が X，descended from immigrants が Y である。　　□ immigrant「（外国からの）移民」　　□ be descended from A「Aの子孫である」

¹Freedom of movement should be the new common sense. ²It is hard to see why people should *not* be allowed to move around the world in search of work or safety or both.

¹移動の自由は新しい常識であるべきだ。²仕事もしくは安全あるいはその両方を求めてなぜ人々が世界中を移動してはいけないのかを理解するのは難しい。

2 □ be allowed to *do*「…するのを許されている」　　□ in search of A「Aを捜して」

---

¹Within the European Union there are growing attempts to secure the principle of freedom for its citizens to live and work in any member country. ²In the U.S. there are no restrictions on the movement of people between states. ³It would be considered an outrage if the inhabitants of a country were not free to travel to another part of that country to get a job there, or if they were not allowed to leave it. ⁴Indeed, it was considered an outrage when this happened in the former U.S.S.R.

¹ヨーロッパ連合の中でも，市民がどの加盟国でも生活し，働く自由があるという原則を確保しようという試みが増えている。²合衆国では各州間の人々の移動には何ら制限はない。³もしある国の住民が職を得るためにその国の別の地域に移動する自由がなければ，あるいは人々がその国を離れることが許されないとしたら，それは人権侵害と考えられるであろう。⁴実際，旧ソ連でこれが起こったとき，それは人権侵害だと考えられた。

1 for its citizens は to live ... member country の意味上の主語。
　□ the European Union「ヨーロッパ連合」　　□ growing「増大する」
　□ attempt to *do*「…する試み」　　□ principle「原理，原則」
　□ any A「〈肯定文で〉どんなAでも」
2 □ restriction「制限」　　□ state「州」
3 It would be ... if the ... は仮定法過去で，or が2つの条件節を結んでいる。
　It は if 節の内容を指している。
　□ inhabitant「住人」　　□ be free to *do*「自由に…できる」
4 □ indeed「実際に」　　□ former「以前の」

--- 第 5 段落 ---

[1]The 1948 Universal Declaration of Human Rights asserts these rights. [2]Yet the Declaration is strangely silent on the question of the right to enter another country. [3]Governments cling to what seems to be one of their last remaining rights: the right to keep people out of their territories. [4]Few people question the morality, legality, or practicality of this right.

[1]1948年の世界人権宣言はこれらの権利を主張している。[2]しかし，その宣言は奇妙なことに他の国に入る権利についての問いには口を閉ざしている。[3]各国政府は残っている最後の権利の1つと思われるもの，つまり人々をその領土から締め出す権利に執着している。[4]この権利の倫理性，合法性，あるいは実用性に疑問を抱く人はほとんどいない。

1 □ assert「を主張する」　　□ right(to *do*)「（…する）権利」

2 □ yet「しかし」

3 what seems ... remaining rights と the right 以下は同格の関係。

　□ cling to A「Aに執着する」　　□ remaining「残っている」

　□ keep A out of B「AをBから締め出す」　　□ territory「領土」

4 of this right は or で結ばれた morality と legality と practicality の3つを修飾している。

　□ question「に疑問を抱く」　　□ morality「道徳性，倫理性」　　□ legality「合法性」

　□ practicality「実用性」

--- 第 6 段落 ---

[1]Nation-states are the agents and enforcers of immigration controls and country boundaries. [2]Most were themselves not fully established until the nineteenth century. [3]Now nation-states are supposed to be on the decline. [4]International institutions such as the United Nations, the International Monetary Fund, the World Bank, and the World Trade Organization attempt to control the actions of national governments. [5]Economic power is concentrated in fewer and bigger corporations. [6]These put pressure on governments to allow goods and capital to move freely around the world, unaffected by considerations of national sovereignty. [7]Sometimes they also press governments to allow the free movement of people, in order to secure the labour they need for expansion. [8]Yet by the 1970s many countries, especially in Europe but not in North America, had more or

less ended the right of people to enter and work.

---

　¹国民国家は移民抑制と国境の主体であり実施者である。²ほとんどの国民国家は19世紀まで
それ自体が十分確立されていたわけではなかった。³今や国民国家は衰退に向かっていると思わ
れている。⁴国連，国際通貨基金，世界銀行，そして世界貿易機関のような国際組織は各国政府
の行動を抑制しようとしている。⁵経済力は少数のより巨大な企業に集中している。⁶これらの
企業は政府に圧力をかけて，商品や資本が国家主権への配慮によって影響を受けることなく，
世界中を自由に移動するのを認めさせようとしている。⁷ときにそれらの企業はまた，その拡大
に必要な労働力を確保するために，人々の自由な移動を認めるように政府に強く要求すること
がある。⁸しかし1970年代までには，多くの国々は，北アメリカはそうではないが，特にヨー
ロッパでは，人々が入国し働く権利を多少なりとも停止していた。

---

1 agents と enforcers を，immigration controls と country boundaries をそれぞれ and が結んで
　いる。
　□ nation-state「国民国家」言語・伝統・歴史の国民的同一性を基盤とする国家のこと。
　□ agent「動因，主体」　　□ enforcer「執行人」　　□ country boundary「国境」
2 □ established「確立された」
3 □ be supposed to be「…であると思われている」　　□ on the decline「衰退して」
4 □ institution「組織，機構」　　□ A such as B「たとえばBのようなA」
　□ the United Nations「国連」　　□ the World Bank「世界銀行」
　□ the World Trade Organization「世界貿易機関」　　□ attempt to *do*「…しようと試みる」
5 □ economic power「経済力」　　□ concentrate「を集中させる」
　□ corporation「企業，会社」
6 These = fewer and bigger corporations
　unaffected 以下は move freely around the world を補足説明する分詞構文。
　□ put pressure on A「Aに圧力をかける」
　□ allow O to *do*「Oが…することを許す，可能にする」　　□ goods「商品」
　□ capital「資本」　　□ unaffected「影響を受けない」　　□ consideration「考慮，考察」
　□ national sovereignty「国家主権」
8 □ more or less「多かれ少なかれ／約，だいたい」

──── 第7段落 ────

　¹Even if it were morally acceptable for the rich nations of the world to use immigration
controls to preserve their disproportionate wealth, it is doubtful whether they achieve this

purpose. [2]There is a mass of evidence to show that immigrants actually make a big contribution to the wealth and prosperity of the countries they go to. [3]Economists have also suggested that the abolition of immigration controls would cause a doubling of world incomes.

[1]たとえ世界の豊かな国々がその不釣り合いに大きい富を保持するために，移民抑制を行うことが道徳的に受け入れられることだとしても，この目的を達成できるかどうかは疑わしい。[2]移民は移住先の国々の富と繁栄に実は多大な貢献をすることを示す大量の証拠がある。[3]経済学者もまた，移民抑制の廃止は世界の所得倍増を引き起こすだろうと言っている。

1 Even if it were ... は仮定法過去で，主節は直説法現在になっている。

it は形式主語で，to use 以下が真主語。for the rich nations of the world は to use の意味上の主語である。

to preserve 以下は目的を表す不定詞句。

□ morally「道徳的に」　　□ acceptable「受け入れられる，許容できる」

□ preserve「を保持する」　　□ disproportionate「不釣り合いな」　　□ doubtful「疑わしい」

□ achieve「を達成する」

2 of the countries they go to は and で結ばれた wealth と prosperity を修飾している。

□ a mass of A「大量のA」　　□ evidence「証拠」

□ make a contribution to A「Aに貢献する」

3 □ economist「経済学者」　　□ suggest that節「…だと示唆する」

□ cause「を引き起こす」　　□ doubling「倍増，倍加」　　□ income「所得」

・・

　　── 第8段落 ──

[1]Immigration is not just good for business. [2]It also improves both the job prospects and the wages and conditions of workers. [3]Without immigration, some sectors of industry would collapse or move abroad, which would result in the loss of many other jobs connected to those industries. [4]The U.S. economy, especially its agriculture, building trades, and services, is heavily dependent on immigrants, including those who have no legal permission to work.

[1]移民はビジネスにとってよいばかりではない。[2]それはまた職が得られる可能性を高め，労働者の賃金と条件が改善する。[3]移民がなければ，産業のいくつかの部門は崩壊するか外国に移

るだろうし，それは結果的にそれらの産業と関連のある多くの他の職が失われることになるだろう。⁴合衆国の経済は，特に農業や建設業，サービス業において，合法的な労働許可を持たない人々も含めて移民に大きく頼っている。

1 not just は第2文の also と not just X but (also) Y「XだけでなくYも」の表現になっている。
2 □ improve「を改善する」
　□ both X and Y「XもYも」 the job prospects が X, the wages and conditions of workers が Y である。　□ prospect「見込み」　□ wage「賃金」　□ condition「条件」
4 □ agriculture「農業」　□ building trades「建設業」　□ services「サービス業」
　□ heavily「非常に」　□ be dependent on A「Aに頼っている」
　□ including A「Aを含めて」　□ those who ...「…する人々」　□ legal「合法的な」
　□ permission to *do*「…する許可」

── 第9段落 ──

¹Many industrialized countries — especially in Europe — have declining and ageing populations. ²Unless immigration is increased, there will not be enough young workers to pay taxes, keep the public sector and industry functioning, and look after old people. ³It has also been shown that on average immigrants contribute more in taxes than they receive in public services.

¹多くの工業国は，特にヨーロッパでは，体力が衰え高齢化が進む国民を抱えている。²移民が増えなければ，税金を払い，公共部門や産業の機能を維持し，高齢者の世話をするのに十分な数の若い労働者がいなくなるだろう。³平均すると，移民は公共サービスで受け取る額よりも税金の点で貢献度が高いこともまた示されている。

1 □ industrialized country「工業国」　□ decline「〈体力・健康などが〉衰える」
　□ age「高齢化する」　□ population「人々，住人」
2 enough＋名詞＋to *do* は「…するのに十分な〜」という意味で，ここでは *do* に pay taxes, keep the ..., look after ... の and で結ばれた3つの動詞句がある。
　keep the public sector and industry functioning は keep O *doing*「Oを…にしておく」の形。functioning は現在分詞。
　□ public sector「公共部門」　□ industry「産業」　□ function「機能する」
　□ look after A「Aの世話をする」
3 □ on average「平均すると」　□ contribute「貢献する」　□ receive「受け取る」

第10段落

¹Those who defend immigration controls often refer to the need to 'preserve national identity'. ²National identity is hard to define, however. ³More or less every country in the world is the product of successive waves of immigration. ⁴While immigrants sometimes acquire the negative image of being unable to assimilate, prone to disease and crime, and so on, most of the migrants and refugees who make it to the rich countries are in fact exceptional people who have to have some money and a great deal of courage and enterprise. ⁵They come because there are jobs, or because they are in desperate danger.

¹移民抑制を擁護する人々はしばしば「国家の独自性を保つ」必要に言及する。²しかし，国家の独自性というのは定義するのが難しい。³世界のほぼすべての国は移民が途切れなく押し寄せてきたことによって生まれた。⁴移民は同化できないとか，病気にかかりやすく，犯罪を犯しがちだなどの否定的イメージを持たれることが時としてあるが，豊かな国にたどり着く移民や難民のほとんどは実際には例外的な人々であり，いくらかの金を持ち，かなりの勇気や進取の気性を備えている必要がある。⁵彼らがやって来るのは，仕事があるからか，または絶望的な危険にさらされているからである。

1 □ defend「を擁護する」　　□ refer to A「Aに言及する」　　□ need to *do*「…する必要性」
　□ identity「独自性，アイデンティティー」

2 National identity is hard to define＝It is hard to define national identity
　□ define「を規定する，定義する」

3 □ successive「連続した」

4 who make it to the rich countries は the migrants and refugees を修飾する関係代名詞節。
　□ while Ｓ Ｖ「…するけれども／ところが一方…」　　□ acquire「を獲得する」
　□ negative「否定的な」　　□ assimilate「同化する」　　□ be prone to A「Aの傾向がある」
　□ crime「犯罪」　　□ and so on「…など」　　□ migrant「(別の地域・国への)移住者」
　□ refugee「難民」　　□ make it to A「Aにたどり着く」
　□ exceptional「例外的な，優秀な」　　□ a great deal of A「多量のA」
　□ enterprise「進取の気性」

5 □ in danger「危険な状態で」　　□ desperate「絶望的な」

[1]A precedent for the opening of borders exists in the European Union. [2]Those who worked for the abolition of European internal frontiers were inspired not only by the interests of big business and free trade, but by an idealistic view of the future of Europe. [3]Contrary to predictions, the introduction of free internal movement within Europe did not lead to mass migration from poor areas to richer areas; on the contrary the authorities would like to have more rather than less labour mobility in the European Union.

[1]国境を開放した先例はヨーロッパ連合に存在する。[2]ヨーロッパ内部の国境廃止のために努力した人々は，ビジネスの拡大や自由貿易という利益によってだけでなく，ヨーロッパの将来の理想像を思い描くことによって奮起したのである。[3]予想に反して，ヨーロッパ内部での自由な域内移動の導入は貧しい地域から豊かな地域への大量の移住につながらなかった。それどころか，EU 当局はヨーロッパ連合での労働移動性を減らすよりむしろ増やしたいと願っている。

1 □ precedent「先例」
2 □ internal「内部の」　　□ frontier「国境（地帯）」　　□ inspire「を奮起させる」
　 □ not only X but Y「XだけでなくYも」　　□ interest「利益／関心」
　 □ free trade「自由貿易」　　□ idealistic「理想の」
3 □ contrary to A「Aとは反対に」　　□ introduction of A「Aの導入」
　 □ lead to A「Aにつながる」　　□ mass「大規模な／大衆の」
　 □ on the contrary「それどころか」　　□ the authorities「当局，関係機関」
　 □ X rather than Y「YよりむしろX」　　□ labour mobility「労働移動性」

[1]The ability of governments to enforce immigration controls is becoming increasingly unsustainable. [2]The costs and suffering caused by these controls are increasing. [3]Clearly it would not make much sense to campaign for immigration controls to be ended only in one country. [4]Their abolition would need to be by agreement among the governments of the world.

[1]各国政府が移民抑制を実施することがますます続けられなくなっている。[2]この抑制によって引き起こされるコストと苦しみは増えている。[3]移民抑制がただ1つの国だけで終わるように運動してもあまり意味がないだろうことは明らかだ。[4]その廃止は世界の政府間での同意による

必要があるだろう。

1 □ enforce「を施行する」　　□ increasingly「ますます」　　□ unsustainable「維持できない」
2 caused by these controls は The costs and suffering を修飾する過去分詞句。
　　□ suffering「苦しみ」
4 □ agreement「同意, （意見の）一致」

- -

第13段落

[1]Abolition of borders implies complete freedom of movement for all, and the right to settle and work in a place of the person's choice, just as people can now do within countries. [2]In a more just world order, movements of capital would be democratically controlled to meet people's needs and to reduce inequalities. [3]But people are not goods or capital — and they should be free to move. [4]The attempt to limit this basic freedom leads to some of the worst abuses of human rights which exist in the world today. [5]The abolition of immigration controls would mean a vast increase in freedom and prosperity for all of us.

[1]国境の廃止は，すべての人に完全な移動の自由があり，国内で人々が今，許されているのとまったく同じように，自分が選ぶ場所で定住し働く権利を持つことを意味する。[2]より公正な世界秩序の中で，資本の移動は人々の必要を満たし，不平等を減らすために民主的に制御されるだろう。[3]しかし，人間は商品や資本ではない。そして人間は自由に移動できるべきなのである。[4]この基本的自由を制限する試みは，今日世界に存在する中で人権蹂躙の最悪の事例につながるものである。[5]移民抑制の撤廃は我々すべてにとって自由と繁栄が大きく増えることを意味するだろう。

1 1つめの and は complete freedom ... for all と the right ... person's choice を結んでいる。
　as は「様態」を表し「…ように」という意味。
　do = settle and ... person's choice
　　□ imply「を意味する」　　□ complete「完全な」　　□ all = all people　　□ settle「定住する」
　　□ choice「選択」
2 □ just「公正な」　　□ order「秩序／順序」　　□ democratically「民主的に」
　　□ meet「を満たす」（= satisfy)　　□ reduce「を減らす」　　□ inequality「不平等」
4 □ limit「を制限する」　　□ abuse「濫用」　　□ human right「人権」

解 答

問1 成人の性格のおよそ半分は遺伝子の産物であり，近所のほかの子どもたちとどのように付き合うかによっても形成されるから。(57字)

問2 しかし，食べ過ぎる両親を持つ子どもが大人になると食べ過ぎるようになるというのは実情ではない。

問3 体罰や離婚，テレビで放映される暴力が子どもに与える影響に関して広く議論される場合，2人以上子どもを持つ親であれば誰でも知っている事実，それぞれの子どもが同じ明白な影響に対して異なる反応をするという事実に触れられることはまずない。

問4 食習慣が乱れていたり，うつ病を患っていたりする親の子どもが同様の傾向があると報告することもあまり役に立たない。というのも，養子の研究のように，遺伝的要素が取り除かれると，そのつながりは普通消えてしまうからである。

問5 子どもが所属する集団の長期的影響は，家庭の長期的影響よりもはるかに強く，一般に認められているよりもはるかに早い時期から始まるという点。(67字)

問6 イ. much less

問7 子どもが身につけるのは，親の行動様式というよりは，男女でまったく異なる行動様式なのである。

問8 エ. a waste of time

▶▶▶ 設問解説 ◀◀◀

問1 下線部(1)の最後の they have は hope と fear に共通する目的語である that 節の that が省略されたもので，have の後ろには，(much) influence over their children を補って考えることができる。したがって，下線部は「親は決して，私たちが望みかつ恐れているほどの影響力を子どもに対して持っていない」という意味。その理由として，直後の文に「成人の性格のおよそ半分は遺伝子の産物なのである」と述べられている。この点について，第3段落から第6段落まで論じられた後，第7段落第1文に「ところが，遺伝子は唯一の決定要因ではない」とあり，同段落第4文には心理学者ジュディス・ハリスの考え

として「成人の性格は，自分たちと親の間で演じられる家族ドラマではなく，近所のほかの子どもたちとどのように付き合うかによって形成される」ことが述べられている。さらに，第8段落から第13段落にジュディス・ハリスの唱えるGS理論を紹介する形で，家庭以外の「子どもの所属する集団」の影響力が強いことが論じられている。したがって，これらの内容を制限字数に留意してまとめればよい。

　　□ have influence over A「Aに対して影響力がある」　　□ not nearly「決して…でない」

問2 be the case は「実情である」という意味。直後の文で「養子にもらわれた子どもは，食べ過ぎる両親の遺伝子を共有しておらず，親の行動をまねることはない」と述べていることから，this は直前の文の that節の内容「食べ過ぎる両親を持つ子どもが大人になると食べ過ぎるようになるということ」を指しているとわかる。

問3 文全体は Public debates ... on television(S) mention(V) a fact(O) という構造。the effect on children of ... は the effect of A on B「AがBに与える影響」が the effect on B of A の語順になったもの。which every ... child knows は a fact を修飾する関係代名詞節。that different ... broad influences は a fact と同格の名詞節。

　　□ debate「討論」　　□ physical punishment「体罰」　　□ divorce「離婚」
　　□ scarcely「ほとんど…ない」　　□ mention「に触れる，言及する」
　　□ respond to A「Aに反応する」　　□ broad「明白な」

問4 It は形式主語で，to report ... the same が真主語。who have ... from depression は parents を修飾する関係代名詞節。as in adoption studies は，省略された語句を補うと，as the genetic element is removed in adoption studies であり，様態を表す副詞節である。

　　□ eating habit「食習慣」　　□ suffer from A「Aを患う，Aで苦しむ」
　　□ depression「うつ病，憂うつ」　　□ tend to *do*「…する傾向がある」
　　□ genetic「遺伝の，遺伝子の」　　□ element「要素」　　□ remove「を取り除く」
　　□ adoption「養子縁組／採用」　　□ link「つながり」

問5 下線部(5)の「社会への適応(GS)理論」とは，ジュディス・ハリスの唱える「性格が子どもの所属する集団の影響で形成される」とする理論である。第13段落第2文に What is original about GS theory is とあるので，補語に当たる its claim ...「集団の長期的影響は，家庭の長期的影響よりもはるかに強く，一般に認められているよりもはるかに早い時期から始まる」という内容をまとめればよい。

　　□ socialisation「社会化」個人が社会に適応すること。

問6 空所(6)を含む文は，GS 理論を唱えるジュディス・ハリスの発話の一部であ
り，GS 理論が「進化という点で道理にかなっている」ことを述べた箇所であ
る。直前の文には「子どもはすでに遺伝的に親と似ている」と述べられてい
る。その上さらに「親の習慣もすべて取り入れるとしたら，外界の変化する状
況に適応するための柔軟性が<u>なくなる</u>」という意味にすれば，文脈が自然につ
ながる。したがって，イが正解。なお，much は比較級を強調している。

問7 pick up の目的語を強調した強調構文である。このように，強調構文で強調さ
れるのが人以外を表す名詞の場合，that の代わりに which が用いられること
がある。なお，these は直前の quite distinct patterns of behaviour を指して
いる。また，their parents' は their parents' patterns of behaviour のことであ
る。

　　例 It was the birth of his grandchild which gave him greatest pleasure.
　　　「彼が最も喜んだのは孫の誕生であった」

　　□ X rather than Y「YよりもむしろX」　　□ pick A up「Aを身につける／Aを拾い上げる」

問8 空所(8)を含む文の主語 These findings は，第2段落から第6段落で述べられ
た「性格のおよそ半分は遺伝子の産物であること」と，第7段落から第13段落
で述べられた「性格が子どもの所属する集団の影響で形成される」という発見
のことである。したがって，これらの発見が示唆しているのは「個々の親を非
難することは<u>意味がない</u>」ということであると考えられる。

　　ア.「メディアでは避けられる」イ.「適切な社会政策」ウ.「事実に基づいている」
　　エ.「時間の無駄」

Outline

要　約

　性格のおよそ半分は遺伝によるものであり，また，性格の形成においては家庭よりも子ども
の所属する集団の影響が強いという考えがある。したがって，親が子どもに与える影響はそれ
ほど強いものではない。(94字)

▶▶▶ 構文・語句解説 ◀◀◀

──── 第1段落 ────

　[1]If a young man committed a serious crime in ancient China his parents were liable to be executed with him, on the grounds that they were also to blame. [2]This logic is reappearing in contemporary social policy: parents are responsible for shaping their children's behaviour; the crime rate among young people is rising; parents must be doing something wrong. [3]If a few were made an example of, the rest might mend their ways and bring up their children properly. [4]But do even the best of parents have that much control?

　[1]古代中国では若者が重大な犯罪を犯すと，親にも責任があるという理由で，その若者と一緒に処刑されることになっていた。[2]このような理屈が，今日の社会政策において再び現れようとしている。親は子どもの振る舞いを方向付けることに対して責任があるのであり，若者の犯罪率が上昇しているのであれば，親が何か間違ったことをしているに違いないという理屈である。[3]何人か見せしめにすれば，残りの親は行動を改め，ちゃんと子どもを育てるであろう。[4]しかし，最もできた親でも，それほど子どもを自由に操ることができるのであろうか。

1 □ commit「を犯す」　　□ ancient「古代の」　　□ be liable to *do*「…する法的責任がある」
　□ execute「を処刑する」　　□ on the grounds that 節「…という理由で」
　□ be to blame「責任がある，責めを負うべきである」
2 □ logic「論理」　　□ reappear「再び現れる」　　□ contemporary「現代の」
　□ shape「を形成する」　　□ crime rate「犯罪率」
3 仮定法過去の文。
　a few were made an example of は made an example of a few の受動態。
　□ make an example of A「Aを見せしめにする」　　□ the rest「残り」
　□ mend「を改める」　　□ bring A up「Aを育てる」　　□ properly「適切に」
4 that much control の that は副詞「それほど，そんなに」という意味。

[1]More and more psychological researchers seem to be suggesting one unexpected theory: parents do not have nearly as much influence over their children as we both hope and fear they have. [2]A decade of research by the geneticist Robert Plomin and others suggest that about half of our adult personality is the result of our genes. [3]Surprisingly, many parents' actions, which you would imagine must make a difference, apparently do not.

[1]ある意外な理論を提唱する心理学の研究者が増えているようである。親は決して，私たちが望みかつ恐れているほどの影響力を子どもに対して持っていないという理論である。[2]遺伝学者のロバート・プロミンらの10年にわたる研究によると，成人の性格のおよそ半分は遺伝子の産物なのである。[3]多くの親の行動は影響があるに違いないと思われているかもしれないが，意外にも，どうやらそうでないようなのだ。

1 □ more and more A「ますます多くのA」　　□ psychological「心理学の」
　□ researcher「研究者」　　□ unexpected「意外な」
2 □ decade「10年」　　□ geneticist「遺伝学者」　　□ personality「性格，個性」
　□ gene「遺伝子」
3 which you would imagine must make a difference は many parents' actions を修飾する非制限
　用法の連鎖関係代名詞節。
　do not＝do not make a difference
　□ surprisingly「〈文修飾で〉意外にも，驚くべきことに」
　□ make a difference「影響がある，違いを生じる」　　□ apparently「外見上は，見たところ」

[1]For example, eating: what could be more obvious than the idea that children whose parents both overeat will grow up to do the same? [2]But this is not the case. [3]Adopted children, who do not share the overeating parents' genes, do not copy their behaviour. [4]The same applies to watching television. [5]Adopted children in a household which watches a lot of television will *not* sit glued to the box, unless watching television is something their biological parents also like to do. [6]Even attitudes to, say, the death penalty or jazz, apparently prime candidates for parental influence, turn out to have a strong genetic component.

¹たとえば，食べることについて考えてみよう。食べ過ぎる両親を持つ子どもが大人になると食べ過ぎるようになるという考え以上に明白なものはあり得るだろうか。²しかし，これは実情ではない。³養子にもらわれた子どもは，食べ過ぎる両親の遺伝子を共有しておらず，親の行動をまねることはない。⁴同じことはテレビを見ることにも当てはまる。⁵よくテレビを見る家庭に養子にもらわれた子どもは，テレビを見ることが生みの親も好んでやることでない限り，テレビに釘付けになることはない。⁶たとえば，死刑や，ジャズといった，親の影響を最も受けそうなことに対する態度でさえ，強い遺伝的要素があることがわかる。

1 that 以下は the idea と同格の名詞節。

 to do the same は結果を表す副詞用法の不定詞句。do the same = overeat
   □ obvious「明白な」　　□ overeat「食べ過ぎる」　　□ grow up「成長する，大人になる」
3 □ adopt「を養子にする／を採用する」
4 □ apply to A「Aに当てはまる」
5 □ household「家庭，世帯」　　□ sit *done*「…された状態で座っている」
   □ glue「を釘付けにする，をくっつける」　　□ the box「テレビ」
   □ biological parent「生みの親」
6 □ say「たとえば」　　□ the death penalty「死刑」　　□ prime「主要な」
   □ candidate「候補」　　□ turn out to *do*「…するとわかる」　　□ component「構成要素」

— 第4段落 —

¹Public debates about the effect on children of physical punishment, divorce or violence on television, scarcely mention a fact which every parent of more than one child knows — that different children respond differently to the same broad influences. ²This is because developmental psychology has resolutely ignored genetics for the past 50 years.

¹体罰や離婚，テレビで放映される暴力が子どもに与える影響に関して広く議論される場合，2人以上子どもを持つ親であれば誰でも知っている事実，それぞれの子どもが同じ明白な影響に対して異なる反応をするという事実に触れられることはまずない。²これは，発達心理学が遺伝学を過去50年にわたり完全に無視してきたからである。

2 □ this is because S V「これは…だからである」　　□ resolutely「完全に，断固として」
　 □ genetics「遺伝学」

¹There are many reasons why the genetic element in the study of personality has been unpopular — from liberal commitment to equal opportunity based on merit, to the shadow of Nazi eugenics. ²Most educators and social commentators have placed responsibility for a child's development on his or her environment, especially on the parents. ³Mountains of books and articles describe how authoritarian and over-protective parents can make a child timid, while a more tolerant approach produces anxious children.

¹リベラル派が能力に基づいた機会均等を重視してきたことから，ナチズムの優生学の影響に至るまで，性格の研究において遺伝的要素がはやらなかった理由は数多くある。²たいていの教育家や社会評論家は，子どもの発達の責任を，その子どもの環境，特に親にあるとしてきた。³権威主義的で過保護な親が子どもを臆病にし，一方より寛大な接し方は心配性の子どもを生むことを述べた本や記事は山ほどある。

1 □ liberal「リベラルな，自由主義の」　　□ commitment to A「Aへの強い関心，係わり合い」
　 □ based on A「Aに基づいている」　　□ merit「能力」　　□ shadow「(悪い)影響」
3 describe how ... child timid の how 以下は describe の目的語となる名詞節で，「…ということ」という意味。
　 □ mountains of A「多数のA，大量のA」　　□ article「記事」　　□ describe「と述べる」
　 □ authoritarian「権威主義的な」　　□ over-protective「過保護な」　　□ timid「臆病な」
　 □ while S V「…するけれども／ところが一方…」　　□ tolerant「寛大な」
　 □ approach「取り組み」　　□ anxious「心配している」

¹Such views, however, now seem rather old-fashioned as genetic influence becomes more accepted among doctors. ²Until the 1970s, for instance, psychoanalysts claimed that autistic children were the result of mothers who were so emotionally distant that their children never learned to form close relationships. ³Now autism is generally accepted to have a strong genetic basis. ⁴Similarly, hardly anyone now believes that the reason why some children have speech problems is that their parents failed to talk to them enough. ⁵The development of language is acknowledged to have a large genetic component. ⁶It is also not very useful to report that children of parents who have bad eating habits or suffer from depression tend to do the same, because when the genetic element is removed, as in adoption studies, the link usually disappears.

¹しかしながら、そのような見解は、遺伝子の影響が医者の間で受け入れられるようになるにつれて、今ではいささか時代遅れのように思われる。²たとえば、1970年代までは、子どもが自閉症になるのは、感情の面でよそよそしいため子どもが親密な関係を築くことができるようにならない母親が原因であると精神分析学者は主張していた。³今では、自閉症には強い遺伝的基盤があると広く受け入れられている。⁴同様に、一部の子どもが言語障害を抱えている理由は、親が十分に話しかけることがなかったからであると考えている者は今ではほとんどいない。⁵言語の発達には大きな遺伝的要素があると認められている。⁶食習慣が乱れていたり、うつ病を患っていたりする親の子どもが同様の傾向があると報告することもあまり役に立たない。というのも、養子の研究のように、遺伝的要素が取り除かれると、そのつながりは普通消えてしまうからである。

1 □ view「見方、考え方、見解」　　□ old-fashioned「時代遅れの」

2 were so emotionally distant that ... は so ... that ～「非常に…なので～する、～するほど…」の構文。

　　□ claim that節「…だと主張する」　　□ distant「よそよそしい／遠い」

　　□ learn to *do*「…できるようになる」　　□ form「を形成する」　　□ relationship「関係」

3 □ basis「基盤」

4 □ hardly anyone「ほとんど誰も…でない」　　□ speech problem「言語障害」

　　□ fail to *do*「…しない、できない」

5 □ acknowledge O to *do*「Oが…すると認める」

第7段落

¹Genes, however, are not the only deciding factor; they rather provide the raw material which a child's environment then forms into different finished material.　²What is it, then, that shapes the child's environment if it is not the parents?　³Recently, a new attempt to answer this question has been made by the American psychologist Judith Harris.　⁴In the journal *Psychological Review*, she suggests that adult character is not shaped by a family drama played out between ourselves and our parents, but by how we get along with other children in the neighborhood.

¹ところが、遺伝子は唯一の決定要因ではない。遺伝子はむしろ原料を提供するだけで、その後子どもの置かれた環境がそうした原料を様々な完成品へと変えていくのである。²それでは、子どもの環境を形成するのは、親でないとすれば、何であろうか。³最近、この問いに答えよう

とする新たな試みが，アメリカ人の心理学者，ジュディス・ハリスによってなされた。⁴『サイコロジカル・レヴュー』誌において，彼女は，成人の性格は自分たちと親の間で演じられる家族ドラマではなく，近所のほかの子どもたちとどのように付き合うかによって形成されると言っている。

1 □ deciding factor「決定要因」　　□ raw material「原料」　　□ form into A「Aになる」

2 What is it ... that ～は疑問詞 what を強調した強調構文。

3 □ attempt to *do*「…する試み」

4 is not shaped by は，not X but Y の not が shaped の前に出た形。Xに当たるのが by a ... our parents，Yに当たるのが by how ... the neighborhood である。なお played out ... our parents は a family drama を修飾する過去分詞句。

　□ journal「(専門的)定期刊行物，雑誌」　　□ suggest that節「…だと示唆する」

　□ play A out「Aを演じる」

　□ get along with A「Aとうまくやっていく」(＝get on with A)

＊＊

── 第8段落 ──

¹Combining evidence from areas of psychological research not usually considered in child development debates, Harris makes a powerful case for group socialisation (GS) theory. ²She starts from the fact that we learn a particular behaviour in a specific context. ³The home is just one of several environments in which children have to learn how to behave, and although you can affect children's behaviour in the way they behave at home, this is not necessarily the case in other situations. ⁴"This makes evolutionary sense," says Harris. ⁵"The parental home is not where children are likely to spend their future. ⁶They are already genetically similar to their parents. ⁷Adopting all their habits as well would give them much less flexibility for adapting to changing conditions in the outside world."

¹子どもの発達の議論では普通検討されることのない心理学の研究領域からの証拠を組み合わせて，ハリスは集団による社会への適応（GS）理論を強く主張している。²彼女は，私たちはある行動を特定の環境で学ぶという事実から出発する。³家庭は，子どもがふるまい方を学ばなければならないいくつかある環境の1つにすぎないのであって，家庭における子どものふるまい方に影響を与えることはできても，他の状況ではこれが必ずしも正しいわけではない。⁴「このことは進化という点で道理にかなっています」とハリスは言う。⁵「親の家というのは，子どもが将来を過ごす可能性が高いところではありません。⁶子どもはすでに遺伝的に親と似ています。⁷親の習慣もすべて取り入れるとしたら，外界の変化する状況に適応するための柔軟性がは

1 Combining evidence ... development debates は分詞構文。

　□ combine「を組み合わせる」　　□ makes a case「主張する」

2 that 以下は the fact と同格の名詞節。

　□ specific「特定の」　　□ context「環境」

3 □ affect「に影響を与える」　　□ the way S V ...「…する方法，様子」　　□ situation「状況」

4 □ make sense「意味をなす，道理にかなう」　　□ evolutionary「進化の」

5 □ parental「親の」　　□ where S V ...「…するところ」

　□ be likely to *do*「たぶん…するだろう，…する可能性が高い」

6 □ genetically「遺伝的に」　　□ be similar to A「Aに似ている」

7 □ as well「…も」　　□ flexibility「柔軟性」　　□ adapt to A「Aに適応する」

　□ condition「状況」

第 9 段落

[1]Humans are social animals. [2]Over millions of years of evolution we have developed mechanisms for getting on with others in the group, as well as competing for status and mates. [3]Those who subscribe to nurture theory concentrate on relationships between two people, typically mother and baby. [4]But learning how to behave with one person does not tell you much about how to behave with someone else quite different — your father, for instance. [5]Far more powerful in shaping behaviour, according to GS theory, is the effect of the group.

[1]人間は社会的動物である。[2]何百万年にもわたる進化を経て，地位や配偶者を求めて競うだけでなく，集団の中で他人とうまくやっていく仕組みを発達させてきた。[3]養育説に同意するものは，二者間の関係，主として母子関係に焦点を絞っている。[4]しかし，ある人に対してどのようにふるまうかを学んだからといって，まったく別の人，たとえば父親に対してどのようにふるまうかについてはあまり役に立たない。[5]GS 理論によると，行動を形成する上ではるかに重要なのは，集団の影響なのである。

1 □ social「社会生活を営む／社会の」

2 □ millions of A「何百万ものA」　　□ evolution「進化」

　□ mechanism「仕組み，メカニズム」　　□ X as well as Y「XもYも／YだけでなくXも」

　□ compete for A「Aを求めて競う」　　□ status「地位」

□ mate「配偶者／(鳥・動物の)つがいの一方」

3 □ those who ...「…する人々」　　□ subscribe to A「Aに同意する」　　□ nurture「養育」

　 □ concentrate on A「Aに注意を集中する」　　□ typically「主として，典型的には」

5 Far more powerful in shaping behaviour ... is the effect of the group は C V S の語順になっている。

第10段落

¹Take gender roles. ²From the nurture viewpoint, gender roles are a key area where parents have an influence — the distant father, the critical mother and a variety of other parenting styles can, it is claimed, significantly affect the development of a child's sexual identity. ³But evidence to the contrary is strong.

¹性別役割について考えてみよう。²養育という観点からは，性別役割は親が影響力を与える重要な領域である。よそよそしい父親とか，口うるさい母親，そのほか様々な親のあり方が，子どもの性的アイデンティティーの発達に大きな影響を与えることがある，と言われている。³しかしそうではないという証拠も有力である。

1 □ gender role「性別役割」

2 the distant ... sexual identity = it is claimed that the distant ... sexual identity

　 □ viewpoint「観点」　　□ critical「口うるさい，批判的な」　　□ a variety of A「様々なA」

　 □ parenting「子育て」　　□ significantly「大きく，著しく」　　□ sexual「性的な」

　 □ identity「独自性，アイデンティティー」

3 □ evidence「証拠」　　□ A to the contrary「それと反対のA，そうではないとするA」

第11段落

¹John Archer of the University of Central Lancashire has been studying how gender differences develop. ²"We have now had about 20 years of a serious attempt by a generation of parents to raise boys and girls in much the same way," he says. ³"Yet, as every school and every parent knows, boys and girls automatically split themselves into single sex groups from an early age." ⁴Once in these groups, they develop quite distinct patterns of behaviour. ⁵It is these, rather than their parents', which children pick up. ⁶Gender roles seem to be under the control of the group.

¹セントラル・ランカシャー大学のジョン・アーチャーは性差がどのように発達するのかを研究してきた。²「およそ20年にわたって，同一世代の親が男の子も女の子もほぼ同じように育てようと真剣に試みてきました」と彼は言う。³「しかし，すべての学校や親が知っていることですが，男の子も女の子も幼い頃から自然と性別ごとの集団に分かれてしまうのです」⁴ひとたびこうした集団に分かれると，男子も女子もまったく異なる行動様式を発達させる。⁵子どもが身につけるのは，親の行動様式というよりは，こうした行動様式なのである。⁶性別役割は，そうした集団に支配されているように思われる。

2 a serious attempt by a generation of parents to raise の to raise 以下は，a serious attempt を修飾する形容詞用法の不定詞句。

　　□ raise「を育てる」　　□ much the same「ほぼ同じ」

3 as every ... parent knows は boys and ... early age を補足説明する関係代名詞節。

　　□ automatically「自然に」　　□ split「を分裂させる」

4 Once in these groups＝Once they are in these groups

　　□ distinct「独特の，異なる」

6 □ under the control of A「Aに支配されている」

- -

第12段落

¹Children do share their parents' beliefs — not because of the parents' careful upbringing, but because of the way that the parents' group affects the children's group. ²You can see the effect clearly when the parents of a child do *not* share the values of the parents of the rest of the children in the group. ³This often occurs with immigrants: GS theory predicts that the children will follow the values of the group, not those of the parents.

¹確かに子どもは親の考えを共有しているが，これは親の注意の行き届いた育て方によるものではなく，親の所属する集団が子どもの所属する集団に影響を与えるやり方によるものなのである。²ある子どもの両親が，集団の他の子どもの親の価値観を共有していないときに，この影響をはっきり見ることができる。³こうしたことは，移民ではよく起きる。GS 理論は，移民の子どもは，自分の親の価値観ではなく，集団の価値観に従うことになると予測している。

1 do share の do は動詞強調の助動詞。

　　□ not because of ..., but because of ～「…だからではなく～だから」

□ upbringing「育て方」

2 □ values「価値観」

3 the values of the group, not those of the parents は not X but Y「XではなくY」が，Y, not X の語順になったもの。なお，those は the values の代用。

　　　□ immigrant「(外国からの)移民」　　□ predict that節「…と予測する」　　□ follow「に従う」

第13段落

¹There is nothing new in the idea that peer pressure influences children. ²What is original about GS theory is its claim that the long-term influence of the group is much greater than that of the home and that it starts much earlier than has generally been acknowledged. ³GS theory does not deny that the way parents behave towards their kids affects the way they behave at home. ⁴But learned behaviour is tied to the situation it was learned in. ⁵The fact that your kids complain and quarrel at home does not mean that they will do so in the playground: the standards of acceptable behaviour, as well as the punishments and rewards, are quite different. ⁶Parents are often surprised when they talk to their child's teacher: "Is she talking about my child?"

---

¹仲間からの圧力が子どもに影響を与えるという考えには，新しい点はない。²GS 理論の独創的な点は，集団の長期的影響は，家庭の長期的影響よりもはるかに強く，一般に認められているよりもはるかに早い時期から始まるという主張である。³親の子どもに対するふるまい方が，子どもの家庭でのふるまい方に影響を与えるということを，GS 理論は否定しない。⁴しかし，学んだふるまいは，それを学んだ状況と結びついている。⁵自分の子どもが家で文句を言い，口論するからといって，遊び場でもそうするということではない。罰と報酬だけでなく，受け入れられる行動基準がまったく異なるのだ。⁶親は，子どもの担任の先生と話をすると驚くことが多い。「先生は私の子どものことを話しているのだろうか」と。

1 that 以下は the idea と同格の名詞節。

　　　□ peer「仲間，同等の人」

2 that the ... the home と that it ... been acknowledged は its claims と同格の名詞節。

　　　□ long-term「長期的な」

3 □ deny that節「…ということを否定する」

4 □ be tied to A「Aと結びついている」

5 that your ... at home は The fact と同格の名詞節。

　　　□ playground「遊び場」　　□ acceptable「受け入れられる，許容できる」

☐ punishment「罰」　　☐ reward「報酬」

- -

―― 第14段落 ――

[1]These findings could lead to a less anxious approach to childraising and a greater appreciation of the role played by schools and seem to suggest that blaming individual parents is a waste of time.

[1]こうした発見は，より不安のない育児への取り組みと，学校の果たす役割のより大きな評価につながるかもしれないし，個々の親を非難することは時間の無駄であると示唆しているようである。

1 ☐ finding「発見」　　☐ lead to A「Aにつながる」　　☐ childraising「育児」
　 ☐ appreciation「評価，認識」

記数法の発達

問1 (1a) エ　　(1b) ア

問2 ア．calendar

問3 MMCCCXXXV

問4 イ．manual

問5 インドの数学者は，今日であれば算術，代数，幾何と言われるであろう分野で進歩を遂げたが，彼らの研究の多くは天文学に対する関心によって動機づけられていた。

問6 ウ．position

問7 位の値がないことを示す追加された記号を，他の9つとまったく同じようにみなすことができなかったから。(49字)

問8 defining it as the result obtained when you

▶▶▶ 設問解説 ◀◀◀

問1 下線部(1a)の「数を記録する印」の短所としては，第2段落第2文に「数を記録する印は，数える項目が4つか5つを超えると，読みづらくなる」と述べられているので，正解はエ。

下線部(1b)の「ローマ記数法」の短所としては，第3段落第6文に「掛け算と割り算を行う唯一許容できる方法は，それぞれ足し算と引き算を繰り返すことである」と，第8文に「この方法はもちろん，掛け算する2つの数字のうち一方が小さいときしか，実用的ではない」と述べられているので，正解はア。

ア．「掛け算と割り算を行うのがやっかいである」

イ．「数を表す60の異なる記号を覚えなければならない」

ウ．「指を使って単純な算術ができない」

エ．「集合の中に4つか5つを超える項目があるとき読むのに苦労する」

問2 空所(2)を含む文にあるイシャンゴの骨は第1段落第5文「アフリカや他の場所で発見された刻み目のある骨の他の例はまた，時間を数量化しようとする初期の試みだったのかもしれない」の事例として取り上げられているので，正解はア。

ア．「カレンダー」イ．「ハンマー」ウ．「コンパス」エ．「定規」

問3 第3段落第1文から空所(3)を含む第4文では，ローマ記数法での足し算の仕方について，MCCXXIII (1,223) ＋ MCXII (1,112) ＝ MMCCCXXXIIIII (2,335) という例を使って説明されており，空所にはその答えをローマ数字で正しく書く必要がある。第3文と空所を含む第4文の前半では「ときに，あるグループの記号を1つ上の記号に変換しなければならないかもしれない。この例では，5つのⅠがⅤに置き換えられ」とあるので，MMCCCXXXIIIII の5つのⅠがⅤに置き換えられ，MMCCCXXXV となる。

問4 空所(4)を含む節の主語 these は Although 節内の「指を使った計算術は1万までの数を伴う計算を行うこと」と「今日計算機を用いるのとほぼ同じ速さでそろばんを使って計算すること」を指している。したがって，頭の技能に加え手の技能が必要であったと考えられるので，正解はイ。
ア.「芸術の」イ.「手の」ウ.「数学の」エ.「言葉の」

問5 make advances in A「Aで進歩を遂げる」の A に関係代名詞 what が導く名詞節がきている。節内では仮定法過去が用いられ，today が条件節に相当する意味を表している。much 以下は意味上の主語を伴った付帯状況の分詞構文。
□ Indian「インドの」 □ mathematician「数学者」
□ describe O as C「OをCだと言う」 □ arithmetic「算術」 □ algebra「代数」
□ geometry「幾何」 □ work「研究」 □ motivate「に動機を与える」
□ astronomy「天文学」

問6 空所(6)を含む文の後の文に，具体例として，ゼロの記号がなければ，「1 3」という表現は13や103，130，1,030という意味にもなることが述べられているので，空所(6)を含む文が「効率的な位取り記数法のためには，特定の位置には入るものが何もない場合にこれを示すことができる必要がある」という意味になるように，空所には position が入る。
ア.「数」イ.「記号」ウ.「位置」エ.「規則」

問7 下線部(7)を含む段落の次の第8段落では，インド人がゼロを作り出した経緯を2段階に分けて説明している。この第1段階を述べた第2・3文に「まず第一に，入るものが『欠けている』空間の周りに円を描くことによって，何もない空間を示すという問題を克服した。バビロニア人もここまではできていた」より，バビロニア人が第2段階まで到達しなかったことが示唆されている。第2段階については，第5文に「第2段階は，その追加された記号（＝位の値がないことを示す記号）を他の9つとまったく同じようにみなすことであった」とあるので，バビロニア人が「0を発見できなかった理由」は，「位の値がないことを示す追加された記号を，他の9つとまったく同じようにみなすことができなかったから」である。

問8 下線部(8)を含む第9段落では，ゼロを発見したブラフマグプタと彼が述べたゼロの性質について紹介している。直前には「ブラフマグプタはゼロという数を導入し」とあり，選択肢には defining があるので，define O as C「OをCと定義する」を分詞構文として用い，defining it as ...「それ(＝ゼロという数)を…であると定義づけた」から始める。また，直後には「ある数からその数を引く」とあるので，「ある数からその数を引くとき得られる結果」という意味になるように，obtained を形容詞用法の過去分詞として用いて，the result obtained when you とする。

要　約

　古代ローマでは数を記録する印に5や10などを表す記号が加えられたが，掛け算と割り算は煩雑で実用的ではなかった。インドでは10進法による10個の数の記号が用いられ，位取りが導入されたが，ある位に入るものがないことを示すために作られた0という記号を他の9つとまったく同じようにみなすことで，数学が発達した。(148字)

▶▶ 構文・語句解説 ◀◀

— 第1段落 —

[1]Humans had been counting things for many thousands of years before the first number system was developed. [2]Early counting was typically carried out by scratching tally marks on a stick, stone, or bone. [3]The oldest known example, consisting of twenty-nine distinct notches deliberately cut into the leg bone of a monkey, was discovered in the Lebombo Mountains of Eswatini and dated to approximately 35,000 B.C. [4]It has been suggested that women used such notched bones to keep track of their monthly fertility cycles. [5]Other examples of notched bones discovered in Africa and elsewhere may also have been early

attempts to quantify time. ⁶The Ishango bone, found in 1960 near the headwaters of the Nile in north-eastern Congo and perhaps twenty thousand years old, bears a series of tally marks carved in three columns running the length of the bone. ⁷A common interpretation is that the Ishango bone served as a calendar.

---

¹人類は，最初の記数法が考え出される以前何千年にもわたって物を数えていた。²初期の数え方は，典型的には棒や石や骨に数を記録する印を刻むことで行われた。³知られている中で最古の例は，猿の脚の骨に意図的に切り込まれた29個のはっきりした刻み目から成り，エスワティニのロボンボ山脈で発見されたもので，紀元前およそ３万５千年までさかのぼる。⁴女性が毎月の受精周期を記録しておくためにそのような刻み目のある骨を使ったとされている。⁵アフリカや他の場所で発見された刻み目のある骨の他の例はまた，時間を数量化しようとする初期の試みだったのかもしれない。⁶イシャンゴの骨は，1960年にコンゴ北東部のナイル川源流近くで見つかったが，これは，２万年ほど前のもので，骨の全長にわたって３列に彫られた一連の数を記録する印がある。⁷一般的な解釈は，イシャンゴの骨はカレンダーとして使われていたというものである。

1 □ humans「人間」　　□ count「を数える」　　□ thousands of A「何千ものA」
　□ number system「記数法」（＝numeral system）

2 □ typically「典型的には」　　□ carry A out「Aを行う，実行する」　　□ scratch「を刻む」

3 consisting of ... a monkey は，The oldest known example を補足説明する現在分詞句で，deliberately cut ... a monkey は twenty-nine distinct notches を修飾する過去分詞句。
　□ consist of A「Aから成る」　　□ distinct「はっきりした，別個の」
　□ notch「（Ｖ字型の）刻み目」　　□ deliberately「意図的に」
　□ Eswatini「エスワティニ」アフリカ大陸南部に位置する絶対君主制国家。
　□ date to A「Aにさかのぼる」　　□ approximately「およそ」

4 □ suggest that 節「…であると示唆する」　　□ notched「刻み目のある」
　□ keep track of A「Aを記録しておく，Aの経過を追う」　　□ fertility cycle「受精周期」

5 discovered in Africa は notched bones を修飾する過去分詞句。
　□ elsewhere「他の場所で」　　□ may have *done*「…したかもしれない」
　□ attempt to *do*「…する試み」　　□ quantify「を数量化する」

6 The Ishango bone を補足説明する過去分詞句 found in 1960 ... north-eastern Congo と形容詞句 perhaps twenty thousand years old が and で結ばれている。
　□ headwaters「源流」　　□ the Nile「ナイル川」
　□ Congo「コンゴ」アフリカ中央部の地域。　　□ bear「を持つ，帯びる」

── 第2段落 ──

[1]With tally marks, a vertical scratch or line is made to record each item in a collection: |, ||, |||, ||||, |||||, ||||||, and so on. [2]However, tally marks become hard to read once you have more than four or five items to count. [3]A common way to reduce the complexity is to group the tally marks in fives, often by drawing a diagonal line across each group. [4]The Roman numeral system, found throughout the Roman Empire and still used today in certain specialized functions, such as the numbering of the early pages of printed books, was a more sophisticated version of this simple idea involving a few additional symbols: V for five, X for ten, L for fifty, C for a hundred, and M for a thousand. [5]For example, using this system, the number one thousand two hundred and seventy eight can be written as MCCLXXVIII (1,000 + 100 + 100 + 50 + 10 + 10 + 5 + 1 + 1 + 1 = 1,278).

---

[1]数を記録する印では，ある集合の中のそれぞれの項目を記録するために垂直の引っかいた跡や線が付けられる。|, ||, |||, ||||, |||||, ||||||といった具合である。[2]ところが，数を記録する印は，数える項目が4つか5つを超えると，読みづらくなる。[3]その複雑さを減らす一般的な方法は，数を記録する印を5つずつグループにすることで，それぞれのグループを横切って斜線が引かれることが多い。[4]ローマ記数法は，ローマ帝国全域で見られ，今日なお書籍の最初の部分でページ番号を振るといった特定の専門的な機能で用いられているが，このような単純な考えを洗練させたもので，5を表す V, 10を表す X, 50を表す L, 100を表す C, 1000を表す M といったいくつか追加の記号を加えたものである。[5]たとえばこの方法を使うと，1278という数は **MCCLXXVIII**（1,000＋100＋100＋50＋10＋10＋5＋1＋1＋1＝1,278）と書くことができる。

4 The Roman numeral system を補足説明する過去分詞句 found ... Roman Empire と still used ... printed books が and で結ばれている。

involving a few additional symbols は a more sophisticated version of this simple idea を修飾する現在分詞句。

☐ Roman「ローマの」　　☐ the Roman Empire「ローマ帝国」

☐ certain A「特定の A，ある A」　　☐ specialized「専門的な，特殊化された」

☐ function「機能」　　☐ A such as B「たとえば B のような A」

☐ numbering「番号を振ること」　　☐ print「を印刷する」

☐ sophisticated「洗練された」　　☐ version「(あるものを少し変えた)もの，…版」

☐ involve「を伴う」　　☐ additional「追加の」　　☐ symbol「記号／象徴」

5 using this system は分詞構文。

<hr>

── 第3段落 ──

[1]Addition in the Roman system is fairly easy, since you simply group all like symbols. [2]For example, to add MCCXXIII to MCXII you simply collect together all the M's, all the C's, all the X's, and all the I's, like this: MCCXXIII (1,223) + MCXII (1,112) = MMCCCXXXIIIII (2,335). [3]Occasionally, you might have to convert one group of symbols to a higher symbol. [4]In this example, the five I's could be replaced by V, to write the answer as MMCCCXXXV. [5]Subtraction, too, is relatively easy. [6]But the only tolerable way to do multiplication and division is by repeated addition and repeated subtraction respectively. [7]For example, V times MCLIII can be computed by adding the second number to itself four times. [8]This method only works in practice when one of the two numbers being multiplied is small, of course.

[1]ローマ式での足し算は，似た記号をすべてグループにまとめるだけなので，かなり簡単である。[2]たとえば，MCXII に MCCXXIII を加えるには，次のようにすべての M，すべての C，すべての X そしてすべての I をひとまとめにするだけである。MCCXXIII (1, 223) + MCXII (1, 112) ＝MMCCCXXXIIIII (2, 335) となる。[3]ときに，あるグループの記号を1つ上の記号に変換しなければならないかもしれない。[4]この例では，5つの I が V に置き換えられ，答えは MMCCCXXXV と書くことになる。[5]引き算も比較的簡単である。[6]しかし，掛け算と割り算を行う唯一許容できる方法は，それぞれ足し算と引き算を繰り返すことである。[7]たとえば，V 掛ける MCLIII は2番目の数字をそれ自身に4回足すことで計算できる。[8]この方法はもちろん，掛け算する2つの数字のうち一方が小さいときしか，実用的ではない。

1 addition「足し算／加えること」　　□ fairly「かなり」　　□ like「似ている，類似の」

2 and は all the M's, all the C's, all the X's, all the I's の4つの名詞句を結んでいる。
　　□ add A to B「AをBに加える」　　□ collect A together「Aをひとまとめにする」

3 □ occasionally「ときに」　　□ convert A to B「AをBに変換する」

4 □ replace「を置き換える，取り換える」

5 □ subtraction「引き算／引くこと」　　□ relatively「比較的」

6 □ tolerable「許容できる」　　□ multiplication「掛け算／増加」　　□ division「割り算／分割」
　　□ repeat「を繰り返す」　　□ respectively「それぞれ」

7 □ A times B「A掛けるB」　　□ compute「を計算する」　　□ ... times「…回」

8 □ method「方法」　　□ work「機能する，うまくいく」　　□ in practice「実際上は」

— 第4段落 —

¹The impracticality of the Roman system for doing multiplication or division meant it was inadequate for many important applications that arose in commerce and trade, such as currency conversion or determining a commission fee for a transaction. ²And there is no way Roman numerals could form the basis for any scientific or technical work. ³Societies that wrote numbers in Roman numerals had to use elaborate systems of finger arithmetic or mechanical devices like the counting board and the abacus to perform the actual calculations, using the numerals simply to record the answers. ⁴Although systems of finger arithmetic could manage calculations involving numbers up to 10,000, and it was possible to carry out a computation on an abacus almost as fast as a person today using a calculator, these required both manual and mental skills of a high order. ⁵Moreover, since there was no record of the calculation, the answer had to be taken on trust.

¹掛け算や割り算を行うにはローマ記数法が実用的ではないということは，通貨の両替や取引の手数料を決定するといった，商業や貿易で起きる多くの重要な利用には向いていないということであった。²また，ローマ数字は科学や技術にかかわる営みの基盤にはなりえなかった。³ローマ数字で数を書いた社会は，実際の計算を行うためには，指を使った複雑な計算術や計算盤やそろばんのような機械的道具を使わざるをえず，数字は答えを記録するためにしか使われなかった。⁴指を使った計算術は1万までの数を伴う計算を行うことができたし，今日計算機を用いるのとほぼ同じ速さでそろばんを使って計算することも可能であったが，どちらのやり方も手と頭の両方の高度な技能が必要であった。⁵さらに，計算の記録はなかったので，答えはそのまま信用するしかなかった。

1 □ impracticality「非実用性」　　□ mean (that) S V ...「ということを意味する」

　□ be inadequate for A「Aにとって不適当である」　　□ application「利用，応用」

　□ arise「生じる」　　□ commerce「商業」　　□ trade「貿易」　　□ currency「通貨」

　□ conversion「両替，転換」　　□ determine「を決定する」

　□ commission fee「手数料，業務委託料」　　□ transaction「取引」

2 □ there is no way S V ...「…ということはありえない」　　□ Roman numeral「ローマ数字」

　□ form「を形成する」　　□ basis「基盤」　　□ technical「技術の」

3 or は elaborate systems of finger arithmetic と mechanical devices ... the abacus の2つの名
詞句を結んでいる。

to perform the actual calculations は目的を表す副詞用法の不定詞句で，using the numerals
simply to record the answers は分詞構文。

　□ elaborate「複雑な，入念な」　　□ finger arithmetic「指を使った計算術」

　□ mechanical「機械的な」　　□ device「道具，装置」　　□ counting board「計算盤」

　□ abacus「そろばん」　　□ perform「を行う」　　□ actual「実際の」

　□ calculation「計算」

4 1つめの and は systems of ... up to 10,000と it was ... using a calculator の2つの節を結ん
でいる。

a person today using a calculator は意味上の主語を伴った動名詞句。

　□ manage「をやってのける」　　□ up to A「Aまで，最大でA」

　□ computation「計算（結果）」　　□ calculator「計算機」　　□ require「を必要とする」

　□ of a high order「高度な」

5 □ moreover「さらに，そのうえ」

　□ take A on trust「Aをそのまま信用する，鵜呑みにする」

・・・

┌─ 第5段落 ─

　¹The number system we use today — the Hindu-Arabic system — was developed in
India. ²It seems to have been completed before 700 A.D., though it did not become
generally known in Europe until at least five hundred years later. ³Indian mathematicians
made advances in what would today be described as arithmetic, algebra, and geometry,
much of their work being motivated by an interest in astronomy. ⁴The system is based
on three key ideas: simple symbols for the numerals, place value, and zero. ⁵The choice
of ten basic number symbols — that is, the Hindus' choice of the base 10 for counting
and doing arithmetic — is presumably a direct consequence of using fingers to
count. ⁶When we reach ten on our fingers, we have to find some way of starting again,
while retaining the calculation already made. ⁷The role played by finger counting in the

development of early number systems would explain why we use the word "digit" for the basic numerals, deriving from the Latin word *digitus* for finger.

---

¹我々が今日用いている記数法，ヒンドゥー・アラビア記数法はインドで作り出された。²紀元700年までに完成したようであるが，一般的にヨーロッパで知られるようになったのは，少なくとも500年後のことであった。³インドの数学者は，今日であれば算術，代数，幾何と言われるであろう分野で進歩を遂げたが，彼らの研究の多くは天文学に対する関心によって動機づけられていた。⁴その記数法は３つの重要な考え，数を表す単純な記号と位の値とゼロに基づいている。⁵基本的な10個の数の記号の選択，すなわちヒンドゥー教徒が数えたり算術を行ったりするため10進法を選択したのは，おそらく指を使って数えていた直接的な成り行きである。⁶我々は指を使って10までくると，すでに終わった計算結果を保持して，また数え始める何らかの方法を見つけなければならない。⁷初期の記数法の発達において指算が果たした役割を考えれば，なぜ我々が指を表すラテン語の **digitus** に由来する **digit** という単語を基本的な数字を表すのに用いるのか説明がつく。

1 □ Hindu-Arabic system「ヒンドゥー・アラビア記数法，インド・アラビア記数法」
2 □ seem to have been *done*「…されていたようである」　　□ complete「を完成する」
　 □ not ... until ～「…するのは～になってからである」　　□ at least「少なくとも」
4 □ be based on A「Aに基づいている」　　□ key「重要な，鍵となる」
　 □ place value「位の値」
5 □ choice「選択」　　□ that is「すなわち，つまり」　　□ Hindu「ヒンドゥー教徒」
　 □ base 10「十進法」　　□ presumably「おそらく」　　□ consequence「成り行き，結果」
6 □ reach「に到達する」　　□ some + 単数名詞「何らかの」　　□ while *doing*「…しながら」
　 □ retain「を保持する」
7 played by ... number systems は The role を修飾する過去分詞句。deriving 以下は the word
　 "digit" for the basic numerals を補足説明する現在分詞句。
　 □ role「役割」　　□ development「発達」　　□ explain「を説明する」
　 □ digit「アラビア数字」　　□ derive from A「Aに由来する」　　□ Latin「ラテン語の」

第６段落

¹The introduction of zero was a decisive step in the development of Hindu arithmetic and came after the other numerals. ²The major advantage of the Hindu number system is that it is positional — the place of each numeral matters. ³This allows for addition, subtraction, multiplication, and even division using fairly straightforward and easily learned

rules for manipulating symbols. [4]But for an efficient place-value number system, you need to be able to show when a particular position has no entry. [5]For example, without a zero symbol, the expression " 1 3 " could mean thirteen (13), or a hundred and three (103), or a hundred and thirty (130), or maybe a thousand and thirty (1,030). [6]One can put spaces between the numerals to show that a particular column has no entry, but unless one is writing on a surface marked off into columns, one can never be sure whether a particular space indicates a zero entry or is merely the gap separating the symbols. [7]Everything becomes much clearer when there is a special symbol to mark a space with no value.

[1]ゼロの導入はヒンドゥー算術の発達において決定的な一歩であり，他の数字の後に行われた。[2]ヒンドゥー記数法の最大の利点は，それが位置によって決まる，つまり，それぞれの数字の位置が重要であるということだ。[3]これによって，記号を操作するためのかなり単純で簡単に学べる規則を使って，足し算，引き算，掛け算，割り算さえできるようになる。[4]しかし，効率的な位取り記数法のためには，特定の位置には入るものが何もない場合にこれを示すことができる必要がある。[5]たとえば，ゼロの記号がなければ，「1　3」という表現は十三（13）や百三（103），百三十（130），ひょっとすると千三十（1,030）という意味にもなる可能性がある。[6]特定の列に入るものが何もないことを示すために数字の間を空けることはできるが，線ではっきりと列に区切られた表面に書いているのでない限り，特定の空間に入るものがないことを示すのか，単に記号と記号を分ける隙間なのか確信が持てない。[7]値がない空間であることを記す特別な記号があれば，すべてがずっと明確になる。

1 □ introduction「導入」　　□ zero「ゼロ」　　□ decisive「決定的な」

2 □ major「最大の，主要な」　　□ advantage「利点」　　□ positional「位置によって決まる」
□ matter「重要である」

3 and は addition, subtraction, multiplication, division の4つの名詞を結んでいる。
□ allow for A「Aを可能にする」　　□ straightforward「単純な，わかりやすい」
□ manipulate「を操作する」

4 □ efficient「効率的な」　　□ place-value number system「位取り記数法」
□ entry「入るもの，記載項目」

5 or は thirteen (13)，a hundred and three (103)，a hundred and thirty (130)，a thousand and thirty (1,030) という mean の目的語である4つの名詞句を結ぶ。
□ expression「表現」

6 separating 以下は the gap を修飾する現在分詞句。
□ unless S V ...「…しない限り」　　□ surface「表面」

□ mark A off「Aを線を引いて分ける」　　□ be sure whether S V ...「…かどうか確信する」
□ indicate「を示す」　　□ merely「単に」　　□ gap「隙間」　　□ separate「を引き離す」
7 □ mark「を印す」　　□ value「値」

━━━ 第7段落 ━━━

¹The concept of zero took a long time to develop. ²The number symbols were viewed as numbers themselves — things you used to count the number of objects in a collection — but 0 would be the number of objects in a collection having no members, which makes no sense. ³Other societies were never able to make the zero breakthrough. ⁴For instance, long before the Indians developed their system, the Babylonians had a positional number system, based on 60. ⁵Today, when we measure time, aspects of their system remain: 60 seconds equal one minute, and 60 minutes one hour. ⁶But the Babylonians did not have a symbol denoting zero, a limitation to their system they were never able to overcome.

¹ゼロという概念は作り出されるのに長い時間を要した。²数の記号は数そのものであると，つまり，集合に含まれる物の数を数えるために使うものだとみなされていたが，0は要素を持たない集合に含まれる物の数であるということになり，これでは意味をなさないのである。³他の社会ではゼロの大発見をすることが決してできなかった。⁴たとえば，インド人が彼らの記数法を作り出すずっと前に，バビロニア人は60に基づく位置によって決まる記数法を持っていた。⁵今日我々が時間を計るとき，彼らの記数法の性質が残っている。60秒が1分，60分が1時間になっている。⁶しかし，バビロニア人はゼロを示す記号を持っておらず，このことは彼らが決して乗り越えることができなかった，彼らの記数法の限界であった。

1 □ concept「概念」　　□ take a long time to *do*「…するのに長い時間を要する」
2 having no members は a collection を修飾する現在分詞句。which 以下は but 以下の節の内容を補足説明する非制限用法の関係代名詞節。
　□ view O as C「OをCとみなす」　　□ make no sense「意味をなさない」
3 □ breakthrough「大発見，飛躍的進歩」
4 based on 60 は a positional number system を修飾する過去分詞句。
5 □ measure「を計る，測定する」　　□ aspect「性質，局面」　　□ remain「残っている」
　□ equal「に等しい」
6 a limitation 以下は前に述べた内容を同格的に言い換えた形になっている。they were never able to overcome は a limitation to their system を修飾する関係代名詞節。

□ denote「を示す，表す」　　□ limitation to A「Aの限界」　　□ overcome「を克服する」

第8段落

¹The Hindus got to zero in two stages. ²First they overcame the problem of indicating empty spaces by drawing a circle around the space where there was a "missing" entry. ³This much the Babylonians had done. ⁴The circle gave rise to the present-day symbol 0 for zero. ⁵The second step was to regard that extra symbol just like the other nine. ⁶This meant developing the rules for doing arithmetic using this additional symbol along with all the others. ⁷This second step — changing the underlying concept so that the rules of arithmetic operated not on the numbers themselves (which excluded 0) but on symbols for numbers (which included 0) — was the key. ⁸Over time it led to a change in the idea of numbers to a more abstract one that includes 0.

¹ヒンドゥー教徒は２つの段階を経てゼロにたどり着いた。²まず第一に，入るものが「欠けている」空間の周りに円を描くことによって，何もない空間を示すという問題を克服した。³バビロニア人もここまではできていた。⁴その円が現代のゼロを表す記号０を生み出した。⁵第２段階は，その追加された記号を他の９つとまったく同じようにみなすことであった。⁶これは，他のすべての記号と一緒にこの追加された記号を使い，算術を行うための規則を作り出すということを意味した。⁷この第２段階は，算術の規則が，（０を除外した）数そのものではなく，（０を含む）数を表す記号で機能するように根底にある考えを変えることであり，鍵であった。⁸やがて，それが数に対する考えにおいて０を含むより抽象的なものへと変化することへとつながった。

1 □ get to A「Aにたどり着く」　　□ stage「段階」

2 □ empty「何もない」　　□ circle「円」　　□ missing「欠けている」

3 This much(O) the Babylonians(S) had done(V) の語順になっている。

4 □ give rise to A「Aを生み出す」　　□ the present-day「現代の」

5 □ extra「追加の」

6 using 以下は付帯状況の分詞構文。

　　□ along with A「Aと一緒に」

7 ——（ダッシュ）以下は This second step の内容を補足説明する動名詞句。

　　□ underlying「根底にある」　　□ so that S V ...「Sが…するために」

　　□ operate「機能する，運用される」　　□ not X but Y「XではなくY」

　　□ exclude「を除外する」　　□ include「を含む」

- 第9段落 -

[1]The zero breakthrough was made by a brilliant mathematician called Brahmagupta, who was born in 598 A.D. in Bhinmal in northwest India, and went on to become the head of the astronomical observatory at Ujjain, then the foremost mathematical center of ancient India. [2]As early as 628 A.D., when he was only thirty years old, Brahmagupta wrote a lengthy text in Sanskrit called *Brahmasphutasiddhanta*, which can be translated as "The Opening of the Universe." [3]In that work, written entirely in verse, Brahmagupta introduced the number zero, defining it as the result obtained when you subtract a number from itself. [4]At the same time, he worked out some basic properties that zero must have. [5]These included the recognition that, when zero is either added to a number or subtracted from a number, the number remains unchanged, and that a number multiplied by zero becomes zero.

[1]ゼロの大発見はブラフマグプタと呼ばれる才能あふれる数学者によってなされたが，彼は紀元598年にインド北西部にあるビンマルで生まれ，長じて当時古代インドで第一の数学の中心地であるウジャイン天文台の所長になった。[2]紀元628年という大昔に，ブラフマグプタはわずか30歳であったが，『宇宙の始まり』と訳すことができるブラーマ・スプタ・シッダーンタと呼ばれる長大な文章をサンスクリット語で書いた。[3]その書は，すべて韻文で書かれ，ブラフマグプタはゼロという数を導入し，ゼロとはある数からその数を引くとき得られる結果であると定義づけた。[4]同時に，彼はゼロが持つに違いないいくつかの基本的な特性を考え出した。[5]それらには，ある数にゼロを加えても，ある数から引いても，その数は変わらないままであることや，ゼロを掛けられた数はゼロになるという認識が含まれている。

1 □ brilliant「才能あふれる」　　□ mathematician「数学者」　　□ go on to *do*「続いて…する」
　□ head「(組織の)長」　　□ astronomical observatory「天文台」　　□ foremost「第一の」
　□ ancient「古代の，大昔の」
2 □ as early as ...「…という昔に」　　□ lengthy「長い」　　□ text「文章」
　□ Sanskrit「サンスクリット語」　　□ translate O as C「OをCと訳す」
3 written entirely in verse は that work を補足説明する過去分詞句。
　□ entirely「すべて，完全に」　　□ verse「韻文」　　□ introduce「を導入する」
4 □ at the same time「同時に」　　□ work A out「Aを考え出す」　　□ property「特性」
5 and は the recognition と同格の関係にある that, when zero ... remains unchanged と that a

number ... becomes zero の 2 つの that 節を結んでいる。

multiplied by zero は a number を修飾する過去分詞句。

☐ recognition「認識」   ☐ remain unchanged「変わらないままである」

9

過食と拒食

解 答

問1　ウ. They are the only problems concerning food in the world today.

問2　イ. the poor — the rich and famous

問3　エ. In our industrial environment the necessity of manual labor has been reduced and heavy bodies have come to be considered unattractive.

問4　自然の厳しい要求に適した物から，現代の世界への適合によって定義される物への身体のこのような変容にとって不可欠なのは，文化の影響を強く受けた新しい身体観である。

問5　ア. You can gain an ideal body when excess weight is removed through rational approaches.

問6　したがって，現代の理想としての痩せた，軽量の人体を生み出すのは単なる流行の変化ではなく，むしろ現代の文化と結びついた基本的な価値観が混ざり合ったものなのである。

問7　科学技術によって多くの物がスリムになっているのに，脂肪を燃焼させる活動が不足する一方で，食欲を刺激する多様な飲食物が入手できるため，身体はスリムになっていないという逆説。(85字)

問8　ウ. use — exchange

▶▶ 設問解説 ◀◀

問1　下線部(1)の both は第1段落第1文の eating too much と eating too little を指している。「過食と拒食が重要である」理由としては，直前に「両者とも過去数十年の間に着実に増加している」ことが，直後の because 以下及び第1段落第3・4文に「極端になると命を奪う」ことが述べられている。また，第1段落第6文に「食行動を歪めかねない複雑な社会的，心理的要因を明らかにしているという点においても重要である」とあり，第2段落以降で，「産業社会において身体と食物に関する考え方が変化したことと関係がある」という点について論じられている。なお，第1段落第5文には there are no other medical problems centered on food とあるが，これは This is not to say that「だからといって…というわけではない」に続いているので，ウは本文に述べられて

いない。よって，ウが正解。

ア.「ここ数十年，それらを思う人が増えている」

イ.「それらは極端な場合，命を奪うこともある」

ウ.「それらは今日の世界で食物に関する唯一の問題である」

エ.「それらは産業社会において身体と食物に関してどのように感じているのかということと関係がある」

問2　空所(2a)(2b)を含む文は強調構文で，「太っている可能性が最も高いのは（　2a　）であり，『どんなに金持ちになっても，どんなに痩せても十分ではない』という教義を身をもって実践しているのは（　2b　），特に女性なのである」という意味。直前の第2段落第8文に today in North America and most of Europe, fat means just the opposite とあり，この just the opposite とは，第7文の「物質的成功と高い社会的地位」の正反対ということである。したがって，「今日太っている可能性が最も高いのは<u>貧しい者</u>であり，痩せているのが<u>富める者</u>である」ことが読み取れるので，イが正解。

問3　下線部(3)の this reversal とは，第2段落第3～9文で述べられた「太っていることが，望ましいことから，望ましくないことになった」という逆転のこと。この問いに対する答えとして，第3段落第1文では，「健康」について触れられているが，続く第2文では否定されている。同段落第3文では「審美的な問題」について述べられているが，さらに重要なこととして「20世紀初頭に北米と西欧で最も劇的に出現した新しい産業環境と都市環境の心理的な影響」が挙げられている。さらに，第7文で「機械の時代の幕開けと共に，重い身体はかつてそれを正当化した手と身体を使った活動と同じくらい時代遅れのものとなった」と述べられている。したがって，エが正解。

ア.「肥満であることで心臓発作の危険性が高くなることが，数十年にわたる医学研究によって証明された」

イ.「審美的価値観に突然の変化が起き，太っていることは流行らなくなった」

ウ.「19世紀とそれ以前には西欧では理想的であるとみなされていた痩せた体が世界中で賞賛されるようになった」

エ.「今日の産業化した環境においては，肉体労働の必要性が減少し，重い身体は魅力的でないと考えられるようになった」

□ reversal「逆転」

問4　ポイントは Essential to ... modern world(C) is(V) a new ... the body(S) という語順が読み取れたかどうかという点。英語では，すでに述べられた情報を文頭に置き，初めて述べる情報を文末に置くことがある。ここでは，this transformation ... modern world が第4段落で述べられた内容であり，a new ... the body がこの文で初めて述べる情報であるため，Ｓ Ｖ Ｃ が Ｃ Ｖ Ｓ の語順になっている。

例 Natural ability is necessary to become an expert in anything, but more important is the willingness to study.

「どんなことでも専門家になるには生まれ持った才能が必要であるが，もっと重要なのは勉強しようという意欲である」

geared to ... of nature は an object を修飾する過去分詞句。defined by ... modern world は one を修飾する過去分詞句で，one は an object の代用。culturally driven は「文化の影響を強く受けた」という意味。

☐ be essential to A「Aにとって不可欠である」

☐ transformation from A to B「AからBへの変容」　　☐ object「物」

☐ geared to A「Aに適している」　　☐ harsh「過酷な，厳しい」

☐ demand「要求」　　☐ define「を規定する，定義する」

☐ fit to A「Aへの適合」　　☐ view「見方，考え方，見解」

問5 下線部(5)の that 以下は a clear ... contemporary body を修飾する関係代名詞節で，represented 以下は the values を修飾する過去分詞句。X, if not Y は「YではないにせよX」という意味。よって，下線部は「今日的身体に関しては，現代のその他あらゆる創造物において表される価値観と軌を一にしている，語られることはなくとも，明らかな基本概念」という意味になる。続く第6段落第1文では，「産業の時代は効率と合理性を理想としていた」ことが述べられ，第4文には「理想的な機械と同様，現代的身体の効率は，余分な重量が取り除かれることを求め，これを成し遂げる手段はダイエットと食品の科学の合理性によって提供される」とある。したがって，アが正解。

ア.「合理的な取り組みによって余分な体重が取り除かれるとき理想的な身体を得ることができる」

イ.「身体は神から贈られたものであり，大切に維持し発達させなければならない」

ウ.「エネルギーを節約する機器だけでなく，身体のエネルギーを効率的に使わなければならない」

エ.「健康で長生きするためには，科学に基づいたダイエットをしなければならない」

☐ unspoken「語られることはない，暗黙の」　　☐ underlying「基本的な，根底にある」

☐ concept「概念」　　☐ contemporary「現代の」　　☐ directly「直接的に」

☐ in line with A「Aと一致している」　　☐ values「価値観」　　☐ represent「を表す」

☐ creation「創造物」

問6 it is ... that ～は強調構文で，no mere change of fashion, but, rather, a blend ... modern culture が強調されている。この no は，not X but Y「XではなくY」の not が no になったもので，but Y の部分が文末に置かれていることに注意。associated 以下は the fundamental values を修飾する過去分詞句。

例 It is not what he says that annoys me, but the way he says it.
「私がいらいらするのは彼が言うことではなく，その言い方である」

□ and so「したがって」　　□ mere「単なる」　　□ lean「痩せた」
□ lightweight「軽量の」　　□ ideal「理想」　　□ blend「混じり合ったもの，混合物」
□ fundamental「基本的な，根本的な」
□ associate A with B「AをBと結びつけて考える，AでBを連想する」

問7 下線部を含む第7段落の第1文に we encounter one of the paradoxes of modern life とあり，続く第2・3文では「科学技術によって，多くの物がスリムになっているのに，身体はスリムになっていない」と述べられている。また，「身体がスリムになっていない」のは「脂肪を燃焼させる活動が不足する一方で，食欲を刺激する多様な飲食物が入手できるため」であることが第4・5文に述べられている。よって，これらの内容を制限字数内でまとめる。
□ paradox「逆説」

問8 空所(8a)(8b)を含む文は「食物に当てはめると，我々の社会では食物が容易に手に入るため，空腹と生物学的欲求を満たすための食物の(8a)価値は当然のものとみなされ，見過ごされやすいのに対して，一方食物の象徴的，あるいは(8b)価値はますます顕著になる，ということになる」という意味。As it applies to food の it は直前の文の the discussion of the contrast between the "use value" of any object and its "exchange value" を指しているので，空所には use か exchange が入ると考えられる。第4段落第5・6文では，「産業社会の興隆に伴い，身体は社会階級の地位を示す象徴的な意味を帯び，重労働や過酷な天候に対する存在価のために評価されることがなくなった」ことが，「身体は exchange value を獲得し use value を失った」と述べられていることから，exchange value とは「象徴的・社会的意味」のことで，use value とは「本来の機能を果たす際の価値」であると推測できる。さらに，第9段落第3文では「ただ空腹を満たすことは，地位の象徴として，または優れた嗜好，美的感性，愛情と愛着，あるいは，民族的，宗教的，さらには政治的信念の印として食物が果たし得る機能に対して，二次的なものになる」と述べられているので，(8a)には use が，(8b)には exchange が入る。
□ nutrition「栄養」　　□ market「市場」

112

要　約

　産業社会の興隆と共に，そこでの生活に適応する中で痩せている身体が望ましく，効率的な身体を個人が合理的に維持し開発するという身体観が生まれた一方で，科学技術の発達に伴い，太るのが避けがたい状況の中で，食物が象徴的意味を持つようになった。このことが，過食と拒食という今日の摂食に関する問題と関係している。(150字)

▶▶▶ 構文・語句解説 ◀◀◀

第1段落

[1]Fundamentally, there are just two major food illnesses in our society: eating too much and eating too little. [2]The former is more prevalent, but both have steadily increased over the past few decades, and both are important because, when pushed to their extremes, they are killers. [3]People who are very overweight may have various health problems, the most deadly of which begins with high blood pressure and can end in death from heart disease. [4]At the other extreme, the rejection of food begins with dieting, can progress to more serious eating disorders, and can end in death from self-starvation. [5]This is not to say that there are no other medical problems centered on food. [6]However, it should be kept in mind that these eating disorders are important not only because they are a problem for many people but also because they reveal the complex social and psychological factors that can distort food behaviors.

[1]根本的に，我々の社会には食に関する大きな病は2つしかない。過食と拒食である。[2]前者の方が広く見られるが，両者とも過去数十年の間に着実に増加しており，極端になると命を奪うため，両者ともに重大な問題である。[3]過度に肥満の人は様々な健康上の問題を抱えているか

もしれず，中でも最も致命的な問題は，高血圧から始まり，心臓病による死に至ることもある。⁴それとは対極的に，食物の拒絶はダイエットから始まり，より深刻な摂食障害へと進行することがあり，最後には自ら飢え死ぬことになりかねない。⁵食にまつわる医学上の問題が他にはないと言っているわけではない。⁶しかし，こうした摂食障害は，多くの人にとって問題であるからだけではなく，食行動を歪めかねない複雑な社会的，心理的要因を明らかにしているという点においても重要であるということを，心に留めておくべきである。

1 □ fundamentally「基本的に，根本的に」

2 when pushed to their extremes ＝ when they are pushed to their extremes

□ the former「前者」ここでは，eating too much のこと。　　□ prevalent「広く見られる」

□ steadily「着実に」　　□ decade「10年」　　□ push「を推し進める」　　□ extreme「極端」

3 the most deadly ... heart disease は various health problems を補足説明する非制限用法の関係代名詞節。

□ overweight「太りすぎの」　　□ deadly「致命的な」　　□ begin with A「Aから始まる」

□ high blood pressure「高血圧」　　□ end in A「Aに終わる」　　□ heart disease「心臓病」

4 □ rejection「拒絶」　　□ progress「進行する」　　□ eating disorder「摂食障害」

□ self-starvation「自ら飢え死ぬこと」

5 □ this is not to say that節「だからといって…というわけではない」

□ medical「医学の，医療の」　　□ center A on B「AをBに集中させる」

6 □ keep A in mind「Aを心に留めておく」

□ not only because ... but also because ～「…からだけでなく～からでも」

□ reveal「を明らかにする」　　□ complex「複雑な」　　□ psychological「心理的な」

□ factor「要因」　　□ distort「を歪める」

― 第 2 段落 ―

¹The most general approach to the mysteries of being overweight has been formulated by the food and diet expert David Booth in the question "Why do we now not like being fat?" ²The question should not be dismissed as mere rhetoric. ³It points to a recent and profoundly significant change in the social and emotional meanings of food and our ideas about our bodies. ⁴Up through the end of the 19th and the early years of the 20th century, we did like being fat. ⁵Fat had obvious survival value as protection against the effects of starvation in a world where local food shortages and widespread famines were not unusual. ⁶And it still does in parts of Africa, Asia, and the former Soviet Union. ⁷In almost all human societies, being fat was also a conspicuous sign of material success and high social status for both men and women. ⁸Yet today in North America and most of

Europe, fat means just the opposite. ⁹It is the poor who are most likely to be fat, and the rich and famous, particularly women, who live out the doctrine "You can never be too rich or too thin." ¹⁰How did this reversal happen? ¹¹Why is possessing a well-padded body or indulging in the joy of eating to the limit no longer desirable in modern societies?

---

¹肥満であることの謎に迫る最も一般的な取り組みは，「今日なぜ私たちは太っていることを好まないのか」という問いかけという形で，食とダイエットの専門家であるディビッド・ブースによって明確に述べられている。²この問いかけはレトリックにすぎないと一蹴してはならない。³それは，食の持つ社会的，感情的意味と，我々の身体に関する考えが近年きわめて大きく変化したことを示唆している。⁴19世紀末及び20世紀初頭までは，我々は太っていることを実際に好んでいたのだ。⁵肥満体は，局地的な食糧不足や広範囲に及ぶ飢饉が珍しくはなかった世界では，飢餓の影響から守ってくれるものとして明白な生存価があった。⁶そして，今でもアフリカやアジア，旧ソ連の一部の地域ではこのことに変わりはない。⁷ほとんどあらゆる人間の社会において，太っていることは，男女双方にとって物質的成功と高い社会的地位を示す明白な印でもあった。⁸もっとも今日，北米とヨーロッパの大半の地域では，肥満体は正反対の意味を持つ。⁹太っている可能性が最も高いのは貧しい人であり，「どんなに金持ちになっても，どんなに痩せても十分ではない」という教義を身をもって実践しているのは金持ちで有名な人，特に女性なのである。¹⁰このような逆転はどのように起きたのであろうか。¹¹でっぷりした身体を持っていることや，お腹いっぱい食べる楽しみにふけることが，なぜ現代の社会ではもはや好ましいことではないのであろうか。

1 □ approach to A「Aへの取り組み」　　□ formulate「を明確に述べる」
　□ diet「ダイエット／飲食物」　　□ fat「太った／脂肪，肥満体」
2 □ dismiss O as C「OをCであるとして退ける」　　□ rhetoric「レトリック，美辞麗句」
3 □ point to A「Aを暗に示す」　　□ profoundly「大いに，深く」　　□ significant「重大な」
　□ emotional「感情的」
4 did like の did は動詞強調の助動詞。
　□ up through A「Aまでずっと」
5 □ obvious「明白な」
　□ survival value「生存価」生物の生存，繁殖を助けるような行動学的特性や生物的特性のこと。
　□ the effect of A「Aの影響」　　□ starvation「飢餓」　　□ local「局所的な」
　□ shortage「不足」　　□ widespread「広範囲に及ぶ，広く行き渡った」　　□ famine「飢饉」
6 does = has survival value
　□ former「以前の」

115

第3段落

¹The politically correct response today would simply be "health." ²But the widespread prejudice, in many cases disgust, against being fat in our society today is not mainly due to the medical risks that have become common knowledge over the past thirty years. ³It is much more a matter of aesthetics and, perhaps even more importantly, a psychological effect of the new industrial and urban environments that emerged most dramatically in North America and Western Europe early in the 20th century. ⁴Most discussions of this topic only note that changes in aesthetic values and fashion styles are responsible for the trend away from the bulky, heavier bodies admired during the 19th century and earlier. ⁵They give little attention to the question of why this trend occurred. ⁶But closer examination suggests that the answer involves a combination of biological, social, and psychological adaptations to modern industrial life. ⁷With the dawn of the machine age and all the technological changes associated with it, including new food processing, distribution, and consumption patterns, heavy bodies became as out-of-date as the manual and physical activities that once justified them.

---

¹今日，政治的に正しい答えは，単に「健康」ということになるだろう。²しかし，今日の社会で太っていることに対する蔓延した偏見は，多くの場合嫌悪となっているが，過去30年の間に常識となった医学上の危険性が主な理由ではない。³審美的な問題の方がはるかに大きく，そしておそらくさらに重要なことには，20世紀初頭に北米と西欧で最も劇的に出現した新しい産業環境と都市環境の心理的な影響なのである。⁴この話題をめぐる議論の大半は，審美的価値観や流行の様式の変化が19世紀以前に賞賛された大きなより重い身体を避ける傾向を生んだと指摘しているにすぎない。⁵なぜこの傾向が生じたのかという問いに注意が払われることはほとんどない。⁶しかし，もっと詳しく検証してみると，その答えには現代の産業化した生活への生物学的，社会的，心理的適応が組み合わさったものが含まれていることが伺える。⁷機械の時代の

幕開けと，それに伴う，新しい食品加工と，流通，消費傾向を含むあらゆる技術の変化と共に，重い身体は，かつてそれを正当化した手と身体を使った活動と同じくらい時代遅れのものとなったのである。

1 □ politically correct「政治的に正しい，公正さを期した，差別的でない」
　□ response「答え／反応」

2 □ prejudice「偏見，先入観」　　□ disgust「嫌悪」　　□ be due to A「Aの原因である」
　□ risk「危険性」　　□ common knowledge「常識，周知の事実」

3 □ aesthetics「美学」　　□ even＋比較級「さらに…」　　□ emerge「現れる」
　□ dramatically「劇的に」

4 aesthetic values と fashion styles が and で結ばれ，共に前置詞 in に続く名詞句となっている。
　□ note that節「…に注目する」　　□ aesthetic「美的な」
　□ be responsible for A「Aを生んだ，Aの原因である」
　□ trend away from A「Aを避ける傾向」　　□ bulky「大きな」　　□ admire「を賞賛する」

5 □ give attention to A「Aに注意を払う」

6 □ examination「検証」　　□ suggest that節「…だと示唆する」　　□ involve「を伴う」
　□ combination「組み合わせ」　　□ biological「生物学上の」
　□ adaptation to A「Aへの適応」

7 □ the dawn「(事の)始まり，誕生，幕開け」　　□ technological「技術の」
　□ processing「加工」　　□ distribution「流通，分配」　　□ consumption「消費」
　□ out-of-date「時代遅れの」　　□ manual「手を使う，手の」　　□ physical「肉体の」
　□ activity「活動」　　□ justify「を正当化する」

── 第4段落 ──

¹A well-fleshed, bulky body with substantial fat reserves is clearly very desirable if you are working outdoors in all sorts of weather or shoveling coal for a living. ²But if you are in a protected indoor environment working at tasks that require little physical effort, such a heavy body is essentially useless. ³And from the standpoint of prevalent social class values, it is also a mark of social status, in the same way that rough work boots and overalls reveal or define a person as low-end working class. ⁴On the other hand, to have a thin body is to be marked as frail: unfit for the heavy outdoor work or frequent childbearing reserved for "the masses," but well adapted to office work and driving cars with automatic transmissions. ⁵In short, with the rise of modern industrial society, the body begins to lose its "use value" while gaining "exchange value." ⁶It takes on a

symbolic meaning revealing social class status and becomes valued less for its survival uses against heavy work or harsh weather than for its decorative or aesthetic functions.

¹かなりの脂肪を蓄えた肉付きのよい，大きな身体は，あらゆる天候のもと屋外で働いたり，生活のために石炭をシャベルですくったりするのであれば，大変望ましいことは明らかである。²しかし，保護された屋内環境で肉体的労力をほとんど要しない作業に従事するのであれば，そのような重い身体は基本的に無用である。³そして，広く認められる社会階級に対する価値観という観点からすると，重い身体は，無骨な作業靴と作業着が人を最下層の労働者階級であると示したり，定義したりするのと同様に，社会的地位の印ともなる。⁴他方，痩せた身体を持つことは，か弱いと印づけられることになる。すなわち，「庶民」のためのものである屋外での重労働や，度重なる出産には向かないが，事務作業や自動変速装置の付いた車の運転には十分適しているということなのだ。⁵要するに，現代の産業社会の興隆と共に，身体はその「使用価値」を失い始めると同時に，「交換価値」を獲得しているのである。⁶身体は社会階級の地位を示す象徴的な意味を帯び，その装飾的あるいは審美的機能によるよりも，重労働や過酷な天候に対して生き延びていくのに使われることで評価されることが少なくなる。

1 □ well-fleshed「肉付きのよい」　　□ substantial「かなりの，相当な」　　□ reserve「蓄え」
　　□ shovel「をシャベルですくう」　　□ coal「石炭」

2 □ essentially「基本的に，本質的に」

3 or は reveal と define を結び，a person as low-end working class が共通して続いている。
　　□ from the standpoint of A「Aの観点から」　　□ social class「社会階級」　　□ mark「印」
　　□ rough「無骨な，粗末な」　　□ overall「作業着，つなぎ」
　　□ reveal O as C「OがCであることを明らかにする」
　　□ define O as C「OをCと定義する」　　□ working class「労働者階級」

4 ：（コロン）以下は，直前の frail の内容を具体的に説明している。reserved for "the masses" は，the heavy outdoor work or frequent childbearing を修飾する過去分詞句。
　　□ on the other hand「それに対して，他方で」　　□ mark O as C「OをCと特徴付ける」
　　□ frail「か弱い」　　□ unfit for A「Aに向いていない」　　□ frequent「頻繁な」
　　□ childbearing「出産」　　□ reserve A for B「AをBのために取っておく」
　　□ the masses「庶民，一般大衆」　　□ adapted「適した」
　　□ automatic transmission「（自動車の）自動変速装置」

5 while gaining ... = while it is gaining ...
　　□ in short「要するに」　　□ rise「興隆，出現」　　□ use value「使用価値」
　　□ exchange value「交換価値」

118

6 □ take on A「Aを帯びる」　　□ symbolic「象徴的な」　　□ valued「高く評価された」
□ decorative「装飾的な」　　□ function「機能」

─ 第5段落 ─

[1]Essential to this transformation of the body from an object geared to the harsh demands of nature to one defined by its fit to the modern world is a new, culturally driven view of the body. [2]The body is now not simply a natural "given" but a form of personal property, an object one owns and is responsible for maintaining and developing. [3]Nor are such maintenance and development merely a matter of individual choice. [4]There is a clear, if unspoken, underlying concept of the contemporary body that is directly in line with the values represented in all the other creations of modern times.

[1]自然の厳しい要求に適した物から，現代の世界への適合によって定義される物への身体のこのような変容にとって不可欠なのは，文化の影響を強く受けた新しい身体観である。[2]今では身体は，自然から「与えられた物」であるだけではなく，個人財産の一形態，すなわち人が所有し，維持し開発することに対して責任を負う物でもある。[3]そのような維持と開発はまた，単に個人の選択の問題でもない。[4]今日的身体に関しては，語られることはなくとも，明らかな基本概念が存在し，現代のその他あらゆる創造物において表される価値観と軌を一にしている。

---

2 an object ... and developing は，a form of personal property と同格の名詞句。one 以下は，an object を修飾する関係代名詞節。
□ not simply X but Y「XだけでなくYも」　　□ given「与えられたもの，所与」
□ property「財産，所有物」
3 Nor are ... は，nor「また…ではない」が文頭に置かれたため倒置が起きたもの。

─ 第6段落 ─

[1]The industrial age idealized efficiency and rationality. [2]The efficiency of any machine is defined by its energy input to output ratio and its power to weight ratio. [3]This ideal can be achieved only through applying rationality, in the form of mechanical engineering. [4]Like the ideal machine, the efficiency of the modern body requires excess weight to be removed, and the means to accomplish this are provided by the rationality of diet and food science. [5]And so it is no mere change of fashion that creates a lean, lightweight human body as the modern ideal but, rather, a blend of the fundamental values associated with modern culture. [6]Nothing, however, is more opposed to those values than excess body

weight. ⁷Living in a culture dedicated almost everywhere to the achievement of light, slim, energy-efficient design, how could we not apply these criteria to ourselves?

¹産業の時代は効率と合理性を理想としていた。²どのような機械であれ効率は，エネルギーの入力対出力の比率と力対重量の比率で定義される。³こうした理想は，機械工学という形で合理性を適用することを通じて初めて達成される。⁴理想的な機械と同様，現代的身体の効率は，余分な重量が取り除かれることを求め，これを成し遂げる手段はダイエットと食品の科学の合理性によって提供される。⁵したがって，現代の理想としての痩せた，軽量の人体を生み出すのは単なる流行の変化ではなく，むしろ現代の文化と結びついた基本的な価値観が混ざり合ったものなのである。⁶しかしながら，余分な重量ほどそうした価値観と対立するものはない。⁷ほとんどあらゆるところで，軽くてスリムでエネルギー効率の良い設計の達成に邁進する文化で暮らしていて，いったいどうしてこうした基準を自分自身に当てはめないでいられようか。

1 ☐ idealize「を理想化する」　　☐ efficiency「効率」　　☐ rationality「合理性」
2 ☐ input「入力」　　☐ output「出力」　　☐ A to B ratio「A対Bの比率」
3 ☐ achieve「を達成する」　　☐ apply「を適用する，当てはめる」
　☐ in the form of A「Aという形で」　　☐ mechanical engineering「機械工学」
4 ☐ require O to *do*「Oに…するように求める」　　☐ excess「余分な」
　☐ means to *do*「…する手段」　　☐ accomplish「を成し遂げる」　　☐ provide「を供給する」
6 ☐ be opposed to A「Aと対立する」
7 how could ... to ourselves? は修辞疑問で，「こうした基準を自分自身に当てはめてしまう」ということを言っている。
　☐ dedicated to A「Aに専念している」　　☐ achievement「達成」
　☐ energy-efficient「エネルギー効率の良い」　　☐ apply A to B「AをBに当てはめる」
　☐ criteria＜criterion「（判断）基準」の複数形。

━━━ 第7段落 ━━━

¹But having applied them, we encounter one of the paradoxes of modern life. ²The same conditions of relative wealth and freedom from the dangers of nature that technology provides for us also make it very difficult for us to avoid becoming fat. ³It is all too obvious that, while many of our objects (telephones, televisions, computers, and so on) have steadily grown slimmer, our bodies have not. ⁴On the one hand, surrounded on all sides by energy-saving devices, we lack the everyday, fat-burning activities that once helped prevent excessive weight. ⁵On the other hand, surrounded by an ever-growing variety of

foods and drinks from all over the world, many of which have been carefully designed and marketed to stimulate our appetites, we are more and more easily led into eating too much. ⁶The way out of this paradox that began to emerge in North America during the 1920s and is still with us is dieting.

¹しかし，それを当てはめると，我々は現代生活の逆説の1つに突き当たる。²科学技術が我々にもたらしてくれる，相対的な豊かさと自然の脅威からの解放という同じ条件のために，我々が太るのを避けることが極めて困難にもなる。³我々の持ち物（電話やテレビ，コンピュータなど）の多くが着実にスリムになっていくのに，我々の身体がそうなっていないのはあまりにも明白である。⁴一方で，エネルギーを使わなくてすむ機器に四方を取り囲まれ，かつては太りすぎの予防に役立っていた毎日の脂肪を燃焼させる活動が不足している。⁵他方では，世界中から押し寄せるますます多様な食べ物や飲み物に取り囲まれ，その多くは食欲を刺激するように入念に作られ売りに出されたものであり，我々はますます容易に食べ過ぎるように仕向けられている。⁶この逆説から抜け出すため，1920年代に北米で出現し始め，今なお我々が行っている方法がダイエットである。

1 having applied them は完了形の分詞構文。

　□ encounter「に出遭う」　　□ paradox「逆説」

2 that technology provides for us は The same ... of nature を修飾する関係代名詞節。

　□ relative「相対的な」

3 our bodies have not = our bodies have not steadily grown slimmer

　□ all too「あまりに」　　□ while S V「…だけれども／ところが一方…」

　□ and so on「…など」　　□ steadily「着実に」

4 surrounded on ... energy-saving devices は分詞構文。

　□ on the one hand「一方で」　　□ on all sides「四方を，至る所に」

　□ energy-saving「エネルギーを節約する」　　□ device「機器，装置」　　□ lack「を欠く」

　□ fat-burning「脂肪を燃焼させる」　　□ help *do*「…するのに役立つ」　　□ prevent「を防ぐ」

　□ excessive「過度の」

5 surrounded by ... the world は分詞構文。many of ... our appetites は，an ever-growing ... the world を補足説明する非制限用法の関係代名詞節。

　□ ever-growing「ますます増加する」　　□ a variety of A「様々なA」

　□ market「を売りに出す」　　□ stimulate「を刺激する」　　□ appetite「食欲」

　□ lead O into *doing*「Oに…するように仕向ける」

6 that began ... with us は The way out of this paradox を修飾する関係代名詞節。

121

[1]By way of conclusion, perhaps the most appropriate thing to emphasize about the food disorders and unhealthy eating behaviors discussed here is that they are a growing problem in our society precisely at a time when, by all objective accounts, we have the safest and most varied food supplies in history. [2]The irony is evident and speaks directly to the fact that psychological meanings of food often have little or no connection with food science or other "objective" facts. [3]Instead, it seems that the very availability of food in our society is what stimulates the growth of the major disorders and the various minor eating problems.

[1]結論として，ここで論じられた食に関する障害や不健康な食行動に関して強調すべきおそらく最も適切なことは，あらゆる客観的な報告からして，史上最も安全で，最も多様な食物が供給されているときにこそ，こうしたことが我々の社会においてますます大きな問題になっているということである。[2]この皮肉な事態は明白であり，食物の心理的意味はしばしば食品科学やそれ以外の「客観的な」事実とはほとんど，あるいはまったく関係がないという事実を赤裸々に物語っている。[3]それどころか，我々の社会において食物が手に入りやすいということ自体が，まさに大きな障害と摂食に関する様々な小さな問題の増大の要因となっているようである。

1 □ by way of A「Aとして」　　□ conclusion「結論」　　□ appropriate「適切な」
　 □ emphasize「を強調する」　　□ precisely「まさに／正確に」
　 □ by all accounts「どの報告によっても，誰の話を聞いても」　　□ objective「客観的な」
　 □ varied「多様な」　　□ supply「供給」
2 that 以下は the fact と同格の名詞節。
　 or は little と no を結び，connection を修飾している。
　 □ evident「明白な」　　□ speak to A「Aをはっきり示す」
　 □ have connection with A「Aと関係がある」
3 □ instead「それどころか，その代わりに」　　□ availability「入手できること」

[1]A convincing explanation for this state of affairs can be drawn from the discussion of the contrast between the "use value" of any object and its "exchange value." [2]As it applies to food, this suggests that, since it is readily available in our society, food's use value for

the satisfaction of hunger and biological needs is easily taken for granted and overlooked, whereas its symbolic or exchange value becomes increasingly prominent. [3]More concretely, the mere satisfaction of hunger becomes secondary to the functions that food can serve as a status symbol or a sign of good taste, aesthetic sensitivity, love and affection, or ethnic, religious, or even political convictions. [4]The social-psychological significance of caviar, for example, is far out of proportion to its ability to satisfy hunger. [5]This fact suggests that the prevalence of eating problems in our wealthy society is closely connected to the increasing importance we have placed on the social and emotional exchange value of food.

---

[1]このような事態に対する納得のいく説明は，いかなるものであれ「使用価値」と「交換価値」の対比をめぐる議論から得られる。[2]食物に当てはめると，我々の社会では食物が容易に手に入るため，空腹と生物学的欲求を満たすための食物の使用価値は当然のものとみなされ，見過ごされやすいのに対して，一方食物の象徴的，あるいは交換価値はますます顕著になる，ということになる。[3]より具体的に言えば，ただ空腹を満たすことは，地位の象徴として，または優れた嗜好，美的感性，愛情と愛着，あるいは，民族的，宗教的，さらには政治的信念の印として食物が果たし得る機能に対して，二次的なものになるのである。[4]たとえば，キャビアの社会的心理的意義は，どれほど空腹を満たすことができるかという点とまったく見合うものではない。[5]このことからしても，我々の豊かな社会において摂食に関する問題が広く見られることが，食物の社会的かつ情緒的交換価値を我々がますます重視していることと密接に結びついていることが伺える。

1 □ convincing「納得のいく，説得力のある」　　□ state of affairs「事態」
　□ draw A from B「BからAを引き出す」　　□ contrast between A and B「AとBの対比」
2 □ apply to A「Aに当てはまる」　　□ available「手に入る」
　□ take A for granted「Aを当然のことと思う」　　□ overlook「を見過ごす，見落とす」
　□ whereas S V「ところが一方…，…する一方で」　　□ prominent「顕著な，目立つ」
3 □ concretely「具体的に」　　□ secondary「二次的な」
　□ serve as A「Aの役割を果たす，Aとして機能する」　　□ sensitivity「感性，感受性」
　□ affection「愛着」　　□ ethnic「民族の」　　□ religious「宗教の」
　□ political「政治の」　　□ conviction「信念，確信」
4 □ social-psychological「社会心理的な」　　□ significance「意義」
　□ caviar「キャビア」チョウザメの卵で高価な珍味。
　□ out of proportion to A「Aと不釣合いで」

5 □ prevalence「広く見られること」　　□ be connected to A「Aと結びついている」
　□ place importance on A「Aを重視する」

名前の音と性格の関係

解 答

問1 m 音は発音する際にとても滑らかに感じられ，象徴的に丸みのある形の滑らかさを連想させるから。(45字)

問2 (2a) round　　(2b) spiky　　(2c) round　　(2d) spiky

問3 人は物事の中にパターンを見出し，物事の間の関係を見つけたいと思うこと。(35字)

問4 そうではなくて，ある種の音は形や大きさに関してだけでなく，味や手触りに関してさえ，一貫した連想を思い浮かべさせることがわかってきている。

問5 呼び名がとても重要であると私たちは考えているが，子どもをボブと呼んだとしても，その子がある一連の性格的特徴を持つことになる可能性が他の一連の性格的特徴を持つことになる可能性よりも高くなることはまったくない。

問6 イ

問7 イ→ウ→エ→ア

問8 外国語の単語の音と意味が合致するときには，意味を推測したり，記憶したりすることがより容易になるという利点。(53字)

問9 イ

▶▶▶ 設問解説 ◀◀◀

問1 下線部(1)は「多くの異なる言語において，人々は b, m, l, および o 音から（ブーバとマルマという造語の場合のように）丸い形を連想しがちである」という意味。m 音が丸い形と結びつけられる傾向がある理由は，第4段落第1・2文「シドゥによれば，こうした広く行き渡っている連想は，これらの音が口の中でどのように感じるかに起源があるのかもしれない。『たとえば，t に対する m の発音を考えてみると，m 音ははるかに滑らかに感じ，それが尖った形に対する丸みのある形の滑らかさを象徴的に捉えているのです』」に述べられているので，これを制限字数内にまとめる。

□ across A「Aの中で／Aを横切って」

□ associate A with B「AとBを結びつけて考える，AでBを連想する」

□ as in A「Aにおけるのと同様に」　　□ made-up「作り上げた／でっちあげた」

問2　第2段落第2・3文より，b, m, l, o を含む単語は「丸みのある(round)」ように聞こえ，k, t, p, i を含む単語は「尖っている(spiky)」ように聞こえることがわかる。したがって，Bob や Molly という b, m, l, o を含む名前の印象を表す(2a)には round が入り，Kirk や Kate という，k, t, i を含む名前の印象を表す(2b)には spiky が入る。また，フランス語でも同じ効果を示していたとあることから，b, o を含む Benoit を修飾する(2c)には round が入り，i, k を含む Eric を修飾する(2d)には spiky が入る。なお，Benoit には i と t が含まれるが，フランス語ではこの名前は「ブノワ」のように発音されるので，i と t は英語の場合と同じようには認識されない。

問3　下線部(3)は「人間は基本的に連想を行う」性質があるという意味。下線部(3)を含む第5段落第3・4文には Pexman の言葉が引用されており，第4文は第3文をより具体的に述べた内容になっているので，第4文の内容をまとめる。ただし，and 以下は音の話に限られているので，より一般的に人間の持つ傾向について述べている and より前の内容を制限字数内にまとめる。

問4　Instead「そうではなくて」は，前文のコロンの後ろの内容を否定して，「音とは恣意的なもので本来備わっている意味などないのではなくて」という意味を表す。文の基本構造は S be found to *do* で，「Sは…することがわかっている」という意味。bring 以下は，bring O to mind「Oを思い起こさせる」の O が mind の後ろに移動した形になっており，O は consistent associations not just with A, but even with B「Aに関するだけでなくBにさえも関する一貫した連想」となっている。

　　□ instead「そうではなくて，その代わりに」　　□ consistent「一貫した」

　　□ shape「形」　　□ flavour「味，風味」flavor のイギリス綴り。　　□ texture「手触り」

問5　not any more ～ than ... は「…よりも～になることは決してない」という意味。no more ～ than で書き換えることができる。

　　例　Snowboarding is not any more difficult than skiing. So just try it.
　　　　(＝Snowboarding is no more difficult than skiing. So just try it.)
　　　　「スノボはスキーより決して難しいことはないよ。だから，試しにやってごらん」

　　なお，another は another set of personality characteristics のことであり，この部分の訳は「彼（＝その子）が一連の性格的特徴を持つことになる可能性が別の一連の性格的特徴を持つ可能性よりも高くなることはまったくない」となる。下線部(5)を含む段落では，名前とその人の性格には，実際には結びつきがないということが述べられているので，if 節が条件を表すと解釈すると，he's not ... than another と意味的につながらないので，even if 節と同意と解釈する必要がある。although that's what we think は譲歩の副詞節であり，if 以下の内容と逆接的になることに注目すると，「私たちが考えていること」である that は前文の that the label matters so much「呼び名がとても重要だ」を指していると考えられる。

□ be likely to *do*「…する可能性が高い，たぶん…するだろう」

□ end up with A「(結果として) A を持つことになる」　　□ one set of A「ある一連の A」

□ personality characteristics「性格的特徴，人格的特性」

問6　空所を含む第12段落第 1 文の that 節は「人々について(6b)を知るにつれて，名前の音は(6a)影響を及ぼす」という意味。同段落第 3・4 文で研究者のシドゥが「名前だけを見せられて，性格について質問されるこうした研究のように，名前しか知らないときには，こうした音が役割を果たすことがあるかもしれません。しかし，その人についてより多くの情報が入るようになると，その人の性格に関する実際の情報がおそらくこうした先入観を消してしまうのでしょう」と述べているので，「人々のことがより多くわかるようになるにつれて，名前の音の影響はより少なくなる」ことがわかる。したがって，(6a)には「より少ない」を表す less，(6b)には「より多くのこと」を表す more が入る。

問7　空所の直前の第18段落第 1 文にある one important real-life lesson「 1 つの重要な現実的な教訓」を表しているのがイの「おそらく私たちは，他人の名前からあまりに多くのものを読み取っているのだ」と考えられるので，イが最初に来る。イの裏付けと考えられるのが，理由を述べるときにも用いられる After all「そもそも，何しろ」で始まるウと考えられるので，ウが 2 番目に来る。ウに書かれている Sidhu と Pexman の研究を their findings「彼らの研究結果」で受けているエがその後に続くのが自然。最後に，第 6 文に ... he says. とあることから，空所の最後にアを置くと he が Sidhu を受けることになる。したがって，イ→ウ→エ→アが正しい順序となる。

問8　外国語学習とブーバ・キキ効果の関連は第 8 段落第 4 文に「大人は新たな言語を学ぶときに連想から恩恵を受け，音と意味が合致するときには，外国語の単語を推測したり，記憶したりすることが容易になる」と述べられているので，これを制限字数内にまとめる。

問9　ブーバ・キキ効果と文字の関連については，本文には述べられていないので，イが正解。アは，第13・14段落に標準中国語話者に，英語話者に生じるようなブーバ・キキ効果が生じないことが述べられているので，不正解。ウは，第16段落に使われる音が英語と異なるシューバ語話者にはブーバ・キキ効果が生じ

なかったことが述べられているので，不正解。エは，第17段落第5文にシドゥという学者が様々な言語における名前と性格の連想については調べてはいないものの，様々な結果が出るだろうと予想していると述べられているので，不正解。

ア.「自分の母語の音声体系における違い」

イ.「音と文字の間に本来備わっている連想」

ウ.「自分の母語で用いられない音の使用」

エ.「様々な言語における名前と性格の連想」

Outline

¶ 1	導入	人は単語や名前の音だけで様々な判断を行う
¶ 2	主題	ある種の音は丸みを帯びているように感じられ，別の音は尖っているように感じられる傾向があり，これをブーバ・キキ効果と呼ぶ
¶3-6	展開1	名前を発音するときの口の中の感触がその人の性格を連想させたり，世界の経験の仕方に影響を与えたりする
¶7-9	補足	音と意味の間の連想は言語を学習したり，未知の単語の意味を類推したりするのに役立つ
¶10-12	展開2	現実には，名前とその人の性格には結びつきはない
¶13-17	展開3	ブーバ・キキ効果は母語の違いによって表れ方が異なり，文化的要因も影響を与える可能性がある
¶ 18	補足	論文などの評価を行う際には，無意識的な連想を防ぐために氏名を取り除いたほうがよい

要 約

　ある種の音は丸みを帯びているように感じられ，別の音は尖っているように感じられるというブーバ・キキ効果と呼ばれる研究結果があり，人は人名の音から性格を推測する傾向があるが，現実には本質的な関係はないようで，母語の影響や文化的要因によっても影響される可能性がある。(130字)

▶▶▶ 構文・語句解説 ◀◀◀

第1段落

¹Picture two cartoon characters, one round and the other spiky. ²Which would you name Bouba, and which one Kiki? ³And which do you then think is more outgoing? ⁴Perhaps surprisingly, most of you will probably attribute the same name and characteristics to each of the shapes. ⁵A growing body of research suggests that people

tend to make a range of judgments based on nothing but the sound of a word or name.

¹一方は丸みがあって，もう一方は尖っている２つのマンガのキャラクターを想像してみよう。²あなたはどちらにブーバという名前をつけ，どちらにキキという名前をつけるだろうか。³それから，どちらがより社交的だと思うだろうか。⁴驚くべきことかもしれないが，おそらくたいていの人は，それらの形のそれぞれに同じ名前と性格を割り当てるであろう。⁵人は単語や名前の音だけに基づいて様々な判断を行う傾向がある，と示唆する研究が増えている。

1 後半は分詞構文で，two cartoon characters の補足説明をしている。one (being) round and the other (being) spiky と考えるとよい。and は one round と the other spiky の２つの句を結んでいる。

　□ picture「を想像する，心に描く」　　　□ cartoon「マンガ」
　□ character「キャラクター，登場人物」　　□ round「丸みのある」　　□ spiky「尖っている」

2 and は Which would you name Bouba? と which one (would you name) Kiki? という２つの疑問文を結んでいる。

　□ name O C「OにCという名前をつける」

3 □ outgoing「社交的な／外向性の」

4 and は name と characteristics という２つの名詞を結んでいる。

　□ surprisingly「驚くべきことに」　　□ attribute A to B「A（性質など）がBにあると考える」
　□ characteristics「特徴」

5 □ growing「増加している」　　□ a body of A「多数のA」　　□ research「研究」
　□ suggest that 節「…ということを示唆する」　　□ tend to *do*「…する傾向がある」
　□ make a judgment「判断を行う」　　□ a range of A「様々なA」
　□ based on A「Aに基づいて」　　□ nothing but A「Aだけ，Aのみ」

第2段落

¹At its most basic, this is known as the *bouba-kiki* effect, or *maluma-takete* effect, because of how our minds link certain sounds and shapes. ²Across many different languages, people tend to associate the sounds "b", "m", "l", and "o" (as in the made-up words *bouba* and *maluma*) with round shapes. ³The sounds "k", "t", "p", and "i", as in the nonsense words *kiki* and *takete*, are commonly seen as spiky. ⁴These associations may be partly rooted in the physical experience of saying and hearing sounds, with some feeling more effortful and rough than others.

¹最も基本的なレベルでは，これはブーバ・キキ効果，またはマルマ・タケテ効果として知られており，その原因は，私たちの心が特定の音と形を結びつけることにある。²多くの異なる言語において，人々は b, m, l, および o 音から（ブーバとマルマという造語の場合のように）丸い形を連想しがちである。³無意味な単語のキキやタケテの場合のように，k, t, p, および i 音は，一般的には尖っているとみなされる。⁴こうした連想は，音を言ったり聞いたりすると，他の音より努力を要し耳障りに感じる音がある，という身体的な経験にある程度は根ざしているのかもしれない。

1 or は *bouba-kiki* effect と *malma-takete* effect という2つの名詞句を結んでいる。

☐ at its most basic「最も基本的なレベルでは」　　☐ be known as A「Aとして知られている」
☐ effect「効果」　　☐ because of A「Aが原因で，Aのせいで」
☐ link A and B「AとBを結びつける」　　☐ certain A「あるA」

3 the nonsense words と *kiki* and *takete* は同格の関係になっている。

☐ nonsense「無意味な，ナンセンスな」　　☐ see O as C「OをCとみなす」
☐ commonly「一般に」

4 1つめの and は saying と hearing の2つの動名詞を結んでおり，sounds はその両方の目的語となっている。2つめの and は more effortful と (more) rough の2つの形容詞の比較級を結んでいる。なお，rough の比較級は正しくは rougher だが，ここでは more effortful と形を合わせるために (more) rough の形で使われている。with some feeling more effortful and rough than others は，with A *doing*「Aが…しながら」という付帯状況を表す。ここでは some が A に相当する。some は some sounds, others は other sounds のこと。

☐ association「連想」　　☐ partly「ある程度は，いくぶん」
☐ be rooted in A「Aに根ざしている，基づいている」　　☐ physical「身体的な，物理的な」
☐ experience of *doing*「…する経験」　　☐ effortful「努力を要する，骨の折れる」
☐ rough「(音が)耳障りな」

⸱⸱

第3段落

¹Surprisingly, the *bouba-kiki* effect even extends into human relationships, and how we imagine the personalities of people we've never met. ²Cognitive psychologist David Sidhu at University College London and psycholinguist Penny Pexman at the University of Calgary have found that people perceive certain personal names such as Bob and Molly as round, and others such as Kirk and Kate as spiky. ³In French, they showed the same effect with the "round" Benoit versus the "spiky" Eric. ⁴In a separate study, participants pictured people with those names as having rounded or spiky personalities. ⁵"The basic

thing we find is that if you compare these very smooth, soft-sounding names like Molly to these harsher-sounding names like Kate, the smoother-sounding names like Molly get associated with things like being more agreeable, more emotional, more responsible, whereas the harsher, spikier-sounding names are thought of as being more extroverted," says Sidhu.

¹驚くべきことに，ブーバ・キキ効果は，人間関係や，一度も会ったことのない人の人柄を想像する場合にまで及ぶ。²ユニバーシティ・カレッジ・ロンドンの認知心理学者デービッド・シドゥとカルガリー大学の心理言語学者ペニー・ペクスマンは，人々はボブやモリーといった特定の個人名を丸いと思い，カークやケイトといった個人名を尖っていると思うことを発見した。³フランス語では，彼らは「丸みのある」ブノア対「尖っている」エリックに関して同じ効果を証明した。⁴ある別の研究では，参加者はそうした名前の人々は丸みのある性格なのか，それとも尖った性格なのかを想像した。⁵「私たちにわかっている基本的なことは，モリーのようなとても滑らかで柔らかく響く名前を，ケイトのようなより耳障りに響く名前と比べてみると，モリーのようなより滑らかに響く名前はより感じがよく，より感情豊かで，より責任感が強いといったことと結びつくのに対し，より耳障りで尖って響く名前は，より外向性が強いと思われているということです」とシドゥは言う。

1 and は human relationships という名詞句と how we … never met という名詞節を結んでいる。we've never met は people を修飾する関係代名詞節。
   □ extend into A「Aに及ぶ」   □ human relationship「人間関係」
   □ personality「性格，人格」

2 1つめの and は，その前後の2人の学者の名前を結んでおり，2つめの and はその前後の2つの名前を結んでいる。3つめの and は，certain personal names such as Bob and Molly as round と others (= other personal names) such as Kirk and Kate as spiky を結んでおり，その両方が perceive の目的語になっている。
   □ cognitive「認知に関する，認識の」   □ psychologist「心理学者」
   □ psycholinguist「心理言語学者」   □ perceive O as C「OをCだと思う」
   □ personal name「人名，個人名」   □ A such as B「たとえばBのようなA」

3 □ with A「Aに関して」   □ A versus B「A対B」

4 □ separate「別の，異なる」   □ study「研究」   □ participant「参加者」
   □ picture O as C「OをCとして心に描く，想像する」   □ rounded「丸い，丸みのある」

5 The basic thing …(S) is(V) that …(C) が文の基本構造。that 節の中は，if S' V' …, S V 〜 という構造。we find は The basic thing を修飾する関係代名詞節。being more agreeable, more

emotional, more responsible は，being の後ろに形容詞の比較級が3つ並列されている。

- □ compare A to B「AをBと比べる，比較する」　□ smooth「滑らかな，スムーズな」
- □ soft-sounding「柔らかい響きの」　□ A like B「たとえばBのようなA」
- □ get associated with A「Aと結びつけて考えられる」
- □ agreeable「感じのよい，愛想のよい」　□ emotional「感情の豊かな」
- □ responsible「責任感の強い」　□ whereas S V ...「ところが一方…，…する一方で」
- □ harsh「耳障りな」　□ spiky-sounding「尖った響きの」
- □ think of O as C「OをCだと思う」　□ extroverted「外向性の強い，外向的な」

── 第4段落 ──

¹These widespread associations may originate in how these sounds feel in our mouth, according to Sidhu. ²"If you think about pronouncing an 'm' versus a 't', for example, that 'm'-sound feels much smoother, and that symbolically captures the smoothness of the rounded shape versus the spiky shape." ³Sounds like "t" and "k" may feel more energetic, capturing an extroverted, cheerful, lively quality.

---

¹シドゥによれば，こうした広く行き渡っている連想は，これらの音が口の中でどのように感じるかに起源があるのかもしれない。²「たとえば，t に対する m の発音を考えてみると，m 音ははるかに滑らかに感じ，それが尖った形に対する丸みのある形の滑らかさを象徴的に捉えているのです」³t や k のような音は，外向的で，明るくて，活発な性質を捉えていて，よりエネルギッシュに感じられるかもしれない。

---

1 □ widespread「広く行き渡っている」　□ originate in A「Aに起源がある，Aから生じる」
　 □ according to A「Aによれば」
2 □ pronounce「を発音する」　□ much + 比較級「はるかに…，ずっと…」
　 □ symbolically「象徴的に」　□ capture「を捉える，捕らえる」
　 □ smoothness「滑らかさ」
3 capturing 以下は分詞構文。
　 □ cheerful「明るい，陽気な」　□ lively「活発な，元気な」

── 第5段落 ──

¹And this mouthfeel of the words we use can influence how we experience the world. ²At any given moment we use a series of subtle cues to pull together information from all our senses, and make judgments and predictions about our environment.

³"There's something about how humans are fundamentally associative," Pexman says. ⁴"We want to see patterns in things, we want to find connections between things, and we'll find them even between sounds and the things those sounds stand for in the world."

¹そして私たちが使用する単語のこの口当たりは，私たちがどのように世界を経験するかということに影響を及ぼすことがある。²どんな瞬間にも，私たちは一連の微妙な手がかりを利用して五感のすべてから来る情報をまとめ，自分の環境について判断や予測をする。³「人間が基本的に連想を行うことに関しては何か大切なことがあるのです」とペクスマンは言う。⁴「私たちは物事の中にパターンを見出したいと思いますし，物事の間の関係を見つけたいと思います，音とその音が世界の中で象徴するものとの間にさえ関係を見つけだそうとします」

1 we use は the words を修飾する関係代名詞節。

  □ mouthfeel「口当たり」   □ influence「に影響を及ぼす」   □ experience「を経験する」

2 to pull ... our senses は目的を表す副詞用法の不定詞句で，use を修飾している。1つめの and は use a ... our senses と make judgments ... our environment を結んでいる。2つめの and は make の目的語となる judgments と predictions を結んでいる。

  □ at any given moment「どんな瞬間にも」   □ a series of A「一連の A」

  □ subtle「微妙な，かすかな」   □ cue「手がかり，ヒント」

  □ pull A together「A＜情報など＞をまとめる，整理する」   □ senses「五感」

  □ environment「環境」

3 □ humans「人間」   □ fundamentally「基本的に，根本的に」   □ associative「連想の」

4 1つめの and は We want ... in things と we want ... between things と we'll find ... the world の3つの節を結んでいる。2つめの and は between A and B の and である。また，those sounds stand for in the world は the things を修飾する関係代名詞節。

  □ connection「関係，つながり」   □ stand for A「A を象徴する，表す」

— 第 6 段落 —

¹The research adds to a growing body of evidence that challenges a long-held view in linguistics: that sounds are arbitrary and have no inherent meaning. ²Instead, certain sounds have been found to bring to mind consistent associations not just with shapes and sizes, but even with flavours and textures. ³Milk chocolate, brie cheese, and still water tend to be perceived as *bouba/maluma*, while crisps, bitter chocolate, mint chocolate, and sparkling water are more likely to be experienced as *kiki/takete*.

133

¹この研究によって，言語学で長年主張されてきた見解に異議を唱える証拠が増えている。それは，音とは恣意的なもので，本来備わっている意味などないというものである。²そうではなくて，ある種の音は形や大きさに関してだけでなく，味や手触りに関してさえ，一貫した連想を思い浮かべさせることがわかってきている。³milk chocolate（ミルクチョコレート），brie cheese（ブリーチーズ），および still water（普通の水）は，ブーバ／マルマとして認識される傾向があるのに対して，crisps（ポテトチップス），bitter chocolate（ビターチョコレート），mint chocolate（ミントチョコレート），および sparkling water（炭酸水）は，キキ／タケテとして感じられる可能性が高い。

1 コロンの後ろの that 節は，コロンの前の a long-held view in linguistics の具体的な内容を表す同格の that 節。

　□ add to A「Aを増やす」（＝increase A）　　□ challenge「に異議を唱える」
　□ long-held「長年主張されてきた」　　□ view「見解／意見」
　□ linguistics「言語学」　　□ arbitrary「恣意的な」　　□ inherent「本来備わっている」

3 □ still water「（発砲性のない）普通の水」　　□ crisps「（英）ポテトチップス」
　□ bitter「苦い」　　□ sparkling water「炭酸水，発泡水」

- -

┌─── 第7段落 ───
│
│ ¹Such associations can help us with important real-life tasks, such as language-learning and guessing the meaning of unfamiliar words. ²In English, words for round things are often round-sounding, as in blob, balloon, ball, marble. ³Words like prickly, spiny, sting, and perky are spiky both in sound and meaning. ⁴Sounds can also indicate size. ⁵An "i"-sound is linked to smallness, while an "o"-sound indicates largeness. ⁶Some of these links exist across thousands of languages, with the "i"-sound excessively popping up in words for "small" around the world.
└──────────────────

¹そのような連想は，言語の学習やなじみのない単語の意味を推測するといった，実生活における重要な課題について私たちの助けとなることがある。²英語では，blob（どろどろした液体の一滴），balloon（風船），ball（球），marble（ビー玉）の場合のように，丸い物を表す単語は丸みのある響きがあることが多い。³prickly（チクチクする），spiny（とげのある），sting（刺す），および perky（きびきびした）のような単語は，音も意味も尖っている。⁴音は大きさも示すことがある。⁵i の音は小ささと結びついているのに対して，o の音は大きさを示す。⁶こうした結びつきの一部は数千の言語にわたって存在し，i 音は世界中で「小さい」を表す単語

に過剰なほど出現する。

1 and は language-learning と guessing the meaning of unfamiliar words を結んでいる。
　□ help A with B「Bに関してAを手伝う，AのBを手伝う」　　□ real-life「実生活の」
　□ task「課題，作業」　　□ guess「を推測する」　　□ meaning「意味」
　□ unfamiliar「なじみのない，よく知らない」
2 □ round-sounding「丸みのある響きがある」
3 □ both A and B「AとBの両方」
4 □ indicate「を示す」　　□ size「大きさ，サイズ」
5 □ link A to B「AをBと結びつける」　　□ while S V「ところが一方…」
6 with 以下は with A *doing* の付帯状況の表現。
　□ link「結びつき」　　□ exist「存在する」　　□ excessively「過度に，度を超えて」
　□ pop up「（急に）現れる」

― 第8段落 ―

　¹For people learning new words, whether babies, young children, or adults, these patterns can be very helpful. ²Young children and even babies already match round sounds with round shapes. ³Parents tend to use sound-shape associations to emphasise the meaning of certain words, such as "teeny tiny." ⁴Adults benefit from associations when they learn a new language, finding it easier to guess or remember foreign words when their sound matches their meaning.

　¹赤ん坊であれ，幼い子どもであれ，大人であれ，新たな単語を学ぶ者にとって，こうしたパターンはとても役に立つことがある。²幼い子ども，さらには赤ん坊でさえ，すでに丸い音と丸い形を組み合わせている。³親は teeny tiny（ちっちゃい）のようにある種の語の意味を強調するために，音と形の連想を利用する傾向がある。⁴大人は新たな言語を学ぶときに連想から恩恵を受け，音と意味が合致するときには，外国語の単語を推測したり，記憶したりすることがより容易になる。

1 learning new words は people を修飾する現在分詞句。whether babies, young children, or adults は whether A, B, or C で「Aであろうと，Bであろうと，またCであろうと」という意味で，直前の people learning new words を補足説明する譲歩の表現。
　□ helpful「役に立つ，助けになる」
2 □ match A with B「AをBと組み合わせる」

135

3 □ emphasise「を強調する」　　□ teeny「ちっちゃい」　　□ tiny「小さい」

4 finding 以下は find O C「OがCだとわかる」を用いた分詞構文。it は形式目的語で，to guess 以下を指しており，easier が C となっている。or は guess と remember の2つの他動詞を結んでおり，foreign words がその共通の目的語となっている。

□ benefit from A「Aから恩恵を受ける」

- -

― 第9段落 ―

[1]Some argue that these instinctive connections between sounds and meaning may even be a leftover from humanity's earliest stages of language evolution and that human language itself started as a string of such expressive, readily guessable sounds.

[1]音と意味とのこのような直観的な結びつきは，人類の言語の進化の最も初期段階の名残でさえあるかもしれず，人間の言語自体がそのような表現力に富んだ，容易に推測可能な音の連なりから始まったのだと主張する人もいる。

1 2つめの and は，argue の目的語となる that these ... language evolution と that human ... guessable sounds の2つの that 節を結んでいる。

□ argue that 節「…だと主張する／論じる」　　□ instinctive「直観的な／本能的な」
□ leftover from A「Aの名残」　　□ humanity「人間，人類」　　□ stage「段階」
□ evolution「進化」　　□ as A「Aとして」　　□ a string of A「Aの連なり，一連のA」
□ expressive「表現力に富んだ」　　□ readily「容易に，たやすく」
□ guessable「推測可能な」

- -

― 第10段落 ―

[1]When it comes to people's personalities, however, sound is not a reliable guide at all. [2]Sidhu, Pexman, and their collaborators tested whether there was a link between a person's name and their personality, perhaps because the round or spiky sound of the name became attached to the wearer. [3]They found no such association. [4]"People worry when choosing baby names. [5]That's because they assume that the label matters so much," Pexman says. [6]"Our data would suggest that although that's what we think, if you call a kid Bob, he's not any more likely to end up with one set of personality characteristics than another."

¹しかし，人格となると，音は指針としてはまったく頼りにならない。²シドゥ，ペクスマンとその共同研究者たちは，人の名前とその性格に結びつきがあるかどうかを検証したが，それはひょっとすると名前が持つ丸みのある，または尖った音が名前の持ち主に付随するようになったのかもしれないという理由からであった。³彼らはそのような結びつきを見つけることはできなかった。⁴「人は赤ん坊の名前を選ぶときに悩みます。⁵それは呼び名がとても重要だという思い込みがあるからです」とペクスマンは言う。⁶「そのように私たちは考えているのですが，子どもをボブと呼んだとしても，その子がある一連の性格的特徴を持つ結果となる可能性は，別の一連の性格的特徴を持つ可能性よりも高くなることはまったくない，ということを私たちのデータは示しています」

1 □ when it comes to A「Aということになると」 □ not ... at all「まったく…でない」
  □ reliable「頼りになる／信頼できる」 □ guide「指針」

2 1つめの and は，Sidhu と Pexman と their collaborators の3つの名詞を結んでいる。2つめの and は，a person's name と their personality の2つの名詞句を結んでいる。
  □ collaborator「共同研究者／協力者」
  □ test whether S V ...「…かどうかを検証する／調べる」
  □ become attached to A「Aにくっつけられる，付随される」
  □ wearer「着用者，使用者」名前の持ち主のこと。

3 □ no such A「そのようなAはない」

4 when choosing ＝ when they are choosing

5 □ That's because S V ...「それは…だからだ」
  □ assume that S V ...「（根拠もないのに）…と思い込む」 □ label「呼び名，ラベル」
  □ matter「重要である」

─ 第11段落 ─

¹Instead, our reaction to a name probably reveals more about our own prejudices. ²"It does suggest that we're prepared to read a lot into somebody's name that probably isn't a cue to what that person is actually like," says Pexman.

¹そうではなく，名前に対する私たちの反応は，おそらく私たち自身の先入観に関してより多くのことを明らかにしている。²「ある人の名前からおそらくその人が実際はどんな人かという手がかりにはならない多くのことを私たちが読み取ろうとしていることを，その反応は確かに示しています」とペクスマンは言う。

1 □ reaction to A「Aに対する反応」　　□ reveal「を明らかにする／暴露する」

□ prejudice「先入観／偏見」

2 It は，直前の文の our reaction to a name を指している。that 以下は，a lot を修飾する関係代名詞節。

□ do＋動詞の原形「確かに…する」do は動詞強調の助動詞。

□ be prepared to *do*「すぐに…しようとする／…する準備ができている」

□ read A into B「BからAを読み取る，Bの中にAを読み取る」

□ cue to A「Aの手がかり」　　□ what A is like「Aはどのようなものか」

□ actually「実際に」

- -

---- 第12段落 ----

[1]Results from an ongoing study by Sidhu, Pexman, and their collaborators suggest that the sound of a name has less of an impact as we find out more about people. [2]When participants were shown videos of people with supposedly round or spiky names, the names made no difference to their judgment of them. [3]"When all you know is the name, like in these studies when you're just shown a name and asked about the personality, then maybe these sounds will play a role," Sidhu says. [4]"But as you start getting more information about the person, then that actual information about the personality is probably going to cancel these biases."

[1]シドゥ，ペクスマンと共同研究者たちによって行われている研究の結果は，人々についてより多くのことを知るにつれて，名前の音はそれほど影響を持たなくなることを示している。[2]参加者たちが，丸みのある，または尖っていると思われている名前を持つ人々のビデオを見せられたとき，名前はその人々に対する彼らの判断にとってまったく重要ではなかった。[3]「名前だけを見せられて，性格について質問されるこうした研究の場合のように，名前しか知らないときには，こうした音が役割を果たすことがあるかもしれません」とシドゥは言う。[4]「しかし，その人についてより多くの情報が入るようになると，その人の性格に関する実際の情報がおそらくこうした先入観を消してしまうのでしょう」

1 □ result from A「Aから得られる結果」　　□ ongoing「進行中の，継続している」

□ impact「影響」

□ find out A about B「BについてAを知る」A には more ／ something ／ anything などがくる。

2 □ show O₁ O₂「O₁ に O₂ を見せる」

□ supposedly「一般に思われているところでは」

□ make no difference to A「Aにとって重要ではない」　　□ judgment「判断」

3 □ all S know is ...「Sが知っているのは…だけだ」　　□ like in A「Aの場合のように」

□ maybe「ひょっとすると／たぶん」　　□ play a role「役割を果たす」

4 □ as S V ...「…するとき」　　□ actual「実際の」　　□ cancel「を取り消す」

—— 第13段落 ——

[1]As widespread as the *bouba-kiki* effect is, it can be changed or cancelled out by different factors, such as the sounds commonly used in our own native language. [2]Suzy Styles and her PhD student Nan Shang tested the *bouba-kiki* effect with Mandarin Chinese. [3]Mandarin is a tonal language, where the meaning of a word can completely change depending on the tone in which it is said. [4]In English, tone can carry some meaning, for example by signalling a question, but not to the extent it does in Mandarin. [5]The researchers presented English- and Mandarin-speakers with two Mandarin Chinese tones, one high and one falling. [6]The English-speaking participants in the experiment perceived the high tone as spiky, and the falling one as rounded. [7]But Mandarin speakers drew the opposite conclusion, picturing the high tone as rounded, and the falling tone as spiky.

[1]ブーバ・キキ効果は広く行き渡っているが，自分の母語でよく用いられる音のような，様々な要因によって変化したり，帳消しにされたりすることがある。[2]スージー・スタイルズと博士課程にいる彼女の学生のナン・シャンは，標準中国語でブーバ・キキ効果を検証した。[3]標準中国語は声調言語であり，単語の意味はそれが話される声調によってまったく変わることがある。[4]英語では，声調はたとえば質問であることを伝えることによって何らかの意味を持つことがあるが，標準中国語ほどではない。[5]研究者たちは英語と標準中国語の話者に，1つは高く，1つは下降調の2つの標準中国語の声調を聞かせた。[6]英語話者の実験参加者は，高い声調を尖っている，下降調を丸みがあると捉えた。[7]ところが，標準中国語話者は正反対の結論を導き出し，高い声調を丸みがある，下降調を尖っていると思い描いた。

1 as＋形容詞＋as S V は「Sは…だけれども」という意味で，though S V＋形容詞とほぼ同意。イギリス用法では最初の as が省略されることが多い。commonly used in our own native language は the sounds を修飾する過去分詞句。

□ cancel A out「Aを帳消しにする」　　□ commonly「一般に，よく」

□ native language「母語」

3 where 以下は a tonal language の補足説明をする非制限用法の関係副詞節。

　□ completely「まったく，完全に」　　□ depending on A「Aによって，A次第で」

　□ tone「声調，抑揚」

4 does = carries some meaning

　□ carry「(意味)を持つ，帯びる」　　□ signal「をほのめかす，伝える」

　□ to the extent that S V「…するほど，…する程度まで」

5 one high and one falling は分詞構文で，two Mandarin Chinese tones の補足説明をしている。
one (being) high and one (being) falling と考えるとよい。

　□ present A with B「AにBを提示する」

6 and は，perceived に続く the high tone as spiky と the falling one as rounded を結んでいる。one は tone の代用。

7 picturing 以下は分詞構文。and は picturing に続く the high tone as rounded と the falling tone as spiky を結んでいる。

　□ draw a conclusion「結論を導く」　　□ opposite「正反対の，逆の」

- -

― 第14段落 ―

[1]One possible explanation is that if we are unfamiliar with tones in a language, as English-speakers are, then we may mainly hear them as high or low, and form associations based on pitch. [2]But if we are familiar with tones, as Chinese speakers are, we may be able to distinguish finer nuances. [3]In the experiment, the Mandarin speakers heard the high tone as smooth, drawn-out, and steady, and therefore, rounded. [4]The falling tone was experienced as sudden because it dropped quickly, making it spiky.

[1]考えられる説明の1つは，英語話者のように言語の声調になじみがない場合は，たいていの場合，それらを音の高低として聞きとり，音の高さに基づいて連想を形成するかもしれない，ということである。[2]しかし，中国語話者のように声調になじみがあれば，より微妙なニュアンスを識別することができるかもしれない。[3]この実験では，高い声調は標準中国語話者には滑らかで，長くて，安定しており，したがって丸みがあると聞こえた。[4]下降調は，急に下がるために唐突と感じられ，尖った感じになった。

1 One possible explanation(S) is(V) that ...(C) が文の基本構造。that 節内の as English-speakers are は，「英語話者のように」という意味で if 節を修飾しており，are の後ろには unfamiliar with tones in a language が省略されている。and は hear them as high or low と form associations based on pitch の2つの動詞句を結んでいる。

□ possible「可能な，考え得る」　　□ explanation「説明」

□ be unfamiliar with A「Aになじみがない，Aをよく知らない」

□ mainly「たいてい，主に」　　□ hear O as C「OがCだと聞こえる」

□ form「を形成する」　　□ pitch「音の高低」

2 □ distinguish「を識別する，区別する」　　□ fine「微妙な，繊細な」

□ nuance「ニュアンス，微妙な違い」

3 1つめの and は smooth, drawn-out, steady の3つの形容詞を結んでいる。2つめの and は，その3つの形容詞と rounded というもう1つの形容詞を結んでいる。

□ drawn-out「(時間的に)長い，長引いた」　　□ steady「安定した」

□ therefore「したがって」

4 making it spiky は分詞構文で，which made it spiky とほぼ同意。

□ sudden「唐突な，突然の」　　□ make O C「OをCにする」

- -

── 第15段落 ──

[1]Other studies also found variations in the *bouba-kiki* pattern. [2]The Himba, a remote community in Northern Namibia who speak the Otjiherero language, judged *bouba* to be round and *kiki* to be spiky, in line with the general trend. [3]But they found milk chocolate to be spiky-tasting, suggesting that our associations with regard to our senses are not universal.

[1]他の研究でも，ブーバ・キキパターンのバリエーションが見つかった。[2]ナミビア北部の人里離れた土地で暮らす，ヘレロ語を話すヒンバ族が，一般的な傾向と同じく，ブーバを丸みがある，キキを尖っていると判断した。[3]しかし，彼らはミルクチョコレートを尖った味がすると感じ，このことは五感に関する私たちの連想が普遍的ではないことを示唆していた。

1 □ variation「バリエーション，変種」

2 The Himba と a remote ... Otjiherero language は同格の関係。

□ remote「人里離れた，へんぴな」　　□ Namibia「ナミビア」アフリカ南西部の国。

□ the Otjiherero language「ヘレロ語」ナミビアの他にアフリカ南部のボツワナ，アフリカ南西部のアンゴラなどで話されている言語。　　□ judge O to be C「OをCと判断する」

□ in line with A「Aと一致して，Aに従って」　　□ general「一般的な」

□ trend「傾向，趨勢」

3 suggesting 以下は分詞構文で，which suggests that ... とほぼ同意。

□ find O to be C「OをCだと思う」　　□ spiky-tasting「尖った味の」

— 第16段落 —

[1]When Styles and the linguist Lauren Gawne tested the *bouba-kiki* effect on speakers of Syuba, a language in the Himalayas in Nepal, they found no consistent response either way.　[2]The Syuba speakers seemed confused by the made-up words, possibly because they did not sound like any actual Syuba words.　[3]This made it hard to form any meaningful associations.　[4]An analogy would be to say the made-up word "ngf" to an English speaker, and ask if it is round or spiky.　[5]It would probably be difficult to make a meaningful choice.　[6]"When we hear words that don't follow the word-pattern of our native language, it's often hard to do things with that word," Styles says.　[7]"We can't hold it in our short-term memory long enough to make decisions about it."

[1]スタイルズと言語学者のローレン・ゴーンは，シューバ語というネパールのヒマラヤ山脈の言語の話者に及ぼすブーバ・キキ効果を調べたが，どちらにも一貫した反応は見られなかった。[2]シューバ語話者はそれらの造語に戸惑うように見えたが，ひょっとすると，それらが実際のシューバ語のどんな単語のようにも聞こえなかったからだろう。[3]このせいで，何らかの意味のある連想を形成することが難しくなったのだ。[4]類例を出すなら，英語話者に ngf という造語を聞かせ，それが丸みがあるか，尖っているかを尋ねるようなものだろう。[5]おそらく意味のある選択を行うのは難しいだろう。[6]「自分の母語の言葉のパターンを踏襲していない単語を耳にするとき，その単語について何かを行うのは難しいことが多いのです」とスタイルズは言う。[7]「私たちはその単語について様々な決断を下すのに十分なほど長く，それを短期記憶に保持しておくことはできないのです」

1 Syuba と a language in the Himalayas in Nepal は同格の関係。
　□ linguist「言語学者」　　□ the Himalayas「ヒマラヤ山脈」　　□ response「反応」
2 □ confused「戸惑った，混乱した」　　□ possibly「ひょっとすると，もしかすると」
3 □ meaningful「意味のある」
4 □ analogy「類例，類似」
5 □ make a choice「選択を行う」
6 □ follow「を踏襲する，に従う」
7 □ hold「を保持する」　　□ short-term memory「短期記憶」
　□ 副詞 + enough to *do*「…するのに十分なほど〜」

[1]Cultural factors are also likely to affect our reactions to the sound of personal names. [2]In English, the sounds "k" and "oo" are perceived as inherently humorous. [3]English female names are more likely to contain sounds that are perceived as small, such as the "i"-sound in Emily, and also feature more soft sounds than male names. [4]But in other languages, names can follow a completely different sound pattern. [5]Sidhu hasn't yet tested the name-personality association across different languages, but expects that it would vary.

[1]文化的要因も，人名の音に対する私たちの反応に影響を与える可能性が高い。[2]英語では，k と oo の音はもともとユーモラスなものとして認識される。[3]英語の女性の名前は，男性の名前に比べて，Emily における i 音などのように，小さいと認識される音を含む可能性が高く，また，柔らかな音が多いという特徴がある。[4]しかし，他の言語では，名前はまったく異なる音声パターンに従うことがある。[5]シドゥは，異なる言語における名前と性格の連想についてはまだ調べていないが，それは様々になるだろうと予想している。

1 □ cultural「文化的な，文化の」　　□ factor「要因，要素」

2 □ inherently「もともと，本来的に」　　□ humorous「ユーモラスな，おどけた」

3 and は are more ... in Emily と feature more soft sounds の2つの動詞句を結んでいる。

　　□ female「女性の」　　□ contain「を含む」　　□ feature「を特徴として持つ」

5 but は hasn't yet ... different languages と expects that it would vary の2つの動詞句を結んでいる。

　　□ not yet「まだ…でない」　　□ vary「異なる，様々である」

[1]Uncovering these hidden associations holds one important real-life lesson. [2]We probably read too much into other people's names. [3]After all, Sidhu and Pexman found no evidence that Bobs are actually friendlier, or Kirks more extroverted. [4]Their findings may add weight to calls to remove names from important documents such as scientific papers under review, to prevent unconscious bias. [5]Sidhu supports the idea. [6]"I think that makes a lot of sense," he says. [7]"When someone is being judged, taking away all of these extra things that could bias the judgment is always a good idea."

¹こうした隠れた連想を明らかにすることには，１つの重要な現実的な教訓がある。²おそらく私たちは，他人の名前からあまりに多くのものを読み取っているのだ。³そもそも，シドゥとペクスマンは，ボブという名の人たちが実際によりフレンドリーであったり，カークという名の人たちがより外向的であったりすることを示す証拠は何も発見しなかった。⁴彼らの研究結果は，無意識的な偏見を防ぐために，審査中の科学論文などの重要な文書から氏名を除いてほしいという声の重要性を増すかもしれない。⁵シドゥはその考えを支持している。⁶「それはとても理にかなっていると思います」と彼は言う。⁷「誰かが審査されているときに，判断を偏らせかねないこうした余分な事柄をすべて取り除くというのは，常によい考えです」

1 □ uncover「を明らかにする，暴く」　　□ hidden「隠れた」　　□ lesson「教訓」

3 Kirks の直後に are が省略されている。

　□ after all「そもそも，何しろ」　　□ friendly「フレンドリーな，人懐こい」

4 □ finding「研究結果」　　□ add weight to A「Aの重要性を増す」

　□ call to *do*「…してほしいという声，要求」　　□ remove A from B「BからAを取り除く」

　□ document「文書」　　□ paper「論文」　　□ under review「審査中の，検討中の」

　□ unconscious「無意識的な，無意識の」

6 □ make sense「理にかなう，意味をなす」

7 that could bias the judgment は these extra things を修飾する関係代名詞節。

　□ take A away「Aを取り除く」　　□ extra「余分な，追加の」　　□ bias「を偏らせる」